THE
LINCOLNS

THE
LINCOLNS

A SCRAPBOOK LOOK AT

ABRAHAM AND MARY

CANDACE FLEMING

schwartz & wade books · new york

Published in the United States by Schwartz & Wade Books, an imprint of Random House Children's Books,
a division of Random House, Inc., New York.
Schwartz & Wade Books and colophon are trademarks of Random House, Inc.

Visit us on the Web! www.randomhouse.com/kids
Educators and librarians, for a variety of teaching tools, visit us at www.randomhouse.com/teachers

Library of Congress Cataloging-in-Publication Data
Fleming, Candace.
The Lincolns : a scrapbook look at Abraham and Mary / Candace Fleming. — 1st ed.
p. cm.
ISBN 978-0-375-83618-3 (trade) — ISBN 978-0-375-93618-0 (lib. bdg.)
1. Lincoln, Abraham, 1809-1865–Juvenile literature. 2. Lincoln, Mary Todd, 1818-1882–Juvenile literature. 3. Presidents–United States–Biography–Juvenile literature. 4. Presidents' spouses–United States–Biography–Juvenile literature. 5. Married people–United States–Biography–Juvenile literature. 6. Presidents–United States–History–19th century–Sources–Juvenile literature. 7. Presidents' spouses–United States–History–19th century–Sources–Juvenile literature. 8. Washington (D.C.)–History–Civil War, 1861-1865–Sources–Juvenile literature. 9. United States–History–Civil War, 1861-1865–Sources–Juvenile literature. I. Title.

E457.905.F58 2008
973.7092'2–dc22
[B]
2007044113

Printed in China
10 9 8 7 6 5 4 3 2 1
First Edition

A NOTE ON THE TYPE

This book was set in a typeface called Old Times American, which was designed by Nathan Williams based on typefaces from the 1800s. In those days, each letter was cast from a piece of metal, and then letters were laid next to each other one by one to make words and sentences. The larger, more decorative letters were made from wood. Once an entire page of type had been laid out, ink was rolled over the faces of the letters and the inked page was pressed onto paper. Because typesetting was done by hand and eye, the spacing between letters and words was not as even as it is today, when most typesetting is done using computers.

✦ ACKNOWLEDGMENTS ✦

Numerous scholars, experts, archivists, and friends helped me during the five years it took to research and write this book. Special thanks go to:

Dr. John Sellers, historical specialist on the American Civil War and the Lincoln curator at the Library of Congress, who navigated me through the Lincoln papers and shared his as-yet-uncataloged documents.

Thomas Schwartz, state historian and interim executive director of the Abraham Lincoln Presidential Library and Museum in Springfield, Illinois, who answered my seemingly endless questions with patience and humor.

Jason Emerson, Mary Lincoln scholar, who took time away from writing his own book to help me with mine.

And most especially Keya Morgan, a widely respected scholar of Lincoln photography and owner of one of the world's largest collections of original Abraham Lincoln photographs, not only for providing hours of fascinating and enlightening Lincoln conversation but also for generously donating several photographs for this book. These images are particularly noteworthy because they were scanned directly from the original 140-plus-year-old, from-life albumen photographs in the Keya Morgan collection.

Thanks also to the amazingly efficient Jennifer Ericson, who unearthed numerous obscure images in the Lincoln Presidential Library's vast holdings; Cindy Van Horn at the Lincoln Museum in Fort Wayne, Indiana, who raided her archives at a moment's notice to find the perfect photo; B. J. Gooch at Transylvania University in Lexington, Kentucky, who constantly emerged with priceless information about the Todd family; and all those amazing librarians at the Lexington Public Library, who despite floods and destroyed records managed to find the very facts and images I needed.

My heartfelt appreciation is again extended to Dr. Herbert Lasky, retired professor of history at Eastern Illinois University, who took on the monumental task of verifying all the facts in this book.

Thanks, too, to those exceptionally talented people at Random House who work so hard to make me look so good—Lee Wade, Ann Kelley, Emily Seife, Lia Brown, Colleen Fellingham, Barbara Perris, and Sue Warga.

And what would I have done without Patti Ratchford, book designer extraordinaire? Not only is she a genius, but she also has the patience of a saint.

But the greatest privilege I have enjoyed in creating this book has been the opportunity to once again work with the indomitable Anne Schwartz, a woman who can find the perfect solution to any dilemma. Anne helped shape my thoughts, offered valuable criticism, and made my dream of telling the Lincolns' story a reality. She has my eternal admiration.

CONTENTS

I'm an Illinois girl, raised in the very heart of the "land of Lincoln." Growing up, I often bicycled out to the old Lincoln place—the farm Abraham and his parents settled when they moved to the state back in 1830. I thought nothing of clambering over the rotting log cabin or exploring the crumbling root cellar. Sometimes, I rode the extra half mile to Shiloh Cemetery to eat peanut butter crackers while leaning against stepmother Sarah's and father Tom's headstones. Other times, I pedaled over to the fairgrounds where Lincoln once debated Stephen A. Douglas, or I rested on the cool, green grass of the county courthouse—the same place Abraham had practiced law when riding the Eighth Circuit. Occasionally, I spent the night at my friend Emily's house. Lincoln had once slept in what later became her bedroom, and we often lay awake hoping to catch a glimpse of his ghost. Sometimes we asked our friend Karen to join us. Karen was a distant cousin of Lincoln, and I couldn't help but wonder if sharing a pizza with her was like sharing one with our sixteenth president. Then, of course, there was the annual field trip to Springfield; every October, my classmates and I boarded the school bus that would carry us along the Lincoln Heritage Trail to the state capital, some seventy miles away. Yet again, I traipsed through the Lincoln home and filed through the Lincoln tomb. Encountering his bust outside the gravesite, I always rubbed his big bronze nose for good luck. At the Lincoln Souvenir Shop, I bought yet another stovepipe hat pencil sharpener. Then I climbed back on the bus and headed home, feeling as if I had just visited an old friend.

A few years ago, when my editor suggested I write a biography of Abraham Lincoln, I hesitated. Perhaps because Lincoln was so familiar to me, I'd never considered writing about him. Still, as I began reading books and articles, that old childhood feeling of connectedness began creeping over me. Suddenly, I longed to peel away the layers of myth and symbol and produce a close,

intimate portrait of the man. More than anything, I wanted to reveal the *real* Abraham Lincoln. But how?

I dove into the wealth of Lincoln material—letters, diaries, speeches, newspapers—and encountered Mary. I admit I didn't know much about his wife when I first began this project. Certainly, I'd heard stories about her extravagant spending sprees, her violent temper tantrums, her time in an insane asylum. Yet few people know the whole truth: that for all her faults, Mary Lincoln was brilliant and restless, her life a string of tragedies, her spirit amazingly resilient. She and her husband were so inextricably bound that a Springfield friend once said, "They were like two pine trees that had grown so close their roots were forever intertwined."

I knew I couldn't completely understand Abraham without acknowledging the shaping presence of his wife—a woman who made his political career the ruling passion of her adult life. Nor could I understand Mary without exploring her relationship with Abraham—an often unconventional man who tacitly encouraged his wife to break society's rules. The more deeply I became involved in their lives, the more I realized that their story not only chronicles some of the most important events in American history but also illuminates the human condition of love and loss, failure and accomplishment, convention and nonconformity, determination and destiny.

This, then, was what I'd been searching for—a unique way of telling the Lincoln story. By presenting *both* their lives, following them from their strikingly different childhoods through Mary's final years alone, I could place them in a new, more intimate light. You will see a man who loved cats and smelled of woodsmoke; who held his secretary of war's hand while awaiting bulletins from the battlefield, and wrestled with his young sons on the White House carpet; a man who resolved to preserve the Union, yet talked of many things besides war.

As for Mary, by delving into the treasure trove of primary sources related to her life, I could bring her back to her place in history. You will meet her as a schoolgirl, rushing eagerly to her lessons before dawn; as a grieving mother, holding séances in the White House; as an old woman, sick and forgotten by almost everyone.

Because my goal is to bring the Lincolns to life, I have chosen to tell their story visually. After all, one of the best ways to get to know people is to pore over photographs of their children, read snippets of their love letters, bake (if you want to) their favorite cake, or even peek at the contents of their pockets. Within the pages of this book, you will be able to do all that, and more.

But these images don't simply chronicle Mary's and Abraham's lives. They also tell us about the Lincolns' America. During the Civil War, when the camera was still a new invention, photographs could not be quickly and easily reproduced. Therefore, newspapers, magazines, book publishers, and print shops depended on artists to depict the important people and events of the day. And the most popular subject was Abraham Lincoln. Americans hungered for pictures of him. In a time when politicians were considered heroes, it was common to find images of the president hanging in people's parlors. But they were not exact portrayals. Instead, they romanticized his homeliness and glorified his accomplishments. In short, they helped turn him into a legend. As you read this book, look for those pictures that present an idealized Abraham Lincoln. While they are not accurate, they do reveal the hopes and fears of nineteenth-century Americans. They are still enlightening, if not entirely truthful.

Besides being chock-full of visuals, this book is organized in a unique fashion. Rather than presenting entries in strict chronological order, I have chosen to divide some of the information by key themes, such as growing up with slavery, being a parent, and political ambition. By my doing so, I hope you will clearly see how specific events unfolded, relationships progressed, and ideas developed. If you wish, you can use the chronology on the following pages to place these entries within the context of the Lincolns' lives.

You will also notice that this book is more about people than battles. Certainly, you will read about such pivotal events as the surrender of Fort Sumter and the Battle of Gettysburg. But mixed in among these sobering entries, you will find mention of Abraham's joke-telling and Mary's dressmaking, Tad's pet goats and Robert's pet peeves. Why mix the mundane with the horrific? Because it is the everyday events—the dinner table conversations and the complaints about ill-fitting boots—that truly bring the Lincolns to life. It is the mundane that makes them real. And it is the ordinary that will, I hope, leave you feeling as if you have just visited old friends.

A NOTE ABOUT NAMES

Because I wish to represent the historical figures in this book as they would want to be represented, I have chosen to use the names they preferred. Thus, Abraham Lincoln is never referred to as Abe, because he detested the name, while Mary is never called Mary Todd Lincoln, because she dropped the *Todd* after her marriage and never used it when signing her name.

I have also done something like this for Elizabeth Keckly. In her published memoir and in the history books her last name is spelled *Keckley*. During my research, however, scholars pointed out that Elizabeth herself spelled it *Keckly*. I have chosen to use Elizabeth's spelling.

Roman text = Abraham's events

Italicized text = Mary's events

Bold italicized text = events shared by Abraham and Mary

1809 Abraham Lincoln is born on February 12 on Sinking Spring Farm in Kentucky.

1811 The Lincolns move to Knob Creek.

1815 Abraham briefly attends a log house school, where he learns to read and write.

1816 In December, the Lincolns move to the backwoods of Indiana.

1818 On October 5, Abraham's mother, Nancy Hanks, dies from milk sickness.

Mary Todd is born December 13 in Lexington, Kentucky.

1819 Abraham gets a stepmother when Thomas Lincoln marries Sarah Bush Johnston.

Abraham briefly attends Andrew Crawford's "blab" school.

1822 Abraham attends James Swaney's school for a few months.

1823 *Five-year-old Mary takes a trip to Frankfort, Kentucky.*

1824 Abraham attends Azel W. Dorsey's school. He creates a "sum" book.

1825 *On July 5, Mary's mother, Eliza Todd, dies while giving birth.*

1826 *Mary gets a stepmother when Robert Todd marries Elizabeth Humphreys. Attends Shelby Female Academy.*

1828 On January 20, Abraham's sister, Sarah, dies while giving birth.

In April, he takes a flatboat to New Orleans, where he observes a slave auction.

1830 In March, the Lincoln family moves to Illinois and settles along the Sangamon River.

Abraham gives his first political speech that summer.

While visiting Henry Clay's home, Mary declares she intends to grow up and marry a president. In the summer she discovers that her mammy is illegally feeding runaway slaves, and begins to think about the moral implications of slavery.

1831 Abraham moves to New Salem, Illinois, where he works as a clerk in a village store. Learns basic math, reads Shakespeare.

1832 Abraham becomes a candidate for the Illinois General Assembly. When the Black Hawk War breaks out in April, he enlists and is elected captain of his rifle company, serving a total of three months. Loses the election in August. Goes into the general store business with his friend William Berry.

Mary completes her education at Shelby Female Academy and is sent to Madame Mentelle's Boarding School for Girls, where, among other subjects, she studies French, learning to speak it fluently. Gets into a hot political debate with a friend over President Andrew Jackson.

1833 The Lincoln-Berry store fails. Abraham is given the position of village postmaster and teaches himself to survey land.

A cholera epidemic strikes Lexington, creating lifelong fears in Mary.

1834 On August 4, Abraham is elected to the Illinois General Assembly as a member of the Whig Party. He begins to study law.

1835 Ann Rutledge, Abraham's love interest, dies in August. In the fall, he begins courting Mary Owens.

1836 Abraham is reelected to the Illinois General Assembly.

Mary completes her education at the Mentelle Boarding School and enters Lexington society.

1837 Abraham receives his law degree. In April, he leaves New Salem and settles in the new state capital, Springfield, to practice law with John T. Stuart. He meets Joshua Speed, who will become a lifelong friend, and ends his relationship with Mary Owens.

In June, Mary Todd visits her sister Elizabeth Edwards, who lives in Springfield, but returns to Lexington at the end of the summer.

1838 Abraham is reelected to the Illinois General Assembly.

1839 Abraham begins traveling the Eighth Judicial Circuit.

Mary moves to Springfield in June.

Abraham and Mary meet at a dance in December.

1840 *The couple becomes engaged.*

1841 *They break off their engagement on January 1.*

Abraham has an episode of severe depression. He ends his partnership with John Stuart and begins work with lawyer Stephen Logan.

Mary is heartbroken but continues social rounds.

1842 *The couple begins courting again. They marry on November 4 and move to the Globe Tavern.*

1843 *The couple's first child, Robert Todd, is born on August 1.*

1844 *In May, the Lincolns buy a cottage on the corner of Eighth and Jackson.*

Abraham dissolves his law partnership with Logan and sets up his own practice with William Herndon.

1846 *The couple's second child, Edward Baker, is born on March 10.*

In May, Abraham is nominated as the Whig candidate for the U.S. Congress, and on August 3 he is elected to the U.S. House of Representatives.

1847 *The Lincolns take a vacation to Lexington, Kentucky, before moving into a boardinghouse in Washington, D.C.*

Abraham takes his seat in Congress on December 6. On the twenty-second, he submits his "Spot Resolutions."

1848 As a congressman, Abraham denounces every bill that tries to spread slavery into new territories.

Disappointed with Washington, Mary takes the children for an extended stay with her family in Lexington.

1849 Abraham returns to Springfield and his law practice. On May 22, he is granted a patent for "an improved method of lifting vessels over shoals."

In July, Mary's father, Robert Smith Todd, dies.

1850 *On February 1, the couple's son Eddie dies of tuberculosis. On December 21, their third son, William (Willie) Wallace, is born.*

Abraham resumes his travels on the Eighth Judicial Circuit. Congress passes the Compromise of 1850.

1851 On January 17, Abraham's father, Thomas Lincoln, dies.

1852 *Uncle Tom's Cabin* by Harriet Beecher Stowe is published.

1853 *The couple's fourth son, Thomas (Tad), is born on April 4.*

1854 Congress passes the Kansas-Nebraska Act. Infuriated by the legislature, Abraham reenters politics. He is elected to the Illinois legislature but declines the seat to try to become a U.S. senator.

1855 Abraham is not chosen by the Illinois legislature to be U.S. senator.

Mary stops talking to her old friends Julia and Lyman Trumbull because of politics.

1856 The explosive issue of slavery causes Representative Preston Brooks to physically attack Senator Charles Sumner on the Senate floor, while in Kansas open warfare breaks out. Abandoning the foundering Whig Party, Abraham joins the new Republican Party of Illinois. He gives a passionate speech in Bloomington, earning the party's political spotlight.

Mary renovates the house at Eighth and Jackson with money inherited from her father.

1857 Abraham speaks out against the *Dred Scott* decision.

1858 In May, Abraham wins acquittal for his friend Duff Armstrong. In June, he is nominated by the Republican Party to be a candidate for Illinois's U.S. Senate seat, opposing Democrat Stephen A. Douglas. Gives "House Divided" speech at the state convention in Springfield. Engages Douglas in a series of seven debates across the state.

1859 The Illinois legislature chooses Douglas for the U.S. Senate over Lincoln. In December, Abraham writes a short autobiography.

1860 In May, Abraham is nominated to be the Republican candidate for president. He grows a beard at the suggestion of an eleven-year-old girl. Abraham wins the presidency on November 6. In December, South Carolina secedes from the Union, followed by Mississippi, Florida, Alabama, Georgia, Louisiana, and Texas.

Mary revels in the national spotlight, giving interviews to the press and entertaining prominent guests.

1861 February: Lincoln gives a brief farewell address to his Springfield neighbors. He receives an assassination threat and sneaks into the nation's capital.

March: Inaugurated on the fourth, he learns about the Fort Sumter crisis hours later.

April: Confederates open fire on Fort Sumter in Charleston, South Carolina, on the twelfth. The Civil War begins. Lincoln issues a proclamation calling for soldiers and authorizes the suspension of the writ of habeus corpus. Virginia secedes from the Union.

July: The Union suffers defeat at Bull Run in northern Virginia. Lincoln writes his "memorandum of military policy" and appoints General George McClellan as commander of the Army of the Potomac.

Mary hires African American seamstress Elizabeth Keckly as her dressmaker, a choice that will result in a close friendship. Mary seeks to undermine protocol by insisting on planning all White House social events herself. She receives unfair criticism from the press for her family connection to the Confederacy. Mary tries to make the White House more of a home for Tad and Willie by inviting the Taft children to play. She begins an extensive and expensive renovation of the White House.

1862 *Willie Lincoln dies on February 20.*

January: Abraham issues his General Order No. 1, calling for a Union advance.

March: McClellan begins his disastrous Peninsula Campaign.

June: Abraham secretly begins writing the Emancipation Proclamation.

July: He reveals his Emancipation Proclamation to the Cabinet.

September: McClellan stops Confederate armies at Antietam. Abraham issues a preliminary Emancipation Proclamation, freeing slaves in the South.

November: He replaces McClellan with General Ambrose Burnside.

December: Burnside leads the army to costly defeat at Fredericksburg.

Mary spends most of the year in mourning for Willie. She begins visiting spiritualists and holding séances in the White House. In November, she becomes involved with the Contraband Relief Association.

1863 January: Abraham issues the Emancipation Proclamation. He appoints General Joseph Hooker commander of the Army of the Potomac, replacing Burnside, and places General Ulysses S. Grant in command of the Army of the Tennessee, with orders to capture Vicksburg.

March: Abraham signs an act introducing the draft.

May: Hooker's troops are defeated at the Battle of Chancellorsville.

June: Abraham appoints General George G. Meade as commander of the Army of the Potomac, replacing Hooker.

July: The Union Army under Meade defeats the Confederates at the Battle of Gettysburg on the third. Grant captures Vicksburg on the fourth.

November: Abraham delivers the Gettysburg Address.

December: Abraham recovers from a mild case of smallpox.

Mary forms the Blue Room salon and begins weekly visits to area hospitals. She continues with renovations of the White House, as well as buying sprees. In February, she hosts a White House reception for General and Mrs. Tom Thumb. In June, she moves her family to the Soldiers' Home, then in July has a carriage accident from which she never fully recovers. In December, she is visited by her Confederate sister Emilie.

1864 *Robert Todd Lincoln graduates from Harvard in June and joins Grant's troops in Petersburg, Virginia.*

March: Abraham appoints General Ulysses S. Grant general in chief of all Union armies. General William Tecumseh Sherman succeeds Grant as commander in the West.

May: Grant begins a series of bloody battles known as the "On to Richmond" campaign.

June: Grant begins the siege of Petersburg. Abraham receives the nomination for president from the Republican Party.

July: Confederate Jubal Early raids Washington.

September: Sherman captures Atlanta.

October: General Philip Sheridan scores a decisive victory in the Shenandoah Valley.

November: Abraham is reelected president, defeating Democrat George B. McClellan. He tells journalist Noah Brooks about his premonition of death.

December: Sherman occupies Savannah.

Mary continues shopping, redecorating the White House, and seeking the advice of spiritualists. She cultivates unsavory but influential politicians to help get her husband reelected.

1865 February: Abraham signs the Thirteenth Amendment to the United States Constitution.

March: He is inaugurated on the fourth. He discusses plans for the future with his wife, then takes a trip with his family to City Point, Virginia, to visit Grant's headquarters on the twentieth.

April: Abraham takes a walk with Tad through Richmond, Virginia, on the fourth. He has another premonition of death. General Robert E. Lee surrenders his Confederate army to Grant on the ninth. Abraham makes his last public speech on the eleventh. On the fourteenth, he is shot while attending a play at Ford's Theater. He dies at 7:22 the following morning. On the twentieth, he is given a funeral at the White House; then his body is loaded onto a train that carries him to Springfield, Illinois, where he is laid to rest in Oak Ridge Cemetery on May 4.

In March, Mary goes to City Point with her husband and son, where she makes a public spectacle of herself. She is at her husband's side when he is shot on the fourteenth, and remains there until his death the following morning, when she returns to the White House. Unable to get out of bed, she does not attend her husband's funeral.

In May, she leaves the White House and with Robert and Tad moves to Chicago. She is placed on a very tight budget because Lincoln died without a will, and she begins writing letters to prominent citizens begging for money.

1866 *William Herndon gives his Ann Rutledge speech, devastating Mary. Money worries consume her.*

1867 *In hopes of raising money, Mary attempts to sell her old clothing, resulting in public humiliation.*

1868 *Robert Todd Lincoln marries Mary Harlan in Washington, D.C. Elizabeth Keckly publishes a tell-all book about the Lincoln family. Mary moves to Frankfurt, Germany, with Tad.*

1869 *Mary's first grandchild, named for her, is born in October.*

1870 *After a heated debate, Congress finally awards Mary a widow's pension of $3,000 a year.*

1871 *Mary returns from Frankfurt, Germany, and settles in Chicago. On July 15, Tad Lincoln dies of pleurisy. Mary moves to a center for spiritualists in St. Charles, Illinois, where she hopes to be reunited with her dead loved ones.*

1872 *Over the next three years, Mary moves constantly.*

1875 *Mary is tried for insanity, found guilty, and committed to Bellevue Place in Batavia, Illinois. She convinces lawyer Myra Bradwell to take her case. Mary is released from the asylum and goes to live with her sister Elizabeth Edwards in Springfield, Illinois, vowing never to speak to her son Robert again.*

1876 *Mary moves to Pau, France, to escape the humiliation of her insanity trial.*

1881 *Because of poor health, Mary returns to Springfield.*

1882 *Mary dies of a stroke on July 15. She is laid to rest in Oak Ridge Cemetery beside her husband and their sons Eddie, Willie, and Tad.*

THE
LINCOLNS

CHAPTER

ONE

BACKWOODS BOY

It is a great folly to attempt to make anything out of my early life. It can all be condensed into a simple sentence, and that sentence you will find in Gray's Elegy—"the short and simple annals of the poor." That's my life, and that's all you can make of it.

—ABRAHAM LINCOLN IN A REMARK TO A NEWSPAPER REPORTER, 1860

A PAINTING SHOWING THE WILDS OF KENTUCKY AS THEY LOOKED AROUND THE TIME OF ABRAHAM'S BIRTH

Kentucky was a young state when Abraham was born there in 1809. Admitted to the Union in 1792, it was still considered the frontier—vast, wild, and untamed. So dense was its wilderness, settlers were forced to cut their way through the forest, felling trees as they went. The lowlands, observed one settler, were so thick with underbrush "one could scarcely get through," and "man-eating bears" lurked in the woods.

Still, signs of civilization were cropping up everywhere. Dozens of small towns dotted the frontier, fields of corn swayed in the breeze, and smoke puffed from hundreds of cabin chimneys. "In a few years," settlers proudly predicted, "liberty will flourish for all."

AN UNDATED PHOTOGRAPH OF ABRAHAM'S FATHER, THOMAS LINCOLN

A stocky, well-built man with a shock of straight black hair and an unusually large nose, Thomas Lincoln was, remembered one neighbor, "a tinker— a piddler—always doing, but doing nothing great."

Thomas began life in Virginia but soon moved with his parents and four siblings (three brothers and a sister) to largely unsettled Kentucky. In 1786, when he was only eight years old, his father was killed by Indians. According to the law in those days, the eldest son would inherit the family farm; little Thomas was left not just fatherless but penniless as well. The next years were a struggle. Moving with his mother to the small town of Beech Fork, he became "a wandering, laboring boy," Abraham recalled. Thomas chopped wood, plowed fields, built cabinets—anything to earn enough to buy his first farm, a 238-acre tract of land near Mill Creek in Hardin County, Kentucky. Nearly illiterate, he "never did more than to bunglingly sign his own name," Abraham said later. Instead, Thomas spent his life searching for a plot of land that would make his life easier. He never found it.

A MODERN-DAY PORTRAIT OF ABRAHAM'S MOTHER, NANCY HANKS

Nancy Hanks was born in 1784 in what is now West Virginia and later moved to Kentucky with her mother, Lucy Hanks. Lucy was a seamstress, but who Nancy's father was, nobody knows. Her cousin Dennis Hanks once described Nancy as a woman with a "remarkable keen perception . . . shrewd, smart . . . highly intelligent by nature." But Nancy could not read or write. Whenever she had to sign a legal document she simply made her mark—that is, she scrawled an *X* in place of her name.

Like all frontier women, Nancy worked hard. She hoed the garden, shelled beans, fetched water from the spring a mile away, milked the cow, made soap, knitted socks, carried wood, and picked berries and crabapples. But no matter how hard or fast she worked, recalled Dennis Hanks, there never "seemed enough time to get it all done."

THIS CHURCH DOCUMENT RECORDS THOMAS AND NANCY'S MARRIAGE.

In 1806, twenty-six-year-old Thomas Lincoln decided it was time he found a wife. Riding into the nearby village of Elizabethtown, he presented himself to a woman he knew named Sarah Bush. But when he proposed marriage, Sarah said no. She thought Thomas "too shiftless, too ever-moving" to be a good husband. Undaunted, Thomas tried again two days later. This time he proposed to twenty-two-year-old Nancy Hanks, a girl he had known while living in Beech Fork. Nancy was willing, and on June 12, 1806, the couple took their vows in a one-room cabin packed with friends and neighbors. Afterward, the entire town celebrated by roasting a sheep over an open fire. One of the guests recalled that bear meat was also served, along with venison, wild goose, duck, and "maple sugar lumps tied on a string to bite off for coffee or whiskey." There was music and singing and dancing until dawn. Then, lifting his bride onto his horse, Thomas rode off toward his farm and a new life.

THE CABIN AT SINKING SPRING FARM, KENTUCKY, WHERE ABRAHAM WAS BORN IN 1809

On the twelfth of February—a Sunday—Thomas Lincoln suddenly appeared at his sister-in-law's cabin nearly two miles away.

"Nancy got a baby boy," he announced. It was the Lincolns' second child.

Ten-year-old Dennis Hanks remembered what happened next. "I cut and run . . . to see my new cousin. After all, babies wasn't as common as blackberries in the wood o' Kaintucky." When Dennis burst into the Lincoln cabin, he found Nancy "layin' thar in a bed o' poles and cornhusks. Tom'd built up a good fire and throwed a bear skin over the [covers] to keep 'em warm. . . . Mother came over and washed [the baby] an' put a yeller flannel petticoat on him, an' cooked some dried berries with wild honey for Nancy, an' slicked things up an' went home. An' that's all the fuss either of 'em got."

The baby—dark-haired and gray-eyed—was named Abraham, after Thomas's pioneer father.

A SISTER . . .

From the minute two-year-old Sarah Lincoln saw her baby brother, she was "crazy fer the tot," claimed Dennis Hanks. She rocked her infant brother in his cradle, and as he grew, she taught him how to pick blueberries and collect kindling. She snuggled next to him at bedtime and told him tales of bear hunts and buried treasure. When she turned eight, Sarah refused to attend school unless "little Abe" could go, too. She cried so long and so loud that her parents finally gave in. Days later, the youngsters set off down the dirt road. Sarah held Abraham's hand so "he didn't feel scaired," and at the schoolhouse she helped him learn his letters and numbers. "Yessiree," recalled Dennis Hanks, "Sairy and Abe was more'n brother and sister . . . [they] was best friends."

Dennis Hanks gave this description of young Abraham Lincoln:

Well, now, he looked just like any other baby at furst—like red cherry pulp squeezed dry. An' he didn't improve none as he growed older. Abe never was much fur looks. I ricollect how Tom joked about Abe's long legs when he was toddlin' around the cabin. He growed out o' his clothes faster'n Nancy could make 'em.

But he was mighty good comp'ny, solemn as a papoose, but interested in everything. An' he always did have fits o' cuttin' up. I've seen him when he was a little feller, settin' on a stool, starin' at a visitor. All of a sudden he'd bu'st out laughin' fit to kill. If he told us what he was laughin' at, half the time we couldn't see no joke.

Most o' the time he went bar'foot. Abe was right out in woods about as soon's he was weaned, fishin' in the creek, settin' traps fur rabbits an' muskrats, goin' on coon-hunts with Tom an' me an' the dogs, follerin' up bees to find bee-trees, an drappin' corn fur his pappy. Mighty interestin' life fur a boy.

ON KNOB CREEK

A PHOTOGRAPH TAKEN IN 1860 OF THE OLD CUMBERLAND TRAIL, THE ROAD THAT BROUGHT THE WORLD INTO THE LINCOLNS' CABIN

Even though Abraham had no memory of the farm where he was born, he remembered well the family's second cabin and the countryside around it. One of the farm's most remarkable features was that it stood on the Old Cumberland Trail, a pioneer road that passed from Louisville, Kentucky, to Nashville, Tennessee. Every day, caravans of pioneers passed by the Lincoln cabin—peddlers, preachers, farmers. And each had a tale to tell.

Night after night, Thomas Lincoln swapped stories with these travelers while his young son sat transfixed in the corner. But because he was a child, Abraham didn't understand everything the grown-ups were talking about. When everyone else had gone to bed, he would spend "no small part of the night," he later said, "walking up and down, and trying to make out what the exact meaning [was] of some of their, to me, dark sayings." Then he would translate their conversations until "I had put it into language plain enough for any boy I knew to comprehend." The next day, he would perform these rewritten stories for his friends, who were "mesmerized." It seems Abraham was already honing his great storytelling skills—skills that would become his stock-in-trade throughout his legal and political careers.

BRIEFLY, A BROTHER . . .

When Abraham was three, his mother gave birth to another boy, Thomas. But the baby lived only a few days. His father made him a grave marker by carving the initials *T.L.* into a fieldstone. Then the family gathered to bury the boy in a nearby cemetery.

◆ A CLOSE CALL ◆

Austin Gollaher, a childhood playmate, told this story of a Sunday with Abraham:

Abe and I played around all day. Finally, we crossed the creek to hunt for some partridges. . . . The creek was swollen by recent rain, and, in crossing on the narrow footlog, Abe fell in. Neither of us could swim. I got a long pole and held it out to Abe, who grabbed it. Then I pulled him ashore. He was almost dead, and I was badly scared. I rolled and pounded him in good earnest. Then I got him by the arms and shook him, the water pouring out of his mouth. By this means I succeeded in bringing him to, and he was soon all right.

Then a new difficulty confronted us. If our mothers discovered our wet clothes they would whip us. This we dreaded from experience. . . . It was June, the sun was very warm, and we soon dried our clothing by spreading it on the rocks about us.

A PHOTOGRAPH OF THE LINCOLNS' INDIANA CABIN TAKEN MANY DECADES AFTER THEY LIVED THERE

On a winter morning in 1816—a year so cold folks remembered it as "eighteen-hundred-and-froze-to-death"—Thomas Lincoln helped his wife onto a horse and mounted another, and with a child before each of them, they set out for Indiana. Troubled by legal disputes over land he had purchased, as well as the fact that Kentucky was a slave state—Thomas was morally opposed to slavery—he was off to start a new life.

The land Thomas claimed was on Little Pigeon Creek in a forest so thick he had to hack out a path for his family to follow. The woods, filled with bears and other threatening animals, scared seven-year-old Abraham. Years later, when he returned for a visit, he wrote a poem about it:

> *When first my father settled here,*
> *'Twas then the frontier line:*
> *The panther's scream, filled night with fear*
> *And bears preyed on the swine.*

Abraham had an ax put into his hands the very day they arrived at Pigeon Creek, and together father and son struggled to build the cabin. "From then until my twenty-third year, I was almost constantly handling that most useful instrument," Abraham recalled.

THE YOUNG SCRIBE

When Abraham arrived in Indiana, he could already read and write. The year before, his parents had sent him (along with Sarah) to a schoolhouse run by their neighbor, Caleb Hazel, who had taken a special interest in the eager, curious boy. For two brief months, he'd taught Abraham his letters and how to read a little. Excited by the learning, the boy had continued to teach himself. "He set everybody a-wonderin'," recalled a Knob Creek neighbor, "to see how much he knowed, and he not mor'n seven."

Now in Indiana, "he wrote words and sentences wherever he could. . . . He scrawled them with charcoal, he scored them in the dust, in the sand, in the snow—anywhere and everywhere," recalled one settler. When the boy's skill with a pen became public, "little Abraham was considered a marvel of learning and wisdom." Letter writing on the frontier, where there were few schoolhouses, was considered an accomplishment for an adult, but for a child it was almost unbelievable. (Historical records do not indicate whether Abraham's sister, Sarah, could write at this time, too.) Soon folks from all over the area traveled to the Lincoln cabin. They begged Abraham to write letters for them, and even paid him a few pennies for his trouble. "It was," said one historian, "a heady experience for such a young boy," and it showed him—early on—the importance of an education.

A WILD TURKEY LIKE THE ONE ABRAHAM SHOT JUST BEFORE HIS EIGHTH BIRTHDAY

One February afternoon in 1817, while Abraham's father was away, a flock of turkeys strutted into a clearing outside his cabin. Inside, Abraham grabbed his father's rifle, "shot through a crack and killed one of them." Proud of his marksmanship, he raced to collect his prize...then stopped short. The turkey, he saw, was beautiful! Guilt washed over him. How could he have killed something so majestic? "My early start as a hunter," he later recalled, "was never much improved afterward." In fact, he never again "pulled a trigger on any larger game."

THIS ENGRAVING PORTRAYS NANCY LINCOLN'S FUNERAL.

In the fall of the Lincolns' second year on Little Pigeon Creek, Nancy fell ill, suffering with dizziness, nausea, and severe stomach pains. Neighbors recognized it as "milk sickness," a mysterious ailment that settlers knew was somehow connected with the milk of their cows. (Years later, scientists discovered that the cows had eaten the poisonous snakeroot plant.) Because there were no doctors nearby, the Lincolns relied on old wives' tales and Native American remedies to cure Nancy. They desperately tried pipsissewa leaves, boneset tea, and a tonic of snake's head and wild cherry bark. Nothing worked. Knowing she was failing, Nancy called Sarah and Abraham to her bedside. "I am going away from you, Abraham," she told her son, "and I shall not return." Then she lapsed into a coma, and on October 5, 1818, she died.

Death in a one-room cabin in the wilderness was a grim experience for the survivors. Because the Lincolns had no near relatives, they assumed all the burial responsibilities themselves. The body was prepared in the very room in which the family lived. To form the crude coffin, Thomas whipsawed logs into planks, while nine-year-old Abraham whittled the wooden pegs to be used for nails. Then Abraham held the planks as his father hammered them together. Father and son put the coffin on a sled and dragged it to the burial site, where friends and neighbors had gathered. After the burial and a few simple prayers, Thomas placed fieldstones at the head and foot of the grave and carved the initials *N.L.* into the headstone. Then he and his two children headed down the hill toward their cold, lonely cabin.

"She was my angel mother," Abraham said years later. "All that I am, or hope ever to be . . . I owe to her."

CONSOLING HIS SISTER

Eleven-year-old Sarah tried to take over her mother's chores—cooking, cleaning, and sewing—but it was impossible. There was simply too much work for one little girl. "She'd get so sad and lonesome missin' her mother," recalled Dennis Hanks, that "she'd set by the fire and cry."

Abraham tried to cheer her up. He read comforting passages from the family Bible, made up funny stories, and even did tricks like standing on his head. Nothing worked. Finally, he decided she needed a pet. He "got 'er a baby coon, an' a turtle, an' tried to get a fawn, but [he] couldn't ketch any." This didn't make her smile, either. What she needed was something her brother couldn't catch her—a mother.

SARAH BUSH LINCOLN, THE STEPMOTHER ABRAHAM ADORED

Within a year of Nancy's death, unable to stand the loneliness of his dreary cabin, Thomas went back to Kentucky to find a new wife among the families he knew. Once more he looked up Sarah Bush, now Sarah Johnston, a widow with three small children of her own. "Well, Miss Johnston," said Thomas, "I have no wife, and you have no husband. I came . . . to marry you [and] I have no time to lose; if you are willin' let it be done straight off." This time Sarah had no arguments. The very next morning, December 2, 1819, the two were married, and that afternoon they headed for Little Pigeon Creek.

The arrival of his stepmother was a turning point in ten-year-old Abraham's life. Not only did she bring with her an amazing collection of household items—a feather bed; a walnut dresser; a table and chairs; knives, forks, and spoons; and a spinning wheel——that made the Lincoln children feel as if they had entered a world of incredible luxury, but she also brought her children: Elizabeth (thirteen), John D. (ten), and Matilda (eight). The youngsters put laughter and excitement back into the lonely Lincoln cabin and helped ease Abraham's sadness.

Touched by the sight of the ragged Lincoln children, Sarah immediately set to work. "She soaped—rubbed and washed the children clean so they looked pretty neat—well and clean," remembered Dennis Hanks, who at nineteen years of age had come to live with the Lincolns after ☞

Nancy died. Next, she turned her attention to the cabin, insisting Thomas finish the roof and put in a wooden floor. She had him cover the window with greased paper, build an upstairs loft for the boys, and make decent beds for all eight of the family members. "Cracky, but Aunt Sairy was some pumpkins," Dennis exclaimed years later. "Pret' soon, we had the best house in the country."

Maybe even more amazing, Sarah managed to blend the two families into one. She and Thomas would have no children of their own, but it didn't seem to matter. She loved Thomas's children, and grew especially fond of Abraham. "I never gave him a cross word in my life," she remembered. "His mind and mine . . . seemed to move together—move in the same channel."

Abraham loved Sarah, too. He called her Mama and took care of her until his dying day. "She had been his best friend in the world," a relative recalled, "and . . . no man could love a mother more than he loved her."

SCHOOL DAYS FOR ABRAHAM

ANDREW CRAWFORD'S SCHOOL, ONE OF THREE ABRAHAM ATTENDED

Sarah believed education was important, so when a teacher named Andrew Crawford opened a school in a cabin just one mile from the Lincolns' house, ten-year-old Abraham and his four siblings were enrolled.

Crawford's school was a "blab school"—that is, students recited their lessons out loud and all at the same time while the teacher listened through the noise for any errors. Abraham loved school, recalled one of his classmates. "He was always early and attended his studies . . . at the head of the class, he kept up his lessons even on Sunday."

Sadly, Abraham attended for only three months before Crawford gave up teaching and moved away. It was a whole year before James Swaney opened a school four miles from the Lincoln farm. Abraham longed to go. Because of the distance, as well as all the farm chores he had to do, he managed it only a few times each month. Seeing him walk into the schoolroom was memorable. "He wore buckskin breeches," remembered one of the girls who sat next to him, "and a cap made of the skin of a squirrel or coon. His breeches were baggy, and lacked by several inches meeting the tops of his shoes, thereby exposing his shinbone, sharp, blue and narrow!"

The next year, for about six months, he went to a school taught by Azel W. Dorsey in the old Crawford cabin. Dorsey taught Abraham to multiply, divide, and do fractions—higher mathematics that most people never mastered. With this solid foundation, he was able to continue teaching himself arithmetic even when his formal education ended. All told, he once said, "my schooling did not amount to one year."

THE TITLE PAGES OF SOME FAVORITE BOOKS READ BY ABRAHAM DURING HIS CHILDHOOD

Once he learned to read, Abraham "hankered after books," recalled his cousin Dennis. "Seems to me now I never seen Abe after he was twelve that he didn't have a book in his hand or in his pocket. . . . When noon came he'd set under a tree, an' read an' eat. An' when he come to the house at night, he'd tilt a chair back by the chimbley, put his feet on the rung, an' set on his back-bone an' read. . . . It didn't seem natural, nohow, to see a feller read like that . . . but Aunt Sairy declared Abe was goin' to be a great man some day, an' she wasn't goin' to have him hindered."

Books were scarce on the frontier. Other than Abraham's classroom texts, his first books were those that Sarah Bush Lincoln had brought with her from Kentucky. One was the family Bible. Abraham read it at times, "though not as much as more congenial books—suitable for his age," Sarah remembered. *The Pilgrim's Progress* was preferred, as was *Robinson Crusoe,* an exciting tale of being shipwrecked on a lonely island. But the book he loved best was *Aesop's Fables.* "He kept . . . Aesop's always within reach," one of his playmates recalled, "and read the [fables] over and over again." He memorized much of what he read. "Abe could easily learn and long remember," Sarah later said. Obviously, some of Aesop became ingrained in his mind, especially the tale of the lion and the four bulls with its moral: *A kingdom divided against itself cannot stand.*

MAN'S BEST FRIEND

Abraham borrowed, read, and returned every book he could get his hands on. Over and over he told his neighbors:

My best friend is the man who'll get me a book I ain't read.

A PAGE FROM THE "SUM" BOOK ABRAHAM MADE WHEN HE WAS FIFTEEN YEARS OLD

Because his time in the schoolroom was so limited, Abraham continued to educate himself. One way he did so was explained by his stepmother: "When he came across a passage [in a book] that struck him, he would write it down on boards if he had no paper, and keep it there till he did get paper, then he would rewrite it, look at it, repeat it. He had a copybook, a kind of scrapbook in which he put down all things and preserved them." In the corner of this book, he wrote the lines:

Abraham Lincoln
his hand and pen
he will be good but
god knows when.

GIFTED

Abraham knew he was different from those around him—unusually gifted and with great potential. Others recognized this, too. Recalled his schoolmate Nathaniel Grigsby, "Abe soared above us. He naturally assumed the leadership of the boys. He read and thoroughly read his books whilst we played. Hence he was above us and became our guide and leader." It was a role Abraham would assume again and again during his life.

This nineteenth-century lithograph shows a grown-up Abraham revisiting a grown-up Little Pigeon Creek.

By 1822—just six years after the Lincolns' arrival—two general stores had sprung up in Little Pigeon Creek. There were a tavern, a mill, and the newly built Pigeon Creek Baptist Church, which also served as the town's meeting hall.

There were plenty of people, too. Forty families with a total of ninety-four children now lived in the area—a far cry from the dark, lonely forest Abraham had moved into. Most came from Kentucky, and they formed a close-knit community that gathered to build barns, pull taffy, and sew quilts. Abraham probably met many of the neighbor children when he went with his father on his carpentry jobs, or when the family had callers.

And they had plenty. Sarah was a good cook, and neighbors flocked to her table, where Thomas told stories and gossiped for hours on end.

The Lincolns now had an impressive garden to help feed all those guests. In it they grew potatoes, turnips, cabbages, beets, and squash. Recalled one neighbor, "They had the best garden in the county—plenty of cucumbers and the largest watermelon I ever seen."

Yes, life in Indiana had grown easier. As Dennis Hanks once said, "By cracky, but Little Pigeon Creek got civilized."

FATHER AND SON

Thomas Lincoln didn't understand his son. Why was the boy so obsessed with books and learning? Whenever he found his son in the field reading a book or interrupting the other workers by reading passages aloud, Thomas would angrily snatch the book away. Then, recalled Dennis Hanks, he "would slash Abe for neglectin' his work" and destroy the book. Whipped by his father, Abraham "never balked, but dropt a kind of silent, unwelcome tear, as evidence of his . . . feelings."

As Abraham grew, his father became dependent on him for "farming, grubbing, hoeing, making fences." The boy resented having to do these heavy chores, and it showed. "He was lazy," said Dennis Hanks. "He was always reading—scribbling—ciphering—writing poetry." The neighbors agreed. "He was awful lazy," said one. "He was jest no hand to pitch in at work."

Perhaps Abraham wouldn't have resented these beatings so much if they had been balanced with hugs, kisses, and an occasional tousle of his hair. But Thomas Lincoln was a stolid man who could not give Abraham emotional support or show compassion. While neighbors described Thomas as a man who was good-humored, "loving everyone and every-

This modern-day sketch shows Thomas teaching Abraham some carpentry skills.

thing," this love didn't seem to extend to his son.

By his late teens, Abraham was itching to get away from his father. He resented everything Thomas represented—poverty, ignorance, dead-end jobs—and he couldn't keep his low opinion to himself. "[My father] grew up literally without education," Abraham later remarked scornfully. He "did nothing more than bunglingly learn to write his name," and he chose to live in a place where "there was absolutely nothing to excite ambition or education."

When Abraham could legally escape from his father's "cramped life," he never looked back. Over the years, he occasionally visited his father and stepmother, and he often sent money. But he didn't try to establish any close bonds, and neither did Thomas. "If we could meet now," a forty-year-old Abraham wrote to his father in 1849, "it is doubtful whether it would be more painful than pleasant."

Two years later, Thomas Lincoln died. Although Abraham, his only son, lived just seventy-five miles away, he did not attend the funeral. "Unable to simulate a grief I do not feel, I shall remain at home," he wrote.

THIS NINETEENTH-CENTURY DRAWING FROM HARPER'S WEEKLY MAGAZINE SHOWS ABRAHAM EARNING HIS FIRST DOLLAR.

As soon as he was old enough to earn wages (around the age of twelve), Abraham was hired out to his neighbors. One ran a ferry along the Anderson River, and Abraham spent a season with him, clearing land, splitting rails, butchering hogs, and doing whatever else was needed. For his labor, he earned about $6 a month (a little over $100 in today's dollars)—an amount he dutifully handed over to his father, as the law demanded.

When he wasn't working, young Abraham often wandered down to the river's edge, where he built himself a little flatboat. Lying on his back on the boat, he listened to the lapping water and dreamed of floating far, far away. One day, a steamship suddenly churned into view and "two men with trunks came down to the shore in carriages," remembered Abraham. " 'Will you take us and our trunks out to the steamer?' they asked." Abraham agreed. He sculled

them out, helped each aboard, and lifted their heavy trunks onto the deck. For his trouble, each gentleman tossed a silver half-dollar into the boat. "I could scarcely believe my eyes as I picked up the money," said Abraham. "I could scarcely credit that I, a poor boy, had earned a dollar in less than a day. . . . The world seemed wider and fairer before me."

BACKWOODS COMEDIAN

Young Abraham's sense of humor was well known to his neighbors, as these stories prove.

One day Thomas Lincoln's calf became mired in a swamp and died. He asked his son to take the calfskin down to the tannery and have it properly treated. Fourteen-year-old Abraham obeyed. Calfskin under his arm, he strolled into the shop and told the keeper, "My father wants his hide tanned."

<hr/>

After Sunday services, Abraham often jumped up on a nearby tree stump and parodied the proceedings. "Abe would take out the Bible and read a verse," recalled his stepsister Matilda, who with the other children would gather around to watch his show. "Then he would pretend to do the preaching, and we would pretend to do the crying." Thomas, however, was not amused, and he "would come out and make Abe quit—send him back to work."

<hr/>

As a teenager, Abraham attended all the dances in the county . . . but to tell stories, not to dance. "He was so odd and original and humorous and witty that all the boys would gather off at one side and listen to him tell jokes and spin yarns," remembered one frontiersman. To further entertain his friends, he did handsprings and cartwheels. These shenanigans annoyed the girls. Because of Abraham, "it was hard to get enough boys to stand a set," recalled one neighbor. "Yep," agreed Dennis Hanks. "Abe was always mighty popular with the boys, but the girls would jest as soon spit in his eye."

<hr/>

When Abraham was sixteen, he played a practical joke on his stepmother that became legendary. Sarah had just whitewashed the inside of the cabin, and everything sparkled—the walls, the floors, the ceiling. Feeling "pleased and proud as punch," she headed off to church. The moment she was out of sight, Abraham called to a barefoot neighbor boy wading outside in a mud puddle. Picking him up and holding him feetfirst, Abraham walked the child up one side of the cabin, across the ceiling, and down the opposite side. When Sarah returned, she took one look at the little footprints on her fresh white surfaces, gasped, and then "laughed to burst a seam," recalled Dennis Hanks. Once the fun was over, Abraham whitewashed the cabin again, the joke well worth the extra work.

THINKING ABOUT GOD

Abraham grew up in an intensely religious community. The Baptists held services three times a week, and in the summer, traveling preachers held fervent prayer meetings in which folks were often "taken with the spirit"—writhing, shaking, falling to the ground in convulsions. His own stepmother, Abraham recalled, "recited certain Bible verses as she went about her household chores." And his father said grace at every meal: "Fit and prepare us for humble service for Christ's sake, Amen."

In 1823, the Lincolns joined the Little Pigeon Creek Baptist church—everyone but fourteen-year-old Abraham. "Abe had no particular religion," his stepmother later said, "and didn't think of these questions at the time, if he ever did."

But Abraham *was* thinking about religion, and he was developing his own belief system—one that stayed with him the rest of his life. He called it the "Doctrine of Necessity," and explained it this way: "The human mind is impelled to action, or held in rest by some power, over which the mind itself has no control." He truly believed in fate—that a divine purpose was at work in his life, and that his destiny had been fixed in advance for all time.

While some people may have used the concept of predetermined fate as an excuse to achieve little, many historians believe it was behind some of Abraham's most beloved traits: his compassion, his tolerance, and his willingness to overlook other people's mistakes. After all, people were fated to make mistakes. Policies were fated to fail. It was all just part of God's plan. Such a faith allowed him to continue aspiring, achieving, and looking toward the future.

On January 20, 1828, twenty-one-year-old Sarah Lincoln Grigsby died in childbirth. Her nineteen-year-old brother, Abraham, heard the news while doing carpentry work at a neighbor's home. "I will never forget that scene," recalled one old-timer. "Abe sat down in the door of the smoke house and buried his face in his hands. The tears slowly trickled from between his bony fingers and his gaunt frame shook with sobs. We turned away."

Her death left a lasting mark on Abraham's mind and spirit. "From that moment on," he later said, "I felt very alone in the world." He began experiencing severe bouts of depression, remembered one neighbor, "laughing, then crying by turns." It was the beginning of a lifelong struggle with the illness.

This sketch shows Abraham grieving for his sister, Sarah.

Abraham was raised in a household that despised slavery. Thomas and Sarah Lincoln opposed it on religious grounds—they believed slavery was a sin—even though they lived in Kentucky, a slave state. When Thomas had difficulties establishing his land title, he looked for a place to live that did not depend on slave labor. That place was the territory of Indiana.

Abraham shared his parents' view. He was, he later said, "naturally anti-slavery . . . I cannot remember a time when I did not so think and feel." But he had little contact with slavery's horrors. None of his neighbors owned slaves or even came from slave-owning families. Though he may have seen slaves being driven south down the Old Cumberland Trail near Knob Creek, almost all his knowledge of slavery came from listening to his parents and reading newspapers and books.

One such book, William Grimshaw's *History of the United States,* which Abraham read at the age of twelve, denounced slavery as barbaric, uncivilized, and immoral. Stressing the importance of the American Revolution, the author appealed to his readers to "not only declare by words, but demonstrate by our actions, that 'all men are created equal.' "

On a trip down the Mississippi River in 1828, nineteen-year-old Abraham saw slavery up close for the first time. That year, he and his friend Allen Gentry filled a flatboat with meat, corn, and flour and floated it down the river for sale in New Orleans. Abraham had never gone beyond his wilderness neighborhood before, and New Orleans was by far the biggest city he had ever seen. He saw busy shops, brick buildings, wide avenues filled with horses and carriages. And everywhere he saw slaves. In those days one-third of all people living in New Orleans were slaves. It had to have been a life-changing experience. But curiously, Abraham left no record of this trip. Why? Some historians have speculated that the sight was too heartbreaking, too "unsettling and overwhelming."

Abraham returned to New Orleans three years later when he piloted yet another flatboat down the Mississippi. This time, he visited the city's slave market, where he witnessed men and women being sold like farm animals. According to one of his travel companions, John Hanks, he saw "Negroes in chains—whipped and scourged." In disgust, he watched as a young girl was auctioned off. Bidders pinched her flesh, pried open her mouth to count her teeth, and forced her to trot around the auction block so they could "satisfy themselves that the article they were buying," said Hanks, "was sound." Abraham found the whole event revolting. "By God, boys," he cried out, "let's get away from this. If ever I get a chance to hit that thing [meaning slavery], I'll hit it hard."

While this story may be more myth than fact (Hanks "remembered" being in New Orleans even though Abraham claimed his friend did not travel that far south), William Herndon, Abraham's future law partner, also claimed he heard his colleague talk about the experience. Said Herndon, "Against this inhumanity his sense of right and justice rebelled."

This nineteenth-century engraving of the New Orleans slave market shows the types of atrocities Abraham would have witnessed.

EARLY IN 1830, Thomas Lincoln decided to move his family again. He had heard glowing reports about the richness of Illinois farmland and believed he could make his fortune there. After selling his land, his hogs, and his corn, he gathered up the household and started off. There were Thomas and Sarah Lincoln in the first wagon, along with her son John D. Johnston. Cousin Dennis Hanks, his wife, and their four children were in the second wagon, while Abraham's stepsister Matilda rode in the third wagon with her husband and daughter. Abraham followed along on the family mule. Although he was now twenty-one and legally an adult, he remained with his father "out of obligation," with his stepmother "out of affection."

ABRAHAM SAVES HIS DOG.

The journey, Abraham later recalled, was "painfully slow and tiresome." Streams were swollen, and there were few bridges. At one crossing, Abraham's yellow dog, Honey, jumped from the wagon and broke through the ice. Because turning back would have taken too much time and been too dangerous, the dog was left to his fate. "But," said Abraham, "I could not bear to lose my little dog so I jumped out of the wagon and waded waist deep in the ice and water, and got hold of him, and helped him out and saved him." The little dog's happiness warmed his shivering master's heart. "His frantic leaps of joy and other evidences of a dog's gratitude amply repaid me for all the exposure I had undergone." Thus, dripping wet and clutching his dog, Abraham Lincoln arrived in Illinois.

HIDDEN GENIUS

In March 1830, the Lincolns settled along the Sangamon River in central Illinois. That summer they cleared fifteen acres of land, and Abraham split the logs to fence them in.

He spoke publicly about politics for the first time, too.

One day, a well-respected, highly educated politician made a campaign stop in a cornfield outside the village of Decatur. In the audience stood Abraham, "shambling and shabbily dressed," and working as a hired hand. At first, Abraham listened closely to the politician. But soon he began arguing, making points that were remarkably intelligent. "I could not believe such logic and reasoning was coming from the uncouth figure of that extraordinary hired hand," the politician recalled. "I was amazed, surprised . . . left breathless."

It was a pattern that would be repeated throughout Abraham's political life. People would form an initial impression based on his homeliness and Hoosier accent, only to be shocked when they recognized his intellectual powers. Recalled one Springfield citizen, "He disguised his genius in his backwoods roots."

GOOD-BY TO MA AND PA

In the summer of 1831–after the cabin had been raised and the fences had been built, and Abraham had taken his second boat trip to New Orleans–he left his parents' home for good. "Saying good-by to his father was easy," wrote poet and historian Carl Sandburg, "but it was not so easy to hug his mother and put his long arms around her, and lay his cheek next to hers and say he was going out into the big world to make a place for himself."

THIS MODERN-DAY PHOTOGRAPH OF A RESTORED NEW SALEM, ILLINOIS, SHOWS HOW THE TOWN LOOKED WHEN ABRAHAM ARRIVED IN JULY 1831.

Abraham always claimed he wound up in the tiny village of New Salem by accident. "I was," he said, "a piece of floating driftwood" accidentally washed ashore by the floodwaters of the Sangamon River. Actually, his flatboat got stuck on a nearby dam, and the whole town had turned out to watch the young giant struggle to save his craft. "He had his boots off, hat, coat and vest off. Pants rolled up to his knees and shirt wet with sweat and combing his fuzzie hair with his fingers as he pounded away on the boat," recalled one spectator. Unable to budge the flatboat, he bored a hole in the bow and unloaded enough of the boat's goods that the stern came up. When the water poured through the hole, the boat rose and floated over the dam. Townspeople marveled at Abraham's ingenuity. Abraham marveled at New Salem. With its one hundred residents, cooper's shop, mill, hatmaker, three general stores, and tavern, it was the biggest community he had ever lived in. Accepting a job as a clerk in Denton Offutt's general store, he cheerfully helped customers and—when no one was there—read and studied.

ABRAHAM ANNOUNCES HIS CANDIDACY FOR THE ILLINOIS STATE LEGISLATURE IN THIS AD FROM THE *SANGAMO JOURNAL*.

Folks in New Salem quickly grew fond of Abraham Lincoln. With the women he was courtly and helpful. With the men he gossiped and told funny stories. "When he talked," remembered one old-timer, "his countenance would brighten up, his eyes would sparkle, and he would explode in unrestrained laughter in which [we were all] compelled to take part." So popular was he that within only eight months of his arrival, his neighbors encouraged him to run for the state legislature.

Could he win? To be sure, the position wasn't an important one. In those days, state legislators needed no special education or previous experience. They dealt with simple issues such as whether or not cattle should be fenced or wells should be dug. Candidates did not even need the backing of a political party. Instead, they appealed directly to the voters, who chose their favorites. Still, Abraham was just twenty-three, with less than a year of formal education and no idea of how state government worked. As one resident of New Salem said, "Lincoln had nothing, only plenty of friends."

He decided to run and appealed directly to the public by placing an announcement in the local newspaper, the *Sangamo Journal,* which was distributed throughout the county. In it he declared himself in favor of local improvements, such as roads and canals. He also spoke in a folksy, down-home way that would become distinctly his own. "I was born and have ever remained in the most humble walks of life," he reminded the voters. If elected, he would work hard for the people. If defeated, he was "too familiar with disappointments to be very much chagrined."

The election was held in August, and Lincoln lost, finishing eighth in a field of thirteen candidates. Yet it pleased him that in New Salem, where folks knew him, he received 227 out of 300 votes.

A DISCHARGE PAPER SIGNED BY CAPTAIN ABRAHAM LINCOLN

In the spring of 1832, New Salem was shocked by news that Chief Black Hawk of the Sauk and Fox tribes had crossed the Mississippi River with five hundred armed braves. He intended, he said, to grow corn on the land stolen from his people almost thirty years earlier. Alarmed, Illinois's governor called for a thousand volunteers to fight them. In a fervor of patriotism (and the need for a paycheck), Abraham answered the call. He enlisted in a militia group made up of his neighbors and friends. To his delight, they elected him captain, even though he knew nothing about military matters. Once, when he saw his company marching directly into a fence, he couldn't remember how to order them to pass through the gate. "Halt!" he cried. "This company will break ranks for two minutes and form again on the other side of the gate."

I CERTIFY, That *David M Pantier* volunteered and served *as a private* in the Company of Mounted Volunteers under my command, in the Regiment commanded by Col. SAMUEL M. THOMPSON, in the Brigade under the command of Generals S. WHITESIDE and H. ATKINSON, called into the service of the United States by the Commander-in-Chief of the Militia of the State, for the protection of the North Western Frontier against an Invasion of the British Band of Sac and other tribes of Indians,—that he was enrolled on the *21st* day of *April* 1832, and was HONORABLY DISCHARGED on the *7th* day of *June* thereafter, having served *48 days*

Given under my hand, this *26th* day of *September* 1832

A Lincoln Capt

For three months his company marched and drilled. In all that time, they never met or fought a single Indian. But Abraham did admit to having "had a good many bloody struggles with the mosquitoes."

This photograph of the restored interior of the Berry-Lincoln store shows how it looks today.

In 1832, the Offutt store went bankrupt, and Abraham had to find another job. That's when his friend William Berry suggested they go into business for themselves. Buying another store's old stock on credit, they soon opened for business.

At the Berry-Lincoln store, people could buy pots, plates, glassware, calico, ox yokes, and a small selection of shoes. But the store had few customers, which left Abraham with lots of time to read. He devoured poetry and developed a deep love for Shakespeare's plays. However, his real interest was in the use and structure of language. When he learned that someone had a copy of *English Grammar* by Samuel Kirkland—considered to be the best guide—Abraham walked six miles to borrow it. For months afterward, he studied every passage, asked his friends to test his mastery, and memorized long sections. This, Abraham said in 1860, taught "[me] to speak and write as well as I do now."

All this study was good for his education but not good for business. Before long, the store "winked out," said Abraham. Jobless once more, he was also saddled with a $1,100 debt (about $25,000 in today's dollars)—a huge amount for someone who earned only $2 to $3 a month (about $45 a month today). Abraham called it "the national debt" and vowed to repay every cent. He would spend the next fifteen years doing just that.

A LETTER FROM POSTMASTER LINCOLN

After both his store and his bid for the state legislature failed, Abraham needed to find work. But where? His New Salem friends solved his problem. They presented him with the position of village postmaster (after persuading the previous postmaster to resign). "I never saw a man better pleased," recalled the town doctor. Abraham would now "have access to all the newspapers of the day."

STRUGGLING TO MAKE ENDS MEET

The position of postmaster provided only a few dollars each month. To supplement his meager income, Abraham split rails, helped in the mill, gave neighboring farmers a hand at harvesting, and took whatever additional work came his way. When John Calhoun, the county surveyor, offered to make him his assistant, Abraham jumped at the chance. He threw himself into studying geometry and trigonometry—knowledge that was important to a surveyor. Then he scraped together enough money to buy a compass and a chain and, as he said, "went at it." Within six weeks he had taught himself enough to start his new job.

Surveying was physically demanding work. On a typical day, Abraham pushed through briar patches and slogged through swamps in order to lay out roads and townsites and to mark off property boundaries. Often he returned home with his clothes ripped and his face scratched. A surveyor usually got $2.50 for each quarter section of land he surveyed. If he worked hard, he could make almost $10 a week (about $230 in today's dollars). Often, though, pay was in goods. For his first surveying job, Abraham received two buckskins, which one of his neighbor's wives "foxed" onto the seat of his pants to "protect his more sensitive parts from the briars."

As Abraham gained experience, he took on jobs that were more and more difficult. Soon he was laying out roads and towns. All of his work was accurate. "When any dispute arose," said one old-timer, "Mr. Lincoln's compass and chain always settled the matter satisfactorily."

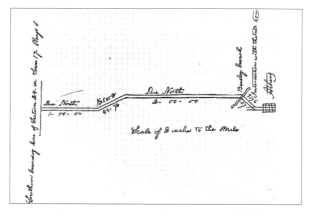

A survey done by Abraham in 1836

ABRAHAM'S FIRST LOVE

When Abraham was twenty-five years old he fell in love with Ann Rutledge, daughter of the man who had founded New Salem. Ann, recalled her cousin, "was a beautiful girl . . . well educated for that early day, a good conversationalist, and always gentle and cheerful."

How their romance developed is a mystery. No letter from Ann is known to exist, and in the thousands of pages of correspondence Abraham left behind, there is not a single mention of her name. Still, most historians believe Ann and Abraham decided to wed sometime in 1835. Since Abraham was still trying to figure out how to make a living, however, the couple agreed to wait a year. Then tragedy struck. In August, Ann fell ill with what was probably typhoid. For weeks she lingered between life and death. New Salem residents later recalled that Ann insisted on seeing Abraham, even though her doctor had prescribed absolute quiet. What did the young lovers say to each other? No one knows. But a few days later she lapsed into a coma and died.

Ann's death plunged Abraham into another deep depression. He "slept not . . . ate not . . . joyed not," recalled one neighbor. He cried often, and confessed to a friend "that he could not bear the idea of its raining on her grave."

A PHOTOGRAPH OF ABRAHAM'S SECOND LOVE, MARY OWENS

Sometime in 1834 or 1835, Abraham met Mary Owens, the daughter of a well-to-do Kentucky family who had come to New Salem for the summer. Mary "was tall, portly, had large blue eyes and the finest trimmings I ever saw," remembered one resident, and she impressed everyone with her wit and charm, especially Abraham. "If ever that girl comes back," he told a friend when Mary returned to Kentucky in the fall, "I'm going to marry her."

Mary did come back about a year after Ann Rutledge's death, and the two began courting. They attended dances, took long walks, and read poetry to one another. But soon small events began to point to differences between them. Once while out horseback riding with a group of young people, they came to a treacherous stream. All the men gallantly helped their ladies across—all but Abraham. He rode on without once looking back.

"I suppose you did not care whether my neck was broken or not?" Mary said when she caught up to him.

Oafishly, he replied, "You're plenty smart to take care of yourself."

Mary soon concluded, "Mr. Lincoln was deficient in those little links that make up a woman's happiness."

Abraham was having second thoughts, too. "Now when I beheld her, I could not avoid thinking of my mother," he later wrote, "and this, not from withered features, for her skin was too full of fat to permit its contracting into wrinkles, but from her want of teeth, her weather-beaten appearance . . . and from a kind of notion in my head that *nothing* could have commenced at the size of infancy, and reached her present bulk in less than thirty-five or forty years."

Although there was no definite understanding between them, Abraham felt honor-bound to marry her. "I had told her sister I would take her for better or worse," he said, "and I made a point . . . to stick to my word."

For six months after Mary returned to Kentucky, Abraham wrote her letters that were "dry and stupid," hoping she would find him so idiotic she would break off their relationship. When she didn't, he tried a more straightforward approach. "I now say that you can drop the subject [of marriage], dismiss your thoughts of me, and leave this letter unanswered without calling forth one accusing murmur from me," he wrote her. This time Mary took him up on his offer. But to his surprise, instead of feeling relieved, Abraham felt mortified. "My vanity was deeply wounded that she who I had taught myself to believe no body else would have, had actually rejected me." The affair, he concluded, had taught him to "never again think of marrying; and for this reason; I can never be satisfied with any one who would be blockheaded enough to have me."

ONE OF ABRAHAM'S PAY STUBS FOR HIS SERVICES AS LEGISLATOR IN THE ILLINOIS GENERAL ASSEMBLY

Financial pressures forced Abraham back into politics—he truly needed the $245 (about $5,000 in today's dollars) that legislators earned yearly—and in 1834 he decided to run for the Illinois legislature again. This time he refused to issue any statements or publish any speeches. Instead, he embarked on a handshaking campaign, stopping to greet and talk with voters in every part of the county. At one farm he went out into the field to meet some thirty men who were at work harvesting grain. The men grumbled that they could never vote for a man who couldn't hold his own in a field. "Boys," said Abraham, "if that is all, I am sure of your votes." And taking up the sickle, he easily led the harvesters all around the field. It was this charm and ease that won him the seat. This time he was chosen, remembered Abraham, "by the highest vote cast for any candidate."

A few weeks after the election, the twenty-five-year-old legislator climbed into a stagecoach and headed for the state capital, Vandalia. For the next three months—from December 1 to February 13—Lincoln lived in a rented room that he shared with two other legislators, and he went to work each day on the ground floor of the dilapidated statehouse. (The building was in such bad shape that lawmakers were occasionally hit in the head by chunks of falling plaster!) Most of his work was routine. During that first session, Lincoln voted to appropriate $2.50 to fix the statehouse stoves, granted permission for a man named Clayton Bell to legally change his name to Clayton Elder Bell, and helped pass a bill encouraging the killing of wolves.

When the session closed, he returned to New Salem. In his pocket was more money than he had ever had before. But it wasn't nearly enough to pay off his debts. Abraham went back to surveying and delivering the mail.

NEW EVIDENCE AT NEW SALEM

As the traditional story goes, Abraham flitted from job to job during his time in New Salem. After years of struggling to make ends meet, he rode off to Springfield—on a borrowed horse and with only a few dollars in his pocket—where he finally made good. But new evidence may change this story. In 2006, Thomas Schwartz, interim director of the Abraham Lincoln Presidential Library, discovered an 1830s legal document in the library's archives. It revealed that Abraham actually owned a half interest in two lots, as well as a house in New Salem. "Lincoln invested in this community in a way the traditional story ignores," said Schwartz. "Obviously, he was much more active than just standing around in the store, telling jokes and going bankrupt. This shows a lot of hard work."

Discovery of the document led to an archeological dig in a vacant lot at New Salem State Park. Scientists searched for evidence that there had indeed been a home where the document claimed Abraham's house once stood. Among the tiny but important pieces of history they eventually unearthed were window and bottle glass, a shell button, pottery fragments, and a slate pencil—proof that a structure had stood there. Taken together, the document and archeological evidence are forcing historians to reconsider Lincoln's early years. "We will have to go back and relook at our whole understanding of him and New Salem," said Schwartz.

LAWYER LINCOLN

While serving in the state legislature, Abraham was encouraged by John T. Stuart—a rising young attorney from Springfield, Illinois—to study law. The idea intrigued Abraham. For years, he had hung around frontier courthouses, watching country lawyers "bloviate and bluster." He had even drafted wills and created deeds for neighbors who were unable to write. The law would allow him to earn a respected place in the community, to live by his intellect instead of by hard physical labor. But could he really become a lawyer with so little formal education?

The answer was yes. In those days, a person did not have to attend law school to become a lawyer. Instead, he simply read law in the office of a practicing attorney until he knew enough to pass the state bar exam, allowing him to practice law on his own. Abraham studied by himself. He "borrowed books from Stuart, took them home, and went at it in good earnest," he later said. For three years he analyzed and memorized Illinois's laws. He still did some surveying to pay his bills until March 1, 1837, when he hung up his compass and chain forever. On that day, he passed the bar exam. Abraham Lincoln was now a full-fledged lawyer.

A PHOTOGRAPH OF LINCOLN'S NEW HOMETOWN, SPRINGFIELD, ILLINOIS, LOOKING MUCH AS IT DID WHEN HE MOVED THERE IN 1837

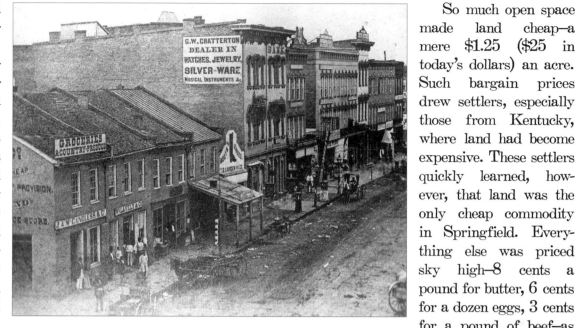

On April 15, Abraham Lincoln rode into Springfield on a borrowed horse. He carried $7 in his pocket and his few belongings—a coonskin cap, a homespun shirt, a comb, several books, and a bowie knife—in his saddlebags. He came not only to continue his old duties as a state legislator (this was the year the state capital had been moved from Vandalia to Springfield) but also to take up new duties as a partner in the law office of his old friend John T. Stuart.

So much open space made land cheap—a mere $1.25 ($25 in today's dollars) an acre. Such bargain prices drew settlers, especially those from Kentucky, where land had become expensive. These settlers quickly learned, however, that land was the only cheap commodity in Springfield. Everything else was priced sky high—8 cents a pound for butter, 6 cents for a dozen eggs, 3 cents for a pound of beef—as

Springfield wasn't much to look at in the early part of the nineteenth century. It remained a raw, unsettled prairie town, with some of its buildings still made of logs. The roads—wide but unpaved—were muddy quagmires in winter and suffocatingly dusty in summer. Wooden slats were used in place of sidewalks, forcing pedestrians to leap from one board to the next so as not to step in the manure left behind by the freely roaming hogs.

The prairie pushed right up to the edge of town, making it feel as if it were an island on a sea of tall grass. Noted one visitor, "It is all prairie, everywhere I look . . . prairie, prairie, and cultivated fields a mere speck on its surface."

merchants attempted to profit from the growing population. And this was at a time when the average laborer earned about $6 a week!

That year, the town boasted a population of around 1,500. The courthouse—soon to be replaced by the new capitol building—was surrounded by nineteen dry goods stores, seven groceries, four drugstores, two clothing stores, and one bookstore. Four hotels catered to the politicians pouring into town, while six churches prayed for their souls. If a citizen needed medical attention, he could choose from among eighteen doctors. And if he needed legal help, twelve lawyers were on hand, including Abraham.

JOSHUA SPEED, ABRAHAM'S FIRST FRIEND IN SPRINGFIELD

THE FIRST THING Abraham did when he arrived in Springfield was stop in at Ellins & Company General Store. One of the proprietors, Joshua Speed, looked up when the bell above the door tinkled and saw one of the saddest-looking men he had ever laid eyes on. "I never saw so gloomy and melancholy a face in my life," he said.

Abraham leaned on the counter and asked how much a single mattress with sheets and pillow would cost. When Speed said $17, Abraham sighed. "It is probably cheap enough," he said, "but I want to say that cheap as it is, I have not the money to pay. But if you will credit me until Christmas, and my experiment here as a lawyer is a success, I will pay you then. If I fail . . . I will probably never pay you at all."

Taking pity on the sad stranger, Speed came up with an alternative plan. "I have a very large room," said Speed, "and a very large double bed in it, which you are perfectly welcome to share with me if you choose."

Abraham perked up. "Where is your room?" he asked.

Speed pointed to the winding stairs that led from the store to the second floor. "Upstairs."

Without another word, Abraham picked up his saddlebags, went upstairs, dropped them in the middle of the floor, came down again, and with a grinning face announced, "Well, Speed, I am moved."

From that moment, recalled Speed, they were "everlasting friends."

Abraham Lincoln's life in Springfield had begun.

CHAPTER TWO
BLUEGRASS GIRL

My whole childhood was desolate.

—MARY LINCOLN IN A LETTER TO A FRIEND,
MAY 1871

A PARADE MARCHES DOWN THE CENTER OF LEXINGTON, KENTUCKY, IN 1818—THE YEAR MARY TODD WAS BORN.

Because Lexington was located in the heart of the wilderness, travelers to the city expected to find savage Indians, wild animals, and wooden shacks. Instead, to their amazement, they found elegant Georgian homes, wide, stately streets, and a city of cultural refinement. In 1780, Lexington's founders had established Transylvania University because, as one settler put it, "I cannot educate my children in the country." The university quickly became the city's center, providing public enlightenment through lectures, debates, and French and Latin lessons. So educated did Lexington's population become that guidebooks of the day referred to the city as the "Athens of the West."

MARY'S FATHER, ROBERT SMITH TODD

Born in 1791, Robert Todd grew up in a twenty-room brick mansion set among formal gardens and cultivated fields. Thirty slaves worked those fields, managed the livestock, polished the silver, wiped the china, and dusted the library's shelves of leather-bound books. After studying law at Transylvania University, Robert set out to make his mark. The name Todd opened doors in Lexington, and he was soon offered a partnership in a lucrative grocery business. He was also elected clerk of the Kentucky House of Representatives, a position that had little to do with politics and everything to do with popularity. So popular was Robert that he held the position for more than twenty years.

A charming man, he enjoyed the good things in life—expensive clothing, private carriages, rare brandies—and he did not scrimp when providing for his own family. All of his children, little Mary included, would learn to consider fashionable dress, piano lessons, Persian rugs, country estates, and mahogany-furnished double parlors a natural part of everyday life.

AND WHAT DID MRS. TODD DO?

Much less is known about Eliza Parker Todd's early life. Like her husband, she grew up in a Lexington mansion, waited on by slaves. From an equally prominent family, Eliza had known and socialized with Robert since childhood. At the age of eighteen, she married him and set about having babies. Firstborn was Elizabeth (1813), followed by Frances (1816), Mary (1818), Levi (1819), Robert (1821), Ann (1824), and George (1825).

Meanwhile, Aunt Chaney, one of the family's slaves, did all the cooking. Nelson drove the carriage, served in the dining room, and did the marketing. Other slaves swept, dusted, polished, and tended the garden. Above all, there was Mammy Sally, who took care of the children's every need. When Eliza wasn't pregnant or nursing, she busied herself with Lexington's social scene—paying and receiving morning calls, taking afternoon drives, shopping on Main Street, attending parties. Like other white women in Lexington, she had little to do except "read a few romances," said one neighbor, "and devote what free time she had to dress, in which she displayed a great deal of taste."

A PHOTOGRAPH OF THE HOUSE WHERE MARY TODD WAS BORN, TAKEN SHORTLY AFTER A FIRE DESTROYED ITS ROOF

Robert and his wife looked forward to the birth of their third child in 1818. When Eliza's time came on December 13—a rainy Sunday—she retired to an upstairs bedroom. Robert quickly summoned the best and most expensive midwife in Lexington, who encouraged Eliza with talk, gave her sips of mulled wine, and caught the baby when the moment finally arrived.

It was a girl—a pink-cheeked, brown-eyed daughter her parents named Mary Ann. (Her middle name was dropped when her sister Ann Maria was born.)

A GLIMPSE OF LITTLE MARY

Mary's cousin Lizzie Humphreys gave this description of Mary as a child:

Mary in those days was called a "tomboy." She was always playing pranks, and was the fearless and inventive leader in every possible kind of mischief. . . . Her cheeks were as pink as tea roses and they dimpled when she smiled. Her blue eyes sparkled with excitement. She chattered busily and constantly about her friends, her family. . . . She told colorful stories, and without meaning to wound, she now and then could not restrain a witty or sarcastic remark that cut deeper than she intended. . . . She was impulsive and made no attempt to conceal her feelings; indeed, that would have been impossible for her face was an index to every passing emotion.

THIS NINETEENTH-CENTURY DAGUERREOTYPE SHOWS A CHILD HOLDING A DOLL SIMILAR TO THE ONE MARY LOVED.

In 1824, Mary's father returned home from a monthlong trip to New Orleans with presents—pewter jacks for Levi, a book of poetry for Elizabeth, and a porcelain-faced doll for six-year-old Mary. Years later, she recalled that it "squeaked entrancingly when pressed on its little stomach." Thinking the squeak "sounded like 'Mama,' I hugged my baby with love and pride."

Mary's doll went everywhere—through the woods in search of mushrooms, under Grandma Parker's front porch, up the big chestnut tree that grew in the front yard. Soon the doll's tiny dress grew shabby. So Eliza bought her daughter some "lovely, sheer, embroidered pink muslin" and directed one of the slaves to teach the girl how to sew. At first, remembered Mary, "I made [the doll] clothes, clumsily put together." But soon she developed a real talent for sewing. Recalled one Todd cousin, "[Mary] used her needle with artistic effect . . . the only one of the family of girls who ever did." This love of sewing would last a lifetime.

ENGRAVINGS LIKE THIS ONE FROM A NINETEENTH-CENTURY MAGAZINE SENSATIONALIZED INDIAN ATTACKS ON KENTUCKY SETTLERS AND TERRIFIED MARY.

One summer day Mary was with relatives at their country estate when a band of friendly Cherokees passed by. All the Todd children had been brought up on gruesome tales of ancestors who had been scalped or tomahawked. Mary had heard how her uncle Sam Todd had been captured by the Shawnee and held for three years before managing to escape, and how her uncle John Todd had been pierced in the back by arrows. So when she glanced out the window and saw the Native Americans approaching, she became hysterical.

Screaming, she tried frantically to find a place to hide. First, she crouched in the open fireplace, "but," said her cousin, "this seemed too big a place for such a slender little girl." She dashed out to find another hiding place. But the Indians were closer now, and her fear was paralyzing. Panicked, all she could do was stand in the center of the room, cover her eyes, and shriek, "Hide me, oh my Savior, hide me!" as the friendly Indians walked by. For the rest of her life, she would shout these words whenever fear overcame her.

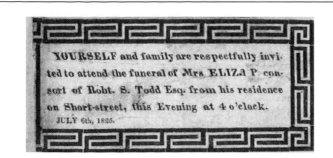

ELIZA TODD'S FUNERAL CARD

On July 4, 1825, while the rest of Lexington celebrated Independence Day, Eliza gave birth to her seventh child—a boy named George. Robert was ecstatic. But his joy quickly turned to sorrow. Within hours of the birth, Eliza developed a fever. Robert immediately sent for two doctors from Transylvania University. They treated Eliza with the prescribed therapies of the day—calomel (a mercury compound) to induce vomiting, laudanum (an opiate) to reduce cramping, and bloodletting to reduce infection. These treatments probably did nothing but make Eliza worse, and by the following morning she was dead.

Six-year-old Mary, along with her brothers and sisters, were brought into the death room to say goodbye. Bewildered, little Mary didn't understand that her mother was gone, and kept asking when she was going to wake up. No one answered her. The other children were too overwhelmed by their own grief to offer much comfort, and Robert was already making burial arrangements. Only Mammy Sally gave any consolation. As she tucked Mary into bed that night, she told her how the ghosts of loved ones came back to protect their family. Ever after, Mary would believe in a spirit world.

The next day Robert sent printed cards inviting friends to his wife's burial "from his residence on Short-street, this Evening at 4 o'clock, July 6th 1825." The funeral began in the family parlor. As family and friends gathered around the coffin, the minister said a few prayers. Afterward, everyone followed as the body was carried to a nearby church cemetery. Here the minister gave a brief eulogy, reminding those present that "resurrection in heaven was better than life on earth." Little Mary couldn't grasp this concept. She clung to the notion that her mother would return, and when she didn't, Mary was left feeling sad, abandoned, and very frightened.

ELIZABETH HUMPHREYS TODD, THE STEPMOTHER MARY DESPISED

After Eliza's death, Robert was left with six children (fourteen-month-old Robert had died the year before of a lung infection), nine slaves, and a twelve-room mansion to manage. He needed a wife—and quickly. But a prominent man such as Robert didn't marry just anyone. It had to be someone suitable in wealth and breeding, someone like twenty-seven-year-old Elizabeth Humphreys of Frankfort, Kentucky.

Robert knew the Humphreys family by reputation. After all, they ruled Frankfort society. Admired for their virtue, intelligence, and good taste, the Humphreys women hosted elaborate tea parties and elegant soirees, while the men held powerful jobs as judges, governors, and United States senators. The family was eager to see their Elizabeth wed to Robert.

On November 1, 1826, the two were married in an elaborate ceremony attended by Elizabeth's friends and family, while the Todd children remained in Lexington. A week later, they met their new mother. Elizabeth may have been elegant and educated, but she wasn't warm or loving. An exacting woman with strict views on proper manners and dress, she found her stepchildren sadly lacking in the social graces. "It takes seven generations to make a lady," she told the Todd girls snootily. "You are six generations short."

Eight-year-old Mary presented a special challenge. Described as a "bundle of nervous energy," Mary had moods that changed so swiftly, one cousin said she was like "an April day, sunning all over with laughter one moment, then crying as though her heart would break the next." She was also "willful and original in planning mischief," recalled a childhood friend. Once, after Mary intentionally put salt in her coffee, Elizabeth called her "a limb of Satan." The label stuck. For the next ten years, Elizabeth humiliated Mary by calling her this name in front of friends and family alike.

Soon, however, Elizabeth had her own children to prefer over the ill-behaved first Todds. Over the next twenty years, she gave birth to nine children—four boys and five girls. No wonder Mary felt "abandoned, unloved and often forgotten."

A FASHION PLATE FROM GODEY'S LADY'S BOOK SIMILAR TO THE ONES THAT FASCINATED MARY

Even as a child, Mary had an interest in fashion. She loved to flip through the pages of *Godey's Lady's Book*—a popular women's magazine of the nineteenth century. One day, recalled her cousin Lizzie, ten-year-old Mary "became fascinated by the lovely bouffant summer dresses that puffed so entrancingly on the hoopskirted ladies of the period." She *had* to have one! But she knew her stepmother would never allow it: hoopskirts were only for grown-up ladies. At last, Mary found a way. Stretching a large skirt over weeping willow branches, she managed to fashion a slightly lopsided dress. Still, Mary was proud of her effort. She could hardly wait to wear it to church the next day.

But in the morning, just as Mary reached the front door, her stepmother came down the hall. "What a fright you are," she cried. "Take that awful thing off." Mary wept angry tears. "She thought she had been treated badly," recalled her cousin, "and freely said so."

The hoopskirt incident soon became "a standing joke in the family," said one of the Todds, "a fine opportunity for the gleeful teasing of the boys who presented her with [willow] switches . . . and made insulting suggestions as to how the switches should be applied."

MARY'S STYLISH STEPGRANDMOTHER, MRS. ALEXANDER HUMPHREYS

One day in June 1828, nine-year-old Mary settled in beside cousin Lizzie on the leather seat of the Todd carriage. Nelson, their slave, lashed their trunks to the back of the rig, then whipped the horses into a sedate trot. The girls were on their way to spend a week with Mary's stepgrandmother in Frankfort, Kentucky.

When they arrived, they were met by a white-gloved butler who led them to their room. For the next seven days, Mary wore white organdy dresses with blue sashes, played in the garden, and drank lemonade from a massive silver tea service.

One evening, her stepmother gave a ball. Mary and Lizzie were allowed to stay up late and admire the ladies in their silk gowns. Grandmother Humphreys, Mary decided, was the height of fashion. She even tried to mimic the woman's elegant manners and haughty airs. "If I can only be, when I am grown up, just like Grandmother Humphreys, I will be perfectly satisfied with myself," she told people when she returned to Lexington.

A PHOTOGRAPH OF THE TODDS' FAVORITE VACATION SPOT, CRAB ORCHARD SPRINGS

Every summer, like other members of fashionable society, the Todds packed their trunks and traveled to the fancy hotel at Crab Orchard Springs, some seventy-five miles away. For four weeks, they swam in the mineral water springs (guaranteed to cure almost every ailment), played croquet on the hotel's front lawn, went for long walks, ate lavish meals prepared by French chefs, and attended balls and plays. Mary always looked forward to this trip. Remembered Lizzie Humphreys, "How exciting we thought it all was . . . the meeting with old friends and acquaintances; the new arrivals each day driving up with jingling harness and prancing horses; the finely dressed ladies stepping mincingly down the carriage steps . . . the Negro fiddlers . . . the flickering candlelight . . . the freedom from school tasks . . . How we hated to go back."

THE TITLE PAGE OF THE BOOK THAT CHANGED MARY'S FUTURE

The Todd family's library was filled with leather-bound books by Shakespeare, Sir Walter Raleigh, and Plato, along with a well-worn copy of *A Vindication of the Rights of Woman* by Mary Wollstonecraft. In this book the author argued that education was a natural right for girls—a radical idea in the first half of the nineteenth century. Only one out of every four American girls received more than four years of formal education, and those who did usually didn't study anything more serious than etiquette, conversation, and the decorative arts.

After reading Wollstonecraft's book, Mary's father was convinced Mary should receive "a substantial rather than ornamental education." While his other daughters were also given formal educations, it was Mary—with her sharp mind—who studied mathematics and philosophy. Of course, Mr. Todd didn't expect his daughter to use this education; she wasn't going to take up a profession. He believed its purpose was to attract a better husband. "If you do not study now," he once threatened, "after your marriage, your mind will collapse and you will fail to amuse your husband."

Still, Mr. Todd's unconventional views guaranteed Mary Todd an education unmatched by her peers. For the rest of her life, she was almost always the most highly educated woman (or person, for that matter) in the room.

A PHOTOGRAPH OF THE FIRST SCHOOL MARY ATTENDED

When Mary turned eight, her father sent her to the innovative Shelby Female Academy, located two blocks from the Todd home. Run by the highly respected Reverend John Ward, it advertised itself as "a complete system of female education." Besides reading, writing, and the basics of mathematics, Mr. Ward also taught geography, philosophy, elocution, and French. His wife and sisters added the necessary female embellishments, teaching painting and embroidery. And every Thursday, Mrs. Ward took the girls into the kitchen, where she taught them to cook from what one pupil described as "her book with many receipts in it."

For the next six years, Mary studied and thrived here. She especially like the early-morning classes Mr. Ward held during the summer months. One morning just before daybreak a watchman saw fourteen-year-old Mary hurrying down Second Street. Since it was not uncommon for girls of this age to marry, he believed he had uncovered an elopement (considered highly immoral in those days) and chased after her. Much to the amusement of the other students and the annoyance of Mr. Ward, a breathless Mary burst into the schoolroom followed by the red-faced watchman, club in hand. Only love, the watchman believed, could make a girl move that fast. But it wasn't love that had sent Mary hurrying down the street; it was the pleasure of putting her quick mind to use, the joy of learning. Mary's cousin remembered how Mary "pored over her schoolbooks by candlelight." And a classmate recalled her as "far in advance over the other girls . . . she had a retentive memory and a fine mind that enabled her to grasp and understand thoroughly."

A CONTINUING EDUCATION

By the time Mary turned fourteen—the age at which most girls ended their formal education—things had changed drastically at the Todd house. Not only was Elizabeth expecting her fourth child, but the family was moving to an even larger home on Main Street. Elizabeth was rapturous. At last she would have a house befitting a Humphreys! The last thing she wanted was temperamental Mary ruining it all. But what to do with her? Elizabeth came up with an unusual idea.

Every Monday for the next four years, Nelson drove Mary the one and a half miles to Madame Charlotte Mentelle's boarding school. While other students from Lexington returned home each evening, Mary stayed over. On Friday Nelson returned in the carriage to bring her home for the weekend.

Poor Mary must have known she was being purposely exiled. Still, she soon fell in love with her new school. There were only twenty-two students, and those who actually lived in Madame Mentelle's home received plenty of attention from the headmistress—something Mary both craved and needed.

Besides reading, writing, history, and philosophy, Mentelle's taught French. Mary became so proficient that she was given the lead in many of the school's French plays. "At different times," Mary's cousin later wrote, "French gentlemen came to [Transylvania] University to study English, and when one was fortunate enough to meet Mary, he was surprised and delighted to find her a fluent conversationalist."

Mary also discovered the joy of reading. She took great pleasure in standing in the Mentelle library and scanning the volumes, choosing books and pulling them off the shelf. She especially loved poetry and was "forever reciting," even though "this was the cause of many a jest among her friends," who thought she was showing off. "Mary Todd," admitted one classmate, "was the brightest girl in Madame Mentelle's school, always had the highest marks, and took the biggest prizes."

But it was the activities outside the classroom that really made Mary's days happy. With her schoolmates, she gossiped and strolled through the school's gardens. At night, Madame Mentelle played the violin while her two daughters taught the girls "cotillions, rounds, and hop waltzes . . . and other graceful dance steps." And on holidays and special occasions, the girls—dressed in white organdy—marched in the local parades. No wonder Mary later admitted that "my early home was truly at boarding school."

A PORTRAIT OF MADAME CHARLOTTE MENTELLE

Opinionated, eccentric, tough-minded, and intellectual, Madame Mentelle became an extraordinary role model for smart, vulnerable Mary Todd. Madame Mentelle never tired of using her own life to terrify and enlighten her students. In bloodthirsty detail, she recalled how she had fled Paris in 1792 after the September massacres—a time during the French Revolution when hundreds of wealthy citizens were being executed. Arriving in Lexington with her husband and two daughters, she had quickly decided that it "has no amiable virtues—its citizens have terrible manners and will never be equal with . . . the sensitive French." Still, Madame continued, her family settled in, and before long she opened a school in hopes of improving the "morals, temper and health of the insipid Lexington females."

With theatrical flair, Madame Mentelle spun other tales, too. She told of being the only child of a rich Paris merchant who raised her as a son, dressing her in trousers and demanding she row across the Seine River before breakfast every morning. And when she told him she feared death, her father locked her in the closet with a corpse—or so she said.

These tales mesmerized Mary. By the end of her four years at the boarding school, she had acquired a lifelong interest in literature, a fluency in French, and more. From her sixty-two-year-old headmistress, she'd absorbed a distaste for Lexington, a love of the theatrical, and a tendency to act both eccentrically and snobbily. Most importantly, she'd absorbed an image of female independence. Mary Todd had learned that a woman can think for herself and take care of herself.

HENRY CLAY, MARY'S FRIEND AND NEIGHBOR

On a bright spring afternoon in 1830, eleven-year-old Mary Todd galloped down a dusty lane. She was headed to Ashland, the palatial estate of the presidential candidate and her father's close friend, Henry Clay. About a mile out of town, she turned up the long driveway and stopped in front of the house. But when she knocked on the door, a slave told her Mr. Clay was busy—he had dinner guests.

"I can't help that," replied Mary. "I've come all the way out here . . . to show Mr. Clay my new pony. You tell him *Mary Todd* would like him to step out for a moment."

A few minutes later, the statesman appeared. After admiring the pony, he said, "You are just in time for dinner."

Unabashed, Mary took Clay's hand and allowed herself to be led into the dining room, where she listened happily to the political discussion swirling around her. Then suddenly she piped up, "Mr. Clay, my father says you will [someday] be . . . president of the United States. I wish I could go to Washington and live in the White House."

"Well," said Mr. Clay, "if I am ever president, I shall expect Miss Mary Todd to be one of my first guests. Will you come?"

Mary nodded, then added, "If you were not already married, I would wait for you."

Henry Clay laughed.

But Mary was serious. Ever after, when telling this story, her family claimed Mary longed to be "mistress of the White House . . . and often said she would marry a president."

PRESIDENT ANDREW JACKSON—THE CAUSE OF MARY'S FIRST POLITICAL ARGUMENT

In December 1832, President Andrew Jackson visited Lexington. As he rode down the street, crowds cheered and shouted. But not Mary. She was not awed by famous men. Ever since she was little, she had been allowed to sit at the dinner table and listen to Kentucky's most prominent men talk politics with her father. To her, recalled a Todd cousin, they were "as ordinary as the air she breathed." Now, fifteen-year-old Mary had her own political opinions. She detested President Jackson, not only for his policies but also because he was running for reelection against her dear friend Henry Clay.

"I wouldn't think of cheering President Jackson, for he is not *my* candidate," said Mary to a friend who was standing beside her. Even though women did not have the right to vote, Mary firmly believed her political opinions had merit. She added, "He is not as ugly as I heard he was."

"Ugly!" exclaimed her friend. "If you call President Jackson ugly, what do you think of Mr. Clay?"

"Mr. Henry Clay," said Mary coolly, "is the handsomest man in town, and has the best manners of anybody—except my father. We are going to snow President Jackson under and freeze his long face so that he will never smile again."

"Humph!" retorted her friend. "Andrew Jackson with his long face is better-looking than Henry Clay and your father rolled into one."

It was too much. Mary huffed away, vowing never to speak to that person again. It was the first of many friendships Mary would end because of political disagreements.

THINKING ABOUT GOD

The Todds didn't take religion seriously. No one fussed about saying grace or learning Bible verses. Church was more of a social event—a place to go dressed up and visit with friends.

Every Sunday Mary attended McChord's Presbyterian Church. From the family pew, she listened to Reverend John Breckinridge preach that heaven was a better place, where there was no sadness; a place where "we will be reunited with our loved ones who have gone before us." Of course, not everyone could get in. If you sinned on earth, warned the reverend, you would be denied "the Kingdom of God."

Mary longed to believe Reverend Breckinridge because she desperately wanted to see her mother again. But was going to heaven the only way? The Todd slaves told her different. Like other blacks, they had kept their African spiritualism alive, mixing it with the required Christianity of their white masters. In black folk religion, the dead returned—sometimes to see their babies, sometimes to leave important messages, and sometimes when they were summoned by a conjurer. According to Mammy Sally, a mourner might walk backward over the departed's grave, or rub dead moles' feet at daybreak to help a dead mother come back—at least for a visit.

Eventually, Mary incorporated both these beliefs into her own view of God. She'd always remain a member of a church—either Presbyterian or Episcopalian, depending on how much she liked the pastor. She often spoke eagerly of dying and going to heaven. Yet she never drew comfort from her Christianity. She prayed but didn't think it helped. "What is to be is to be," she once told her half sister Emilie, "and no amount of prayer can divert our fate." Meanwhile, she continued to believe in a punishing God who caused her to suffer because of her sins. Her greatest comfort came from Mammy Sally's lessons, and the idea that her beloved dead ones hovered nearby, visiting her in her dreams and protecting her while she was awake. They were, as she later said, "always with me."

$150 REWARD.

R ANAWAY from the subscriber, on the night of Monday the 11th July, a negro man named

TOM,

about 30 years of age, 5 feet 6 or 7 inches high; of dark color; heavy in the chest; several of his jaw teeth out, and upon his body are several old marks of the whip, one of them straight down the back. He took with him a quantity of clothing, and several hats.

A reward of $150 will be paid for his apprehension and security, if taken out of the State of Kentucky; $100 if taken in any county bordering on the Ohio river; $50 if taken in any of the interior counties except Fayette; or $20 if taken in the latter county.

july 12-84-tf   B. L. BOSTON.

*Lexington's newspapers were full of ads for runaway slaves, such as
this one, which appeared in the* Lexington Observer & Reporter.

Slavery was at the very center of Mary Todd's life. From her house on Short Street she could see the market square where slaves were auctioned. She could see the whipping post where they were punished and the jail where they were held. On certain days, young Mary could even see gangs of slaves being driven down Main Street, headed for the Mississippi flatboats that would take them to slave markets in Natchez and New Orleans.

Meanwhile, inside her own house there were nine slaves to wipe her tears, iron her skirts, and tie her bootlaces. There was Aunt Chaney, who baked Mary treats and sometimes let her help in the kitchen. There was Nelson, who took her for carriage rides. And there was Sally,

Slaves being driven to the market

"a jewel of a black mammy," who was the center of Mary's world. Not only did Sally nurse Mary through illnesses, comfort her after nightmares, correct her manners, and make sure she ate everything on her plate, but she met Mary's emotional needs as well.

On Sunday, Mammy Sally attended the "white folks' church," where she kept an eye on the Todd children from the balcony—the only place blacks were allowed to sit. But the rest of the week she stuffed Mary with folk wisdom and slave tales. She told the girl about the jaybirds in the backyard and how they flew to hell every Friday night to report to the devil all the bad things Mary had done that week. She impressed Mary with tales about "ole Satan," who had horns "just like an old male cow," and she entertained her with the popular slave stories about Brer Rabbit, who managed to survive by outwitting the bigger, stronger Mr. Fox. "Am I a fox?" Mary supposedly asked one day. Mammy grinned. "You a smart girl," she replied.

Mary sometimes wondered if Mammy Sally wanted to be free, but concluded she did not. "How could we do without Mammy, and how could she exist without us?" Mary once asked her father. He didn't answer.

Mary didn't give the question any more thought until the summer of her twelfth year. One night, while trying to read, she heard a persistent knocking. Mary asked who was at the door. Mammy Sally decided to trust the girl. "That," she confessed, "might be a runaway. . . . We have a mark on our fence—I made it myself—to show that if any runaway is hungry he can get vittles right here. All of 'em knows the sign. I have fed many a one." These were fugitive slaves bound for the Ohio River, where they could cross into the Ohio Territory and be free. Mary knew that helping runaway slaves was illegal. But because she loved her mammy, she offered to bring corn bread and bacon to the runaway herself. "He would hide from you like a rabbit," Sally explained. "Nothing but a black hand reaching out can help him." Mary was shocked. Why would slaves be afraid of her? Then she realized the truth. It didn't matter how kindly her family treated their slaves—the Todds were still white.

Mary kept Sally's secret, but she must have felt very conflicted about slavery. The Todd family's position on the issue didn't make things easier. Even though they owned slaves, the Todds had a long history of antislavery leanings. Mary's grandfather Colonel John Todd had introduced legislation back in 1777 that would have freed Kentucky's slaves if it had passed. Both Mary's grandmothers had freed their slaves in their wills. And when Mary's father ran for the state senate, his opposition had labeled him the "Emancipation Candidate" because of his abolitionist sympathies.

A slave family

Mary began reading newspapers, listening to public debates, asking questions, and discussing (much to her stepmother's dismay) the topic over dessert at the dinner table. Above all, she took a good, hard look at Mammy Sally, Nelson, and Aunt Chaney. By her sixteenth birthday she was firmly convinced slavery was "a monstrous wrong." But what to do about it? Mary had no idea.

A slave auction house

A slave auction in Lexington's courthouse yard

THIS NINETEENTH-CENTURY ENGRAVING SHOWS THE AGONY OF A FAMILY STRUCK DOWN WITH CHOLERA.

IN JUNE 1833, fourteen-year-old Mary arrived home from school for the weekend, expecting to spend her days in her usual pursuits—reading in the library, strolling to Monsieur Girion's Confectionery Shop for one of his hot ginger cakes. But a torrential rain put an end to her plans. For twelve straight hours it poured, overflowing privies and contaminating the stream that ran through town. The next day, a woman living on low-lying Water Street became ill with stomach cramps, diarrhea, and vomiting. By nightfall she was dead, a victim of the dreaded disease cholera.

Caused by bacteria and spread through unwashed hands, uncooked fruits and vegetables, and sewage-contaminated drinking water, cholera had made its first appearance in the United States in 1832. Sweeping across the country, it killed thousands in New York City, Philadelphia, and New Orleans. Folks in Lexington had hoped they would be spared. But in that one week ten people died, and ten times that many were ill.

There was no cure for cholera in the nineteenth century. Believing the disease was airborne, people heaved their dead out the windows, then quickly reshuttered the windows before any bad air could infect those inside. The few doctors who stayed in town tried their usual, useless remedies, such as bloodletting.

The Todd family locked themselves up in their big new house on Main Street and refused to allow in anything from outside—fresh produce, flowers, packages, or people. "They would not let us eat fruit or vegetables," Mary later recalled, "just beaten biscuits, eggs, boiled milk and boiled water." Desperate for "something different," Mary sneaked a handful of mulberries. "Then such a to-do," she recalled. "Mother sent for the doctor posthaste, and Mammy made me take ipecac [to induce vomiting] . . . she had to hold my nose to make me take it."

Terrified of the outdoors, the Todds burned so much tar to destroy the germs they believed were floating in the air that it was hard to breathe. "But what was worse than all," said Mary, "everybody was frightened half to death, talking in whispers, almost afraid to breathe." Looking out the window, she could see that there was "nothing on the streets but the drivers and horses of the dead carts with the bodies of those who died. Toward the last there were not even coffins. Father had all the trunks and boxes taken out of the attic to serve as coffins."

The epidemic lasted three weeks and killed more than five hundred people. Happily, no one in the Todd family caught the disease. Still, Mary was affected. She was left with a deep fear of disease and death, and often had nightmares about coffins and cemeteries.

A NINETEENTH-CENTURY ENGRAVING SHOWING ONE OF LEXINGTON'S NUMEROUS COTILLIONS

By the summer of 1836, Mary had completed ten years of school. What was she expected to do with all that education? Enter Lexington society, of course. Reluctantly returning to the Todds' mansion on Main Street, Mary dutifully attended a whirlwind of tea parties, cotillions, and late-night suppers. She dined on Maryland oysters and Spanish pickles, dressed in the finest silks, and danced with boys from the best families.

Not only did Mary dance divinely and have impeccable manners, but people thought she was very pretty. She had, said one suitor, "clear blue eyes, long lashes, light brown hair with a glint of bronze and a lovely complexion." When she was a teenager, "her figure was beautiful," remembered an acquaintance, "and no master ever modeled a more perfect arm and hand." Wildly flirtatious and charming, Mary also had the advantage of being a Todd.

But for all these virtues, Mary was not the toast of the town. She spoke "too sharply, and too intelligently," recalled one childhood friend, and especially liked to discuss politics and current events. Once she got into a heated argument with a dance partner about the virtues of Kentucky government. "She won the debate," recalled her cousin, "but shocked our genteel society." Later, Mary remembered this time as one of failure—a time, she said, "when friends were few."

While other girls her age scrambled to find suitable husbands, Mary turned her nose up at any man who showed interest in her. She called them "hypocritical," "frivolous in their affection," "uninteresting," and "hard bargains." "Among [those] who came calling were scholarly, intellectual men. But Mary never at any time showed the least partiality for any of them," recalled her cousin Lizzie.

One of these suitors—a theology student from Massachusetts attending Transylvania University—called on Mary every Sunday afternoon. She detested him. "His manners were assuming and dictatorial and offensive," Lizzie said later, "but we all tried to be polite"—all but Mary. She laughed at him, teased him, and "impersonated him with wicked accuracy." Still, the young man kept coming back—until the afternoon Mary called him a "Yankee." It was the last straw. Leaping to his feet, the student cried, "Miss Mary, there is a point beyond endurance which I cannot and will not stand!" Remembered Lizzie, "He looked so fierce and his wrath was so great for such a small amount of teasing that Mary leaned back in her chair and laughed merrily." This only made the young man sputter more. Without another word, he swept from the Todd house, never to return.

No wonder her stepmother once wailed, "That limb of Satan will never find a husband!"

INTO ILLINOIS

MARY'S SPRINGFIELD FAMILY

Sister Elizabeth, sister Frances, and brother-in-law Ninian Edwards

ON JUNE 3, 1837, a stagecoach carrying eighteen-year-old Mary Todd bounced into the tiny prairie town of Springfield, Illinois. With her came three trunks overstuffed with skirts, blouses, bonnets, slippers, and parasols—three trunks for a six-week stay.

Mary had come to visit her two older sisters, Elizabeth and Frances. Elizabeth had settled in Springfield five years earlier with her wealthy husband, Ninian Edwards, a businessman and son of a former Illinois governor. Within months, Frances had joined her big sister, taking up residence in the Edwards home. Now, Mary followed, eager, as she said, to escape her stepmother's "relentless persecution."

She quickly found herself at the center of Springfield society. The Edwardses lived in not only the best house (a two-story brick mansion) but the most *important* house as well. From their spot on "quality hill," Elizabeth and her husband entertained judges, senators, and wealthy businessmen. Their soirees set the social and political tone. "Anyone with ambitions," admitted one guest, "sought entree into the Edwards' lofty circle."

Mary found her new world exhilarating. She danced and took carriage rides. She made friends with Mercy Levering, who lived next door, and with Julia Jayne, who lived just down the hill. For hours each day, the girls giggled and gossiped together, making these weeks "the happiest of my girlhood."

With regret, Mary returned to Lexington. But once at home, she refused to join her peers as they made calls, went to parties, and—in increasing numbers—got married. Instead, she returned to her first school, the Shelby Female Academy, as an apprentice. Teaching was the only respectable job a woman could have in those days, and Mary hoped to pay her own way as a schoolteacher. But she never had to take up the career, because on May 21, Frances married a Springfield pharmacist and moved out of the Edwards home. Now there was room for Mary to return indefinitely. Eager to be off, she packed a single trunk and boarded the train for the first leg of her two-week journey. By early June 1839, she had arrived.

Mary Todd's life in Springfield had begun.

CHAPTER

☞ THREE ☜

THE HAPPIEST STAGES OF LIFE

Nothing new here, except my marrying, which to me, is [a] matter of profound wonder.

—ABRAHAM LINCOLN IN A LETTER TO A FRIEND, NOVEMBER 11, 1842

I believe a nice home, a loving husband and a precious child are the happiest stages of life.

—MARY LINCOLN IN A LETTER TO HER DAUGHTER-IN-LAW, MARY HARLAN LINCOLN, MARCH 22, 1869

ABRAHAM LINCOLN AS HE LOOKED
WHEN MARY TODD MET HIM

AND MARY AS SHE LOOKED
WHEN SHE MET ABRAHAM

"This thing of living in Springfield," Abraham wrote soon after arriving, "is rather a dull business. . . . I am quite as lonesome here as I ever was anywhere in my life." Nearly thirty years old, he remained an awkward farmer's son with few social graces. He rarely attended church or parties, he confessed, "because I should not know how to behave myself." Once, he turned up for an elegant evening affair wearing muddy boots and too-short pants. Looking around the room, he shocked the satin-draped ladies by declaring, "Oh boys, how clean these girls look!" Ninian Edwards—Mary Todd's brother-in-law—was so appalled by these crude manners that he declared Abraham "a mighty rough man." Still, as Abraham's law practice grew more and more prominent, the ambitious Edwards began inviting him to soirees at his mansion. By 1839, Abraham had earned a reputation for being smart and honest even if, sniffed Ninian, he was "utterly classless."

With Springfield now her home, twenty-year-old Mary quickly established herself as the centerpiece of a lively group of young people who gathered in the evenings at the Edwards mansion. Proudly calling itself "the Coterie" (those excluded from the group sourly called it "the Edwards clique"), the group included the town's richest, most fascinating young women and most promising young men. While femininity was appreciated, they were more interested in intelligent conversation, and there was an easy equality between the men and women. Mary could speak her mind on subjects ranging from Paris fashions to religion without being ridiculed or ignored. Her conversational skills flourished, and she soon discovered a zest for political gossip. Imitating her former schoolmistress, Madame Mentelle, she could milk the last drops of drama from any story she told, silence a fool with one pithy retort, or make a roomful of people burst into laughter. Ninian Edwards succinctly described her charms: "Mary could make a bishop forget his prayers."

COTILLION PARTY.

E PLURIBUS UNUM.

The pleasure of your Company is respectfully solicited at a Cotillion Party, to be given at the "American House," on to=morrow evening at 7 o'clock, P.=M.

December 16th, 1839.

N. H. RIDGELY,	J. F. SPEED,
J. A. M'CLERNAND,	J. SHIELDS,
R. ALLEN,	E. D. TAYLOR,
M. H. WASH,	E. H. MERRYMAN,
F. W. TODD,	N. E. WHITESIDE,
B. A. DOUGLASS,	M. EASTHAM,
W. S. PRENTICE,	J. R. DILLER,
N. W. EDWARDS,	A. LINCOLN,
	Managers.

AN INVITATION TO THE COTILLION WHERE ABRAHAM AND MARY MET

On a bitterly cold evening in December 1839, Mary Todd looked across the crowded ballroom and for the first time laid eyes on "the plainest man in Springfield," as her sister described him. Certainly, Mary knew of Abraham Lincoln. She had read about his court cases in the newspaper and had heard her brother-in-law talk about him. But she had never met him.

Tall and gawky, wearing a swallowtail coat that was too short, shabbily patched trousers, and mismatched socks, Abraham made his way to Mary's side. "Miss Todd," he said, "I want to dance with you in the worst way." And, as Mary remembered it, "he certainly did."

WHY MARY?

Abraham was obviously enchanted by Mary's vivaciousness and intelligence. He danced with her again and again that first evening, and the next week called on her at home. Soon he was abandoning those lazy talkfests with his friends at Joshua Speed's store to spend time with the girl he affectionately nicknamed "Molly." He escorted her on horseback rides and accompanied her on jaunts to neighboring towns. She had, he told his friends, "the most congenial mind he had ever met." Recalled Lizzie, "Mary led the conversation—Mr. Lincoln would sit at her side and listen. He scarcely said a word, but gazed on her as if irresistibly drawn toward her by some superior and unseen power."

WHY ABRAHAM?

Apparently, Lincoln made an impression on Mary, too. She became "almost immediately intrigued by him," claimed her niece Katherine Helm. She "admired his moodiness, his sincerity, his ambition and his honesty." Whenever he came calling, she turned the full force of her charm on him, laughing at his stories and talking earnestly with him about poetry and politics.

People noticed their relationship. When a friend wondered what she saw in "such a rough diamond of a man," Mary replied, "Imagine what joy it would bring to see his beauty and brilliance shine out more clearly each day. After all, the important thing is the diamond itself, clear and flawless under its film."

Throughout the spring, summer, and fall of 1840, the two were inseparable. Slowly, they moved from friendship to what Mary called having "lover's eyes." By Christmas, Abraham and Mary were engaged.

WHY NOT MARY?

Within days, Lincoln was having second thoughts about his engagement. How could he possibly support a wife? he wondered. He was a man without a reliable income (his law partnership with John Stuart was about to be dissolved). He had no savings. And he didn't own a house. He knew he could never give Mary the life of wealth and luxury she was used to.

WHY NOT ABRAHAM?

Meanwhile, Mary's family was not happy with the engagement either.

"Unsuitable," declared Elizabeth. "Opposite in nature, and education and raising. They had no feelings alike. They were so different, they could not possibly live happily as man and wife."

"I am opposed to him on principle," brother-in-law Ninian said. "He is not a warm hearted man . . . and not capable."

"His future," sister Frances opined, "is nebulous."

Suddenly, Lincoln "was panic-stricken," recalled Katherine Helm. Desperate, he wrote Mary telling her he didn't love her, hoping this would cause her to break the engagment. (In those times, only the lady could end an engagement.) Before sending the letter, however, he showed it to his friend Joshua Speed. "Don't write, that will give her an advantage over you," advised Speed as he tossed the letter into the fireplace. "If you have the courage . . . go see Mary yourself, tell her that you will not marry her; but be quick about it, say little and leave soon."

Lincoln took his friend's advice. But after he had revealed his feelings, Mary burst into tears. Pulling her into his lap, he kissed her. And suddenly, he no longer wanted to end their engagement. He seemed to have realized, said one family friend, that "he loved Mary—he wanted to marry her . . . to please and support a wife."

Mary, however, brooded over Abraham's change of heart. Finally, sadly, on January 1, 1841 (what Lincoln would grimly call the "Fatal First"), she wrote him a letter. In it she released him from their engagement because she thought he wanted it. But she also reminded him that she had not changed her mind, but "felt as always."

Instead of feeling relieved, Lincoln was devastated. As one acquaintance recalled, he went "crazy as a loon."

ABRAHAM'S "SUICIDE POEM" IS PUBLISHED IN A SPRINGFIELD NEWSPAPER.

After the "Fatal First," Lincoln sank into a deep depression once again. "I am the most miserable man living," he sobbed to a friend. And although he had never missed a legislative meeting before, he now missed six consecutive days during the January session. When he reappeared, claimed one observer, he was "reduced and emaciated . . . and seems scarcely to possess the strength to speak above a whisper." Joshua Speed later confessed to feeling obliged "to remove razors from his room—take all knives and other such dangerous things." In this mood, Abraham may have written the poem excerpted below, which some scholars have dated to 1841:

> Yes! I've resolved the deed to do,
> And this the place to do it:
> This heart I'll rush a dagger through,
> Though I in hell shall rue it!
>
> Sweet steel! come forth from out your sheath,
> And glist'ning, speak your powers;
> Rip up the organs of my breath,
> And draw my blood in showers!
>
> I strike! It quivers in that heart
> Which drives me to this end;
> I draw and kiss the bloody dart,
> My last—my only friend!

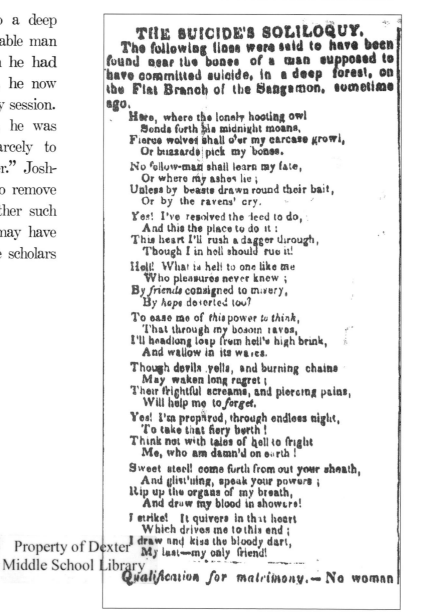

THE SUICIDE'S SOLILOQUY.

The following lines were said to have been found near the bones of a man supposed to have committed suicide, in a deep forest, on the Flat Branch of the Sangamon, sometime ago.

Here, where the lonely hooting owl
  Sends forth his midnight moans,
Fierce wolves shall o'er my carcase growl,
  Or buzzards pick my bones.

No fellow-man shall learn my fate,
  Or where my ashes lie;
Unless by beasts drawn round their bait,
  Or by the ravens' cry.

Yes! I've resolved the deed to do,
  And this the place to do it:
This heart I'll rush a dagger through,
  Though I in hell should rue it!

Hell! What is hell to one like me
  Who pleasures never knew;
By friends consigned to misery,
  By hope deserted too?

To ease me of this power to think,
  That through my bosom raves,
I'll headlong leap from hell's high brink,
  And wallow in its waves.

Though devils yells, and burning chains
  May waken long regret;
Their frightful screams, and piercing pains,
  Will help me to forget.

Yes! I'm prepared, through endless night,
  To take that fiery berth!
Think not with tales of hell to fright
  Me, who am damn'd on earth!

Sweet steel! come forth from out your sheath,
  And glist'ning, speak your powers;
Rip up the organs of my breath,
  And draw my blood in showers!

I strike! It quivers in that heart
  Which drives me to this end;
I draw and kiss the bloody dart,
  My last—my only friend!

Qualification for matrimony.—No woman

BROKEN-HEARTED MARY

Mary was suffering, too. Six months after the breakup, she wistfully wrote, "[Abraham] deems me unworthy of notice, as I have not [seen] him for months...how I wish he would show himself again." Not bothering to conceal her loneliness, the once vivacious belle spent her days reading and sewing. "I was much left to the solitude of my own thoughts," she later wrote, and to "lingering regrets over the past."

MATCHMAKING

A year after their breakup, Mrs. Simeon Francis—a good friend of Abraham's—decided to invite both Abraham and Mary to lunch. She sat them on the sofa and insisted, "Be friends again." At first embarrassed and uncomfortable, they eventually began talking about the one subject they both loved—politics. Politics led to a discussion of poetry, and poetry to a discussion of deeper feelings. By the end of the afternoon, they knew they had to see each other again. Because of the Edwardses' strong opposition to their relationship, however, they began meeting regularly and secretly at the Francis house. It wasn't long before they were engaged.

ABRAHAM AND MARY'S MARRIAGE CERTIFICATE

The couple chose a date for their forthcoming marriage but kept it secret until the last possible moment. Not until the very morning of the wedding did they tell the Edwardses. As Mary's guardian, Ninian insisted she be married in his front parlor. And Elizabeth insisted she have a proper wedding supper. While the women hurried off to instruct the servants on the preparation of the wedding cake (when it was served that night, it would still be warm), Lincoln went to work. Late that afternoon—just hours before the event—he asked his friend James Matheny to be his best man. Matheny later recalled that as the two dressed for the ceremony Lincoln "looked and acted as if he were going to the slaughter." Then they headed out the door, but not before the landlord's son asked where Abraham was going.

"To hell, I suppose," he gulped.

Yet hours later on that rainy November night in 1842 he stood proudly beside his bride. She looked radiant in her sister Frances's white satin dress and pearl necklace. Joining hands before the Episcopalian minister, they promised to take each other "for better for worse, for richer for poorer, in sickness and in health, to love and to cherish" until death parted them. Then Lincoln slipped a simple gold band onto his young bride's finger. Inside the ring were engraved the words *Love is eternal.*

MARY AND ABRAHAM'S FIRST HOME, THE GLOBE TAVERN

The newlyweds did not go on a honeymoon (not unusual in those days). Instead, they drove through a blinding rainstorm to a boardinghouse called the Globe Tavern. There, for four dollars a week, the Lincolns lived in a tiny room on the second floor and took their meals in the crowded dining room on the first floor. The tavern was the most comfortable place Lincoln had ever lived. But for Mary—used to gracious mansions—it was a real comedown. It was the first time in her life that she had no personal servants or slaves, no place to store or display her personal items, no place to receive visitors. Still, she didn't complain, not even when her sisters dropped her from their social circle because of her unsuitable match. Instead, recalled Mary's niece, "she lived quietly, contentedly and deeply in love with her husband."

Mr. and Mrs. Lincoln's favorite newspaper—the <u>Lexington Observer & Reporter</u>

Both Mary and Abraham were avid newspaper readers. Abraham had acquired the habit back in his days as New Salem's postmaster—he read every newspaper that passed through his office before delivering it. And Mary's father had not only encouraged her to read the papers but also refused to let her express a political opinion unless she had the knowledge and information to back it up. It was hardly surprising, then, that one of the first things the couple did after their wedding was to subscribe to the *Lexington Observer & Reporter*. Not only did they both agree with the paper's position on public policy, but from its pages they learned about events affecting their home state of Kentucky. Many evenings Mary read the newspaper aloud while Abraham listened intently, his chair tipped back against the wall, his feet cozy inside the huge black velvet carpet slippers on which Mary had painstakingly embroidered the initials *A.L.*

On February 12, 1843, Mary bustled with activity. She begged Mrs. Beck, owner of the Globe Tavern, to bake a small cake. She wrapped a few gifts (contents unknown). And she invited a handful of friends to the Lincolns' room to celebrate her husband's birthday. That night, before cutting the cake, she made a loving little speech that ended: "I am so glad you have a birthday. I feel so grateful to your mother."

Little did their guests know that Mary would soon be a mother herself.

A GROWING FAMILY

THE EARLIEST KNOWN PHOTOGRAPH OF ABRAHAM AND MARY'S FIRST SON, ROBERT TODD, TAKEN WHEN THE BOY WAS SEVENTEEN

On August 1, 1843—nine months after her wedding—Mary gave birth to her first "precious son." After the baby's birth, she remembered, she awoke to see "my darling husband bending over me with love and tenderness." They called the boy Robert Todd, after Mary's father.

He was wildly rambunctious. Bob, as he was nicknamed, was described at age three by his father in a letter to a friend: "He has a great deal of that sort of mischief that is the offspring of much animal spirits." One of Bob's favorite ways of attracting attention was to run away. Neighbors recalled how time and again Mary would race to the front door and scream, "Bobbie's lost! Bobbie's lost!" Finding him became a neighborhood affair, and his father was even called from work. But Bob was always found eventually, wearing a smug look.

As Bob grew, his parents couldn't help but recognize his intelligence. He had a natural talent for mathematics and "learned his sums all by himself." Anything mechanical fascinated him, and he was constantly taking things apart to see how they worked—door hinges, wagon axles, his mother's teakettle. "He is quite smart enough," said Lincoln. "I some times fear he is one of the little rare-ripe sort, that are smarter at about five than ever after."

At the age of seven, Bob was sent to school. He resisted learning his letters and had to be pushed to apply himself. He was also the butt of his classmates' jokes. Because of an inward-turning eye, he was called "cockeye" by the other students. This taunting, claimed his aunt Elizabeth, resulted in the "uncomfortable reserve and shyness that became so marked a trait in his personality."

Another personality trait revealed itself around this time, too. As one Springfield citizen put it, Bob had a tendency to "act a bit of a snob." Embarrassed by his father's poor beginnings, Bob professed a close kinship with his Todd relatives. The Todds had the things Bob liked—high standards of social correctness, prosperity, and the comfortable style of living that goes with it. This attitude opened a gulf between father and son that was never bridged.

A NEW HOME . . .

The Globe Tavern was not the best place for a couple with a baby. Not only was the room too cramped for three people, but the other guests complained about the infant's crying. So in the fall of 1843, the family rented a three-room cottage on Fourth Street. Little is known of the winter they

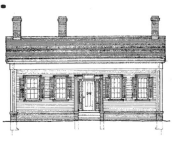

The house on the corner of Eighth and Jackson as it looked when the Lincolns bought it

spent there, and they were soon eyeing a small place on the corner of Eighth and Jackson. Only four blocks from Lincoln's law office, the house had one story, five rooms, some outbuildings, and an eighth of an acre of land. Scraping together $1,500 for the place, the Lincolns moved in by the spring of 1844. Yes, they were still on the wrong side of the tracks—miles from the Edwards mansion—but Mary didn't care. Happily, she hung oval-framed pictures on the wall, placed vases on the mantel, and sewed curtains for the windows. Because their income was limited, they did not have anything of particular value. "Our furnishings," wrote Mary, "remain more practical than decorous."

. . . AND A NEW BUSINESS

William H. Herndon, Lincoln's new law partner

Practicing law alongside the respected Springfield attorney John T. Stuart had helped Abraham build his professional reputation, but it didn't provide job security. When Stuart decided he no longer needed a partner, Lincoln was forced to find a new position.

Eventually, he formed a partnership with Stephen T. Logan, a top-notch trial attorney. From Logan, Abraham learned to prepare his cases carefully, consult with authorities, and effectively sum up for the jury. He also began appearing before the Illinois Supreme Court. But just three years after going into practice together, the two men split. Logan wanted to go into business with his son. Lincoln decided it was time to go into business for himself.

And so it was that one morning in 1844, Abraham headed up the stairs of the Tinsley Building, where the offices of Logan & Lincoln had formerly been, and found William Herndon studying. "Billy," he asked the young law student, "do you want to enter into a partnership with me?"

"Mr. Lincoln," Herndon stammered, "this is . . . unexpected . . . an undeserved honor, and yet I will gladly and thankfully accept the . . . offer."

"Billy," replied Lincoln, "I can trust you, if you can trust me."

Many people found this new partnership puzzling. Now an established and prominent lawyer (though still a financially struggling one), Abraham could have had his pick of any attorney. Why did he choose young, inexperienced Herndon? Because he was tired of being the junior partner and wanted to head his own firm. Besides, Lincoln genuinely liked Herndon. He thought he was "a laborious, studious young man . . . far better informed on almost all subjects than I have been."

Lincoln treated his new partner in a fatherly manner, affectionately calling him "Billy." In return, Herndon gave Abraham unswerving loyalty, always calling the senior partner "Mr. Lincoln."

The reconstructed exterior of the Lincoln & Herndon law office as it looks today

Lincoln's office occupied two dusty rooms on the second floor of a brick building located directly across the street from the courthouse. It was shabbily furnished and wretchedly bare. One visitor recalled that there was "a somewhat dilapidated . . . desk, and a table, a sofa . . . and a half-dozen plain wooden chairs." Apparently, the lawyers overlooked the need for files or filing cabinets. Neither man was orderly, and documents were strewn everywhere. In one corner lay a pile of papers with a note in Lincoln's handwriting that read, "If you can't find it anywhere else, look in this." Sometimes Abraham took legal papers home, where they occasionally met their fate at the hands of his high-spirited sons. And he stuffed documents into his stovepipe hat so often that Herndon called it "his desk and his memorandum-book." As a result, the partners were constantly searching for things—and constantly confessing to their clients that what had been sent to them had been "lost or destroyed and cannot be found after a search among the papers of Lincoln & Herndon."

Whether Abraham was disorganized or not, his name drew clients. Within months, the partners had all the business they could manage. Soon they were handling more than a hundred cases a year, ranging from disputes over runaway pigs to murder. Although they charged the typical client $5 to $20 (about $100 to $400 in today's dollars), Lincoln occasionally provided his services for free. "The Widow Reed is suing for the return of eight dollars," he once told Herndon. "My conscience does not allow me to take the larger portion of that sum." Abraham was also careless about collecting money due. Luckily, the only records Herndon kept in order were lists of fees due the partners. When the fees were collected, he carefully marked them paid.

THE SHADED PORTION OF THIS ILLINOIS MAP SHOWS THE EIGHTH CIRCUIT, WHERE LINCOLN PRACTICED LAW.

On a crisp fall day in 1851, a party of fifteen men made their way across the prairie toward the tiny town of Paris, Illinois, the seat of Edgar County. Among the travelers was Judge David Davis. Weighing close to three hundred pounds, he was too heavy to ride a horse, and so traveled in a carriage drawn by two very strong horses. The group also included a handful of local lawyers, as well as David Campbell, the state's attorney. And riding alongside them was Abraham Lincoln on his horse, Old Bob.

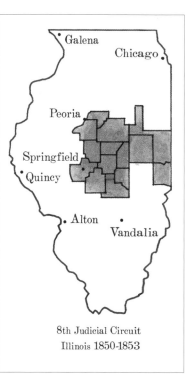

8th Judicial Circuit
Illinois 1850–1853

Where was this group going? They were traveling the vast Eighth Judicial Circuit, which spread across fourteen counties—11,000 square miles and two-thirds of Illinois's width. Each spring and fall, Judge Davis traveled around this circuit, holding court in each remote and tiny county seat where judges were not available. Lincoln and his fellow lawyers went along to try the cases. The whole trip took three months.

Because of the distance and time involved, most lawyers traveled only part of the circuit. But Lincoln, eager to earn money, always made the entire tour, and he made it in both the fall and the spring. This meant he was away from his family six months a year for the almost twenty years he practiced law. And while some lawyers came home on weekends, he did not. "Indeed," noted a friend, "he was desperately homesick and turning his head frequently towards [Springfield]," but he did not give in to his heart's desire. Instead, he kept his eyes on the prize—a growing bank account.

For his troubles, Abraham made an average of $150 a week (about $3,000 in today's dollars)—an enormous sum compared to the $16 a week earned by the average worker. But Abraham was doing more than earning money. He was earning a reputation, growing in prominence, and making statewide political connections. Most important, he was meeting Illinois's voters.

THIS LATE-NINETEENTH-CENTURY PAINTING SHOWS LINCOLN ENDURING THE HARDSHIPS OF TRAVELING THE EIGHTH CIRCUIT.

Life on the circuit was not easy. In winter, the roads were deep with snow; in spring, they were soft with mud. Abraham and his fellow travelers had to drive through unbroken prairie where the grass grew as tall as their horses. When they came to swollen streams without bridges, Judge Davis would ask Lincoln to look for a crossing; if he could get over, the others would safely follow. In this manner they could travel thirty or forty miles each day. Rarely did they see another passing rider.

At night they stopped wherever they could find lodging—inns, cabins, and the occasional hayloft. Sometimes, remembered one lawyer, they slept "with 20 men in the same room." One lawyer remembered Abraham sleeping "in a homemade flannel undershirt" that another friend described as reaching "halfway between his knees and his ankles." In this getup, "he was the ungodliest figure I ever saw." After a breakfast of greasy food and what one lawyer called "pretty tough coffee," they moved on.

COURT DAYS WERE EXCITING, AS THIS PHOTOGRAPH TAKEN IN PARIS, ILLINOIS, IN 1850 PROVES.

Court days were red-letter days in Illinois's backwoods towns, and folks from neighboring areas flocked to their county seats. They held marketplaces on courthouse squares, packed the courtrooms, and listened to the cases. The legal battles both enthralled and entertained them.

Lincoln did lots of business on court days. Settling himself beneath a tree if the weather was nice, he would wait to be approached by folks who needed his services. Most of these cases, one friend recalled, involved "assault and battery—suits on notes—small disputes among neighbors—slander—warranties on horse trades—larceny of a small kind."

With little time to prepare and no books to look up legal precedents, Lincoln mainly based his arguments on common sense. He always spoke plainly and simply to a jury, said Judge Davis, and "he took pains [they] should never be confused." In this way, he won more cases than he lost.

MURDER!

On May 6, 1858, Abraham threw a few things into his carpetbag, tucked some papers into his stovepipe hat, and set out to make the forty-five-mile journey to Beardstown, Illinois. He was going to defend William "Duff" Armstrong, son of some New Salem friends, against a charge of murder.

Duff was accused of killing a young man named James Metzker by deliberately striking him in the eye with a "slung shot"—a solid metal ball encased in leather. Lots of people had seen the attack and testified to the fact in court. One eyewitness, Charles Allen, swore he saw Duff "in the bright moonlight strike [Metzker] down."

No one knows if Lincoln thought his client was guilty, but if he did, he didn't show it. In cross-examination during the trial the next day, he slowly and with seeming casualness had Allen go over his story a dozen times. Again and again he asked him to describe what he'd seen and how he'd seen it. When he finished, Lincoln turned to the jury. "Now I will show you that this man Allen's testimony is a pack of lies," he said. Producing a copy of that year's almanac, he opened it to the date of the murder and read the entry aloud. The almanac showed that at the time Allen claimed he saw the attack, the moon had already set, and it would have

been impossible to see anything. The courtroom exploded into laughter, and Allen's credibility was destroyed.

Usually Lincoln's closing arguments were low-key and logical. But this time he made a gushing, sentimental bid that "took the jury by storm," remembered the trial's prosecutor. Since it was a hot day, Abraham took his coat off and unbuttoned his vest. One of his suspenders—homemade and knitted from wool—fell from his shoulder. But the lawyer pretended not to notice. Instead he locked eyes with the jury and said, "Gentlemen, I appear here without any reward for the benefit of that lady sitting there." He pointed to Duff's sobbing mother, Hannah, "who washed my dirty shirts when I had no money to pay her." He told the jury how he had arrived in New Salem as a penniless young man and had been given food and shelter by Duff's parents. He said he did not believe the son of such kind people could be a murderer. And he begged for Duff's life because God willed that in this small way he could repay his debt to the friends who had been so kind to him in his youth.

His words brought the twelve-man jury to tears. They found Duff Armstrong not guilty.

This nineteenth-century drawing shows Lincoln (inaccurately portrayed with a beard) arguing his most celebrated case; to Lincoln's left sits the defendant, Duff Armstrong, beside his weeping mother.

RULES FOR BEING A GOOD LAWYER

Lincoln once summed up what he believed made a good lawyer:

Persuade your neighbors to compromise whenever you can. Point out to them how the nominal winner is often a real loser—in fees, expenses and waste of time. As a peacemaker, the lawyer has a superior opportunity of being a good man. There will be business enough. . . . There is a vague popular belief that lawyers . . . are dishonest. Let no young man choosing the law . . . yield to this belief. Resolve to be honest at all events; and if, in your own judgment, you cannot be an honest lawyer, resolve to be honest without being a lawyer.

A HARDWORKING WOMAN

After she moved to her own home, Mary's world narrowed. Behind the front door with the now-famous marker engraved *A. Lincoln*, life became an endless routine of domestic chores. As one popular mid-nineteenth-century saying went:

Illinois is Heaven for men and horses,
but Hell for women and oxen.

AN 1860 ENGRAVING FROM *GODEY'S LADY'S BOOK* DEPICTS THE WOMAN AS "THE LIGHT OF THE HOME."

Like millions of other middle-class American women in the nineteenth century, Mary took her domestic cues from the magazine *Godey's Lady's Book*. Along with bestselling books such as *The Master at Home* and *The Young Housekeeper, Godey's* shaped opinions about the proper role of respectable women. "The perfection of womanhood is the wife and mother," gushed one issue of *Godey's*. "The center of the family, the magnet that draws man to the domestic altar, that makes him a civilized being, a social Christian. The woman is truly the light of the home."

It was a new idea. Once, the family had been the center of production and economic activity. Farms and businesses were family-owned and family-run, with women often working alongside their husbands. But by the first half of the nineteenth century, independent shops and factories replaced this family function. Now Americans began to distinguish between public and private spheres. For the middle class,

the public sphere—the man's world—was a jungle where men fought for economic survival in business and politics. The private sphere—the home—was a refuge from that jungle. Governed by women, it was supposed to be the source of spirituality and purity, a religious and moral institution where selflessness and cooperation ruled. Women were expected to be passive and submissive to men in public. They were not supposed to express opinions, make financial decisions, or act with any independence.

To help women understand their role, ladies' magazines employed a series of self-appointed experts who instructed their readers on everything from toilet training to keeping their houses tidy and their tempers under control. They advised women to promote the health, morality, comfort, and prosperity of their husbands and children, and to do it all with an "angelic countenance." And what if their husbands failed in business or their children grew ill? Women took the blame. They must not have sacrificed enough. They must not have focused all their energies on their home. "Your error," *Godey's* warned one such "delinquent" mother, "lies in the false idea that your happiness was to come from outside you and your home."

Burdened with all these restrictions, Mary enthusiastically and energetically tried to seek joy within the four walls of her home. But it wasn't easy. "I feel exhausted after such desperate exertions," she once admitted.

MARY IN THE KITCHEN

Mary's workday began in the tiny kitchen at the back of the house. Cooking was a laborious task that took up most of her day. Everything had to be made from scratch. If she wanted to serve fried chicken, for example, she had to kill the chicken, pluck the feathers, clean the carcass, cut up the meat, and fry it—all the while peeling potatoes, rolling biscuits, and churning butter. Some days the coals in her cast-iron Thompson stove went out. It was her husband's job to start them, but because he was away so much she often did it herself. She used a dry sink for washing dishes and cleaning fruits and vegetables: the water had to be carried in from a pump in the backyard. ☞

FRICASSEED CHICKENS.

Having cut up your chickens, lay them in cold water 'till all the blood is drawn out. Then wipe the pieces, season them with pepper and salt, and dredge them with flour. Fry them in lard or butter; they should be of a fine brown on both sides. When they are quite done, take them out of the frying-pan, cover them up, and set them by the fire to keep warm. Skim the gravy in the frying-pan and pour into it half a pint of cream; season it with a little nutmeg, pepper and salt, and thicken it with a small bit of butter rolled in flour. Give it a boil, and then pour it round the chickens, which must be kept hot. Put some lard into the pan, and fry some parsley in it to lay on the pieces of chicken; it must be done green and crisp.

To make a white fricassee of chickens, skin them, cut them in pieces, and having soaked out the blood, season them with salt, pepper, nutmeg and mace, and strew over them some sweet marjoram slired fine. Put them into a stew-pan, and pour over them half a pint of cream, or rich unskimmed milk. Add some butter rolled in flour, and (if you choose) some small force-meat balls. Set the stew-pan over hot coals. Keep it closely covered, and stew or simmer it gently till the chicken is quite tender, but do not allow it to boil.

You may improve it by a few small slices of cold ham.

———————

CHICKEN CROQUETS AND RISSOLES.

Take some cold chicken, and having cut the flesh from the bones, mince it small with a little suet and parsley; adding sweet marjoram and grated lemon-peel. Season it with pep-

Recipe from Miss Leslie's Directions for Cookery, a popular cookbook used by Mary.

☞ Because she had grown up pampered, Mary had almost no training in cooking. One of the first purchases she made as a married woman was *Miss Leslie's Directions for Cookery.* For eighty-seven cents, she learned to make some of her Kentucky favorites: "waffles, batter cakes and egg cornbread . . . not to mention buckwheat cakes." The Lincolns were on a tight budget, so she served very little beef and pork. Instead, she cooked local game—woodchuck, pheasant, and prairie chicken. She also preserved fruit, made cheese, roasted coffee, and baked bread, pies, and cakes every Wednesday and Saturday. She even made her own rouge, face powder, and perfume. What her mother and stepmother had *never* done, Mary now did daily.

FROM THE KITCHEN OF MRS. LINCOLN

A RECIPE FOR WHITE CAKE

Mary often made this cake for her husband. Occasionally, she served it with fresh strawberries, but she never frosted it. Said Abraham, "Mary's white cake is the best I've ever eaten." Below is her recipe:

1 cup butter

2 cups sugar

3 cups flour

2 teaspoons baking powder

1 cup milk

1 teaspoon vanilla

1 teaspoon almond extract

1 cup chopped blanched almonds

6 egg whites

1/4 teaspoon salt

Cream butter and sugar until light and fluffy. Sift together flour and baking powder; remove 2 tablespoons and set aside. Add sifted ingredients, alternating with milk, to creamed mixture. Stir in vanilla and almond extract. Combine almonds with reserved flour and add to batter.

Beat egg whites until stiff; add salt. Fold into batter. Pour into greased and floured tube pan. Bake at 375 degrees until a cake tester comes out clean, about 55 minutes. Cool 5 to 10 minutes; remove from pan and finish cooling on rack.

———————

ALL ALONE

When Mary and Abraham married, they cut themselves off from parents and relatives. He rarely visited his father and stepmother. And Mary had been dropped by her disapproving sisters. This left her all alone when Lincoln was on the circuit—alone with her worries about the children's health, and her terror of thunderstorms; alone to deal with finances, and social commitments, and milking the cow; alone with her feelings of abandonment. "If my husband stayed at home as he ought to," a neighbor recalled her saying, "I could love him better."

This frontispiece from Mrs. Lydia Green Abell's 1853 book, <u>Ladies Guide; or, Skillful Housewife</u>, depicts the many duties of a nineteenth-century homemaker.

"When it comes to house cleaning," remarked one Springfield housewife, "I am little more than a slave." Indeed, housekeeping in the nineteenth century was an almost impossible task. Because the town's windows did not have screens, the Lincolns' house crawled with insects—bedbugs, moths, flies, mosquitoes, and cockroaches. The only way to get rid of these pests was to "boil the roots of a pokeberry plant . . . then mix with molasses and set about in old saucers." Mary followed these directions religiously. Every night she set out fresh saucers, and every morning she scraped the roach-encrusted mess into the trash.

Mary's cooking and heating stoves also added to her work. Not only did they frequently need to be emptied of ash and soot, but they left black dust on the walls and ceilings, which Mary was forever wiping. Additionally, she constantly refilled the house's lamps and lanterns—its only source of light—with oil and refitted them with wicks. And all the while she buffed furniture, scoured hardwood floors, dusted knickknacks, washed dishes, polished windows, hauled wood, made beds, did the shopping, knitted socks, tended her backyard garden, and devoted four days of every week to doing laundry—washing, bleaching, and ironing. It was, said Mary, "unspeakably dull and terrible drudgery."

PATTERNS LIKE THIS ONE FROM <u>GODEY'S LADY'S BOOK</u> HELPED MARY MAKE CLOTHES FOR HER FAMILY.

Besides cooking and cleaning, Mary had to sew for her family. In midcentury Springfield, she was able to buy some ready-made clothes—socks, shirts, coats, and pants for her sons. And if she couldn't find a particular item in town, she could look for it elsewhere. From a St. Louis storekeeper she requested "a white fur hat for a boy of six months—with white trimmings and white feather—of the prettiest quality." But she made her family's pillows, sheets and curtains, all her own dresses, and Abraham's elaborate shirts. Mary claimed she "could not endure the thought of my husband wearing shirts made by any hands except my own."

Charge accounts in Springfield's stores show that Mary bought endless pieces of "calico . . . cross barred swiss . . . opera flannel . . . wool delaine"

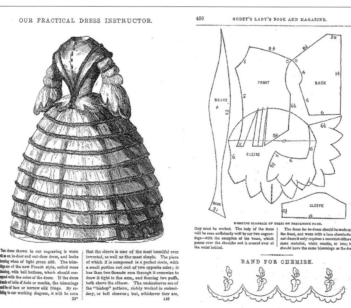

to make her own dresses, as well as the spools of thread, buttons, lace, and ribbons to go with them. It was a time of elaborate dress, and Mary tried to keep up with the styles. Using patterns found in *Godey's Lady's Book,* she took extraordinary care with her creations, adding flowers, tucks, bows, and ribbons. It took Mary months to finish a gown. One—a "white silk with blue brocaded flowers"—was completed just in time for a supper party given by the Edwardses, who had finally readmitted the Lincolns into their social circle. When Abraham saw her wearing it, he said, "Fine feathers enough to make fine birds of us both." His compliment pleased her. Not only had her sewing skills resulted in something stylish, but they had caught the eye of her husband, who could often be distant.

AMBITIOUS ABRAHAM

Abraham liked to pretend he had no great aspirations for himself, but people who knew him best knew the truth. As William Herndon remarked, "His ambition was a little engine that knew no rest." Abraham once half-jokingly told a men's group that he aspired "to nothing beyond a seat in Congress, or a gubernatorial, or a presidential chair." Never during his twenty-four years in Springfield did he lose interest in politics or completely withdraw from public life. He worried about the nation's problems and knew the only way he could change things was through national office. "How hard, oh how hard," he once moaned to Herndon, "it is to die and leave one's country no better than if one had never lived for it."

AMBITIOUS MARY

Mary insisted the road to prominence ran toward Washington, not through Illinois's dusty little courtrooms. With her eye on her husband's political career, she poked, prodded, encouraged, consoled, and applauded his every effort. She was, admitted one family member, "very ambitious."

"My husband is to be President of the United States one day," she was often heard to say. Lincoln tried to lower her expectations. "But nobody knows me," he once told her. "They soon will," she replied confidently.

To live with such a woman was a perpetual kick in the pants for Abraham, and he laughed to think of "such a sucker as me President." Still, Mary's constant encouragement fed his own ambitions and kept him going through the ups and downs of his political career. Acknowledged Lincoln, "[Mary] is my dearest partner of greatness."

➤ WHAT IS A WHIG? ➤

When Abraham entered politics, there were two major political parties in the United States—the Democrats and the Whigs.

As the nation's majority party at the time, Democrats usually controlled Congress, the presidency, and many state offices. They opposed strong, centralized government, believing it would threaten individual liberties, and instead claimed that states had greater legal authority, or rights, than the federal government. (This belief was called "states' rights.") Democrats also denounced the greed, unfairness, and domination of the nation's elite class, making them the party of the common man. Their supporters came from every part of the nation and included Irish and German immigrants and even outsider groups such as Catholics and Jews. But for all their "everyman appeal," the core of Democratic support came from powerful Southern slave owners. They led the party toward proslavery policies, including the promotion of states' rights, which protected the institution. Southerners knew that if states held the

This 1846 Whig ticket, showing various Illinois offices, lists Lincoln for Congress.

highest authority, the federal government could never pass a law making slavery illegal.

The Whig Party, on the other hand, championed banks, businesses, and corporations. They believed in a strong federal government and limited states' rights, and they strongly opposed the expansion of slavery. Although the Whig Party was not antislavery, free blacks and abolitionists overwhelmingly preferred it to the more ardently proslavery Democratic Party. Whigs drew supporters from small farmers, shopkeepers, owners of small businesses, and clerks. People unhappy with the treatment of African Americans and Native Americans also rallied around the Whig Party, as did those who believed in prison reform, public education, and a government-sponsored program of internal improvements (the building of roads, railroads, canals).

Which party did Abraham Lincoln join?

"[I am] always," he declared, "a Whig in politics."

GUESS WHO WANTS TO GO TO CONGRESS?

Abraham had served in the Illinois state legislature ever since his first successful election in 1834. But when his fourth term expired, in 1842, he decided not to run again. "That assemblage," he told a friend, "offers no new worlds to conquer."

The problem was, Illinois offered few political opportunities for a Whig. Democrats held a hefty majority in the state; it had never elected a Whig governor or United States senator, and it had never voted for a Whig presidential candidate. Only in the Seventh Congressional District—an area that included Springfield—did the Whigs hold a solid majority, consistently sending one of their own to the House of Representatives. Wondered Lincoln, "Why shouldn't I be one of the chosen?" Taking an active role in Whig politics, he wrote pamphlets, gave speeches, and wooed party leaders. He was not shy about his goal. "Now if you should hear anyone saying that Lincoln don't want to go to Congress," he wrote a fellow Whig in 1846, "I wish you would tell him he is mistaken. The truth is, I would very much like to go."

IN THE MIDST OF POLITICS . . . A NEW BABY

The only known photograph of Edward Baker Lincoln, age three

On March 10, 1846, Eddie—as his parents called him—was born. "He is very much such a child as Bob was at his age—rather of the longer order," Lincoln wrote to a friend. By all accounts, little Eddie was a happy baby. But he was also in fragile health, alternating between coughing fits and high fevers. Nowadays many historians believe Eddie suffered from tuberculosis, a deadly lung infection.

✦ THE CAMPAIGN MUST GO ON! ✦

Just two months after Eddie's birth, Lincoln finally got his chance for distinction: the district Whig Party nominated him its candidate for the United States House of Representatives.

It was a tough campaign. Lincoln's Democratic opponent was Peter Cartwright, a Methodist preacher and formidable vote-getter. Cartwright spoke well and had lots of friends in the district.

Knowing he needed to face his opponent head-on, Lincoln walked into one of Cartwright's Bible meetings, where the preacher-politican was giving a hell-raising sermon. When he finished, Cartwright turned to his congregation. "All who desire . . . to give their hearts to God and go to heaven will stand!"

Almost everyone in the room stood.

"All who do not wish to go to hell will stand," cried Cartwright.

The rest of the congregation stood—everyone, that is, except Abraham.

Cartwright looked at him. "May I inquire of you, Mr. Lincoln, where are you going?"

Reverend Peter Cartwright, Lincoln's opponent for Congress

"If it's all the same to you," drawled Abraham, "I am going to Congress."

The congregation burst into laughter.

Cartwright sputtered with anger.

And weeks later, Lincoln was elected by a margin of more than fifteen hundred votes.

FUNDING A CAMPAIGN

Abraham was scrupulously honest when it came to money—especially money collected on behalf of his campaigns. After winning his seat in Congress in 1847, he returned $199.25 of the $200 received from his supporters. He gave this explanation:

I made the canvass on my own horse; my entertainment, being at the houses of friends, cost me nothing; and my only outlay was 75 cents for a barrel of cider, which some farmhands insisted I should treat to.

SHOCKING!

Springfield was all abuzz. "Mrs. L., I am told, accompanies her husband to Washington next winter," tattled one of the town's elite.

How shocking! How incredible! How unheard of! In the mid-nineteenth century, congressmen's wives rarely went to the nation's capital, and certainly not wives with small children. Freshman congressmen didn't earn enough to comfortably support a family in Washington, D.C. Only those rich enough to pay the exorbitant rents charged by landlords on Capitol Hill or Pennsylvania Avenue brought their families. As a result, Washington's boardinghouses were crowded with men—unseemly places for a lady and children.

But Mary didn't care what her neighbors thought. She intended to share her husband's success. "She wishes to loom largely," observed Judge David Davis, Lincoln's friend from the Eighth Circuit.

Abraham indulged his wife. "Will you be a good girl in all things, if I consent?" he asked her. "Then come along."

A FAMILY VACATION

IN OCTOBER 1847, the Lincoln family set out for Washington, D.C. On their way, they stopped in Lexington to visit their Todd relatives. When they arrived, the mansion's front door was wide open, and the whole Todd family stood waiting—children and parents in front, Mammy Sally and the other slaves in back. Mary stepped forward, baby Eddie in her arms. "To my mind she was lovely," recalled her littlest half sister, nine-year-old Emilie Todd. "Clear, sparkling blue eyes, lovely smooth white skin . . . glossy light brown hair . . . She was about twenty-nine."

Carrying Bobby, Lincoln followed his wife into the hall. Emilie was frightened of this tall man dressed in black coat and fur hat. "I remember thinking of Jack and the Beanstalk, and feared he might be the hungry giant from the story. . . . Expecting to hear 'Fee, fi, fo, fum!' I . . . tried to hide behind [my mother's] skirts."

But Abraham just smiled and lifted Emilie high into the air. "So this is [Mary's] littlest sister," he said, and kissed her cheek.

As the Todd family greeted their guests, Mrs. Todd's nephew, Joseph Humphreys, slipped out. By chance he had been traveling on the same train as the Lincolns and had arrived at the Todd house before Abraham and Mary. "Aunt Betsey," he'd gasped as he burst into the front parlor, "I was never so glad to get off a train in my life. There were two lively youngsters on board who kept the whole train in turmoil, and their long-legged father, instead of spanking the brats, looked pleased as Punch and aided and abetted [them] in their mischief."

A train similar to the one the Lincolns would have taken

At that moment, he glanced out the window and saw Lincoln alighting from a carriage. "Good Lord," he exclaimed. "There they are now!" He was not seen again until the Lincolns left.

For the next three weeks, the Lincolns enjoyed Lexington. They visited Mary's many relatives, took long walks through the town's fine brick streets, and attended teas and dinners held in their honor.

While Mary shopped and gossiped with the ladies, Abraham poked about in Robert Todd's well-stocked library. Book in hand, he often stretched out on the first-floor landing, where the bright sunlight streamed in through a nearby window. He also spent a lot of time at the courthouse, loafing, swapping stories, and talking politics with the judges and lawyers—friends of his father-in-law. And he took time to romp with Bobby, Eddie, and Emilie. Everyone—Todds and Lincolns—enjoyed the visit. At the end of their time together, said Emilie, "we hated to let them go."

When Mary and Abraham (along with Robert, age four, and Eddie, one and a half) first arrived in Washington, they felt they were on a shared adventure. Here was the biggest, most cosmopolitan city either of them had ever seen. Of course, the place was not perfect. Pigs wandered freely through the unpaved streets, and garbage, dead animals, and human waste littered every neighborhood. Only the lower part of Pennsylvania Avenue was paved, there wasn't a single streetlight, and cowsheds leaned against the Capitol. Only blocks from that building stood the crowded slave pens where congressmen from Southern states sometimes shopped for humans. Still, for all its shortcomings, Washington was on its way to becoming a world-renowned city—the first city created solely to serve as a center of government.

But living in Mrs. Spriggs's boardinghouse—the Lincolns' first Washington home—left much to be desired. The family shared a room on the second floor "with a bed, a bureau, table, chairs, closets and a good fireplace." The dining room, which overlooked the Capitol, served hearty meals of "graham bread, apples, dinner potatoes, spinach with eggs, various meats, figs, raisins and bread puddings." When the Lincolns arrived, there were ten other boarders, all men, and meals took on an especially manly atmosphere. Amid the tobacco spitting and dirty jokes, Mary was remembered as being "very retiring." She quickly decided to take all her meals in their room, but Abraham continued eating downstairs. He enjoyed the camaraderie and the political gossip.

This engraving shows Washington's citizens engaged in such common social activities as promenading along the avenue and listening to a band in the park.

During the day, Mary cared for the boys while Abraham worked at the Capitol. When the government offices closed at three, Abraham met her, and they joined the other citizens in promenading along the avenue before dinner at four. There were plays, concerts, lectures, and art exhibitions. The Lincolns listened to the Marine Band, went to Carusi's Saloon to see the blackface minstrel shows, and took the boys to puppet shows. They attended President Polk's New Year's Eve reception and a ball honoring George Washington's birthday. Mary found it all very exciting . . . at least for a while.

Mary was bored. The first weeks in Washington had been exciting, but now . . . there was nothing to do. Her husband, busy with the work of Congress, had little time to spend with her. And because there were few representatives' wives in Washington, she did not have any female friends with whom to socialize.

Perhaps to console herself, Mary shopped. She discovered how much "going out and getting what I want" suited her. She bought toys for Robert, clothes for Eddie, a pair of kid gloves for Abraham. For herself she splurged on a new deep-brimmed "Neapolitan Bonnet"—the most expensive item in the milliner's shop on Pennsylvania Avenue. She spent recklessly, with a slippery regard for debt. And she kept it from her husband.

The Washington adventure had turned into a disappointment. No one had made the slightest fuss over the wife of the freshman congressman from Illinois. The humid weather was aggravating Eddie's cough. And Bobby was constantly at her skirts. She had to get away. But where? She couldn't return to the house in Springfield, because they had rented it out. And so, while her husband and other members of Congress wrestled with the difficult issue of slavery, Mary took the children to her parents' home in Lexington. There she sank back into a life of comfort—comfort provided by slavery.

Mary had lasted only four months in Washington.

ABSENCE MAKES THE HEART GROW FONDER.

Abraham and Mary in 1847, the year they went to Washington.

While separated, husband and wife wrote each other often. They obviously missed each other, as the following excerpts from their letters show:

He wrote: *"What did Bobby and Edd[ie] think of the little letters Father sent them? Don't let the blessed fellows forget Father."*

She wrote: *"Do not fear the children have forgotten you. . . . Even Edd[ie]'s eyes brighten at the mention of your name."*

He wrote: *"I want to see you, and our dear boys very much."*

She wrote: *"I feel very sad away from you."*

He wrote: *"In this troublesome world we are never quite satisfied. When you were here, I thought you hindered me some in attending to business; but now, having nothing but business—no variety—it has grown exceedingly tasteless to me. . . . I hate to stay in this old room by myself."*

She wrote: *"How much I wish instead of writing, we were together this evening."*

LINCOLN'S HANDWRITTEN SPEECH LATER KNOWN AS THE "SPOT RESOLUTIONS"

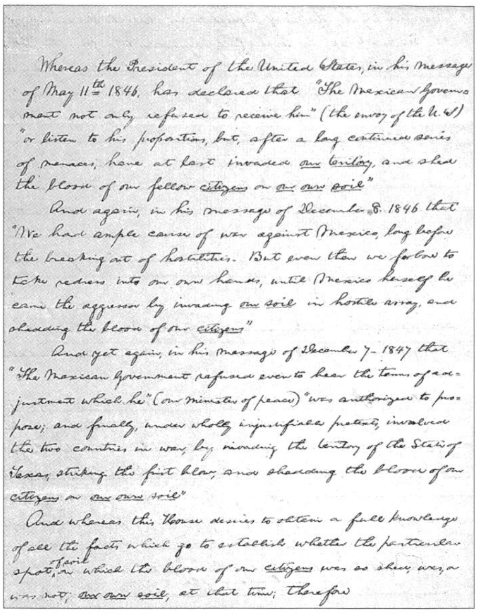
Whereas the President of the United States, in his message of May 11th 1846, has declared that "The Mexican Government not only refused to receive him" (the envoy of the U.S.) "or listen to his propositions, but, after a long continued series of menaces, have at last invaded our territory, and shed the blood of our fellow citizens on our own soil"

And again, in his message of December 8. 1846 that "We had ample cause of war against Mexico, long before the breaking out of hostilities. But even then we forbore to take redress into our own hands, until Mexico herself became the aggressor by invading our soil in hostile array, and shedding the blood of our citizens"

And yet again, in his message of December 7 - 1847 that "The Mexican Government refused even to hear the terms of adjustment which he" (our minister of peace) "was authorized to propose; and finally, under wholly unjustifiable pretexts, involved the two countries in war, by invading the territory of the State of Texas, striking the first blow, and shedding the blood of our citizens on our own soil"

And whereas this House desires to obtain a full knowledge of all the facts which go to establish whether the particular spot of soil on which the blood of our citizens was so shed, was, or was not, our own soil, at that time; therefore

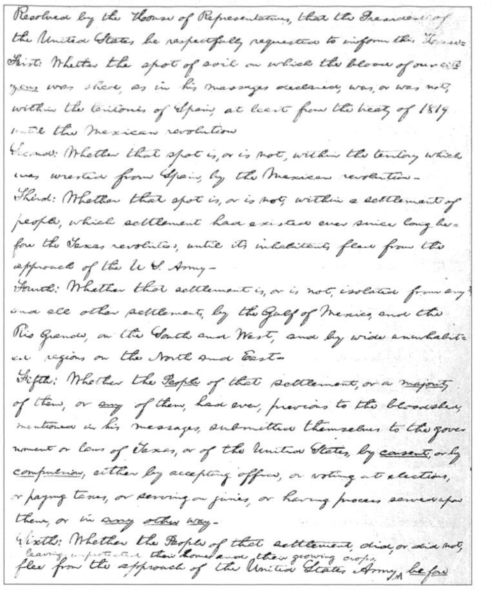
Resolved by the House of Representatives, that the President of the United States be respectfully requested to inform this House—

First: Whether the spot of soil on which the blood of our citizens was shed, as in his messages declared, was, or was not, within the territories of Spain, at least from the treaty of 1819 until the Mexican revolution

Second: Whether that spot is, or is not, within the territory which was wrested from Spain, by the Mexican revolution—

Third: Whether that spot is, or is not, within a settlement of people, which settlement had existed ever since long before the Texas revolution, until its inhabitants fled from the approach of the U.S. Army—

Fourth: Whether that settlement is, or is not, isolated from any and all other settlement, by the Gulf of Mexico, and the Rio Grande, on the South and West, and by wide uninhabited regions on the North and East—

Fifth: Whether the People of that settlement, or a majority of them, or any of them, had ever, previous to the bloodshed, mentioned in his messages, submitted themselves to the government or laws of Texas, or of the United States, by consent, or by compulsion, either by accepting office, or voting at elections, or paying taxes, or serving on juries, or having process served upon them, or in any other way—

Sixth: Whether the People of that settlement, did, or did not, flee from the approach of the United States Army, leaving unprotected their homes and their growing crops, before

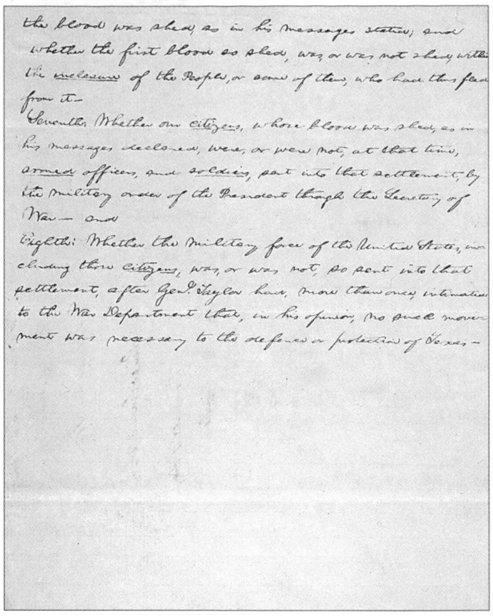
the blood was shed, as in his messages stated; and whether the first blood so shed, was, or was not shed, within the enclosure of the People, or some of them, who had thus fled from it—

Seventh: Whether our citizens, whose blood was shed, as in his messages declared, were, or were not, at that time, armed officers, and soldiers, sent into that settlement, by the military order of the President through the Secretary of War— and

Eighth: Whether the military force of the United States, including those citizens, was, or was not, so sent into that settlement, after Genl. Taylor had, more than once, intimated to the War Department that, in his opinion, no such movement was necessary to the defence or protection of Texas—

At the time Lincoln was elected to Congress, the United States was at war with Mexico over land. President James K. Polk had been determined to add what would eventually become New Mexico, Arizona, Colorado, Nevada, Utah, and California to the United States' territory, expanding the nation to the Pacific Ocean. After a failed attempt to buy the land, Polk had asked Congress to declare war in April 1846.

Polk claimed that Mexico struck the first blow by shedding "the blood of our citizens on our own soil." From the start, Whigs had claimed that the president was lying, and that the United States had actually begun the war by opening fire on a Mexican settlement. But by the time Lincoln arrived in Washington, the fighting had ended and the peace treaty was about to be signed. At this point, Lincoln later admitted, it would have been easier to remain silent. But when Democrats in the House introduced resolutions blaming the war on Mexican aggression, the Whigs were forced to respond.

Lincoln led the assault. On December 22, 1847, he gave a fiery speech in the House, demanding that the president pinpoint the exact "spot" where Americans had been attacked; "whether the particular spot" had been in Mexico or the United States; and whether that "spot had existed before the approach of the United States army."

Not surprisingly, the president did not respond to the freshman congressman from Illinois. But Lincoln's constituents did. The majority of voters—Democrat and Whig alike—were delighted by the outcome of the war: the huge addition of land to American territory. So when they read Lincoln's speech, they were furious. The *Illinois Register* claimed he had disgraced his district with "treasonable assault" and asserted he would "henceforth" be known as a "second Benedict Arnold." The *Springfield Register* demanded, "Out, damned Spot!" The nickname stuck. Folks began calling Lincoln's resolutions the "Spot Resolutions" and him "Old Spotty."

Lincoln tried to clarify his position. He argued that to simply accept President Polk's words without question was to "allow the President to invade a nation whenever . . . he says it is necessary."

But with the American flag waving over both the Atlantic and Pacific shores, no one listened. Instead, members of Congress were busy debating whether the territories would be slave or free. Lincoln denounced every bill that tried to spread slavery into the new lands.

At the end of his first term in 1849, Lincoln returned to Springfield. Response to his "Spot Resolutions" had kept him from running for a second term.

ABRAHAM'S PATENT FOR AN "IMPROVED METHOD OF LIFTING VESSELS OVER SHOALS"

Before leaving Washington, Lincoln applied to patent a device he had invented to lift boats over sandbars and shoals.

The idea had come to him in 1848, when a boat he was traveling on ran aground in shallow water. It reminded Abraham of his youthful days on the Mississippi River when vessels were stuck on sandbars for hours, days, even weeks. Wasn't there some way to stop these irritating delays? He wondered if a kind of bellows could be attached below the water line on each side of the boat's hull. Whenever the boat got stuck, the bellows could be filled with air, which would buoy up the boat, allowing it to float free.

Abraham soon began constructing a model of his invention. He "whittled away on the device," recalled William Herndon, "while waxing poetic about its merits." Lincoln received his patent, but he did nothing with it. He never tested the invention under working conditions or tried to sell the idea.

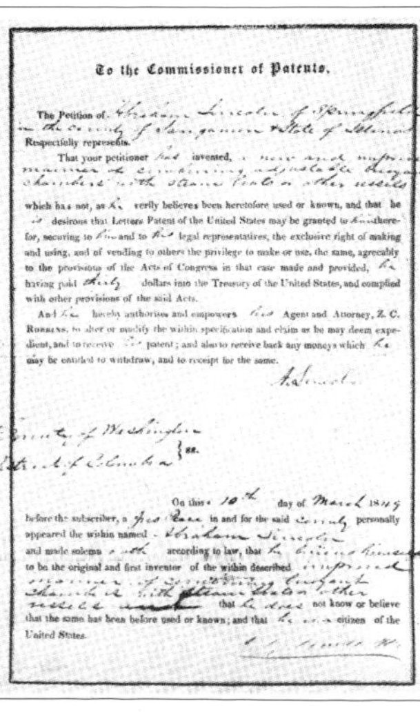
To the Commissioner of Patents.

The Petition of Abraham Lincoln of Springfield in the county of Sangamon & State of Illinois

Respectfully represents.

That your petitioner has invented, a new and improved manner of combining adjustable buoyant chambers with steam boats or other vessels

which has not, as he verily believes been heretofore used or known, and that he is desirous that Letters Patent of the United States may be granted to him therefor, securing to him and to his legal representatives, the exclusive right of making and using, and of vending to others the privilege to make or use, the same, agreeably to the provisions of the Acts of Congress in that case made and provided, he having paid thirty dollars into the Treasury of the United States, and complied with other provisions of the said Acts.

And he hereby authorises and empowers his Agent and Attorney, Z. C. Robbins, to alter or modify the within specification and claim as he may deem expedient, and to receive the patent; and also to receive back any moneys which he may be entitled to withdraw, and to receipt for the same.

A. Lincoln

County of Washington
District of Columbia } ss.

On this 10th day of March 1849 before the subscriber, a Justice of the Peace in and for the said County personally appeared the within named Abraham Lincoln and made solemn oath according to law, that he believes himself to be the original and first inventor of the within described improved manner of combining buoyant chambers with steam boats or other vessels that he does not know or believe that the same has been before used or known; and that he is a citizen of the United States.

SAD NEWS

MARY'S FATHER DIES.

In July 1849, Mary's father, Robert Smith Todd, was suddenly stricken with cholera. Growing worse despite all the doctors gathered at his bedside, he made a will (in which he left Mary $750), then signed it with a tremulous hand. Hours later, he died.

News of his death could not have reached Mary and Abraham at a worse time. Eddie was desperately ill, and they could not leave his bedside. There was, Mary later said, "no time, nor room to grieve [for him]."

EDDIE LINCOLN'S HEADSTONE

When Eddie was three, his always fragile health took a turn for the worse. Mary's brother-in-law Dr. William Wallace prescribed Wistor's Balsam of Wildcherry, a medicine full of cough-suppressing opium. Desperately, Mary spooned the elixir into her weak son's mouth while rubbing his bony chest with spirits of camphor and feeding him an invalid diet of oatmeal gruel and rice jelly. Nothing worked. On February 1, 1850, little Eddie died.

The funeral was held the next day. Rain pattered on the roof as the Reverend James Smith said a few words in the Lincolns' parlor. Then Abraham, along with their friends and neighbors, followed the tiny casket to the cemetery. Mary chose not to go. Instead she stayed in bed, weeping so long and so hard that it scared six-year-old Bobby.

"Eat, Mary," Lincoln urged his wife a few days after the funeral, "for we must live too."

Mary expressed her grief by writing a poem that appeared in the *Springfield Journal* a week after Eddie's death. The last stanza read:

Angel boy—fare thee well, farewell
Sweet Eddie, We bid thee adieu!
Affection's wail cannot reach thee now
Deep though it be, and true.
Bright is the home to him now given
For of such is the Kingdom of Heaven.

Lincoln was grief-stricken, too. But he spoke little about the loss. "We miss him very much," he said simply.

CHAPTER

FOUR

TUMULTUOUS TIMES

As a nation, we began by declaring that "all men are created equal." We now practically read it, "all men are created equal except Negroes."

—ABRAHAM LINCOLN IN A LETTER TO JOSHUA SPEED, AUGUST 24, 1855

You must not include [my husband] with so many of those, who belong to *that party*, an *Abolitionist*. In principle he is far from it—All he desires is, that slavery, shall not be extended, let it remain, where it is.

—MARY LINCOLN IN A LETTER TO EMILIE TODD, NOVEMBER 23, 1856

◆ SLAVERY TAKES CENTER STAGE. ◆

The war with Mexico added vast amounts of new land to the United States. As Americans moved into these places, Congress was prompted to create territories from which new states would eventually be carved. But the admission of each new state raised a crucial question: would it be admitted to the Union as a free state or a slave state?

Since its beginnings, America had been equally divided between Southern states, where slavery was legal (known as slave states), and Northern states, where slavery was illegal (free states). This uneasy balance had been maintained through a series of compromises, including the Missouri Compromise of 1820, which allowed slavery in some Western territories and barred it from others.

Now Southerners wanted to move into these new Western territories, bringing with them slaves by the hundreds of thousands. The North, meanwhile, insisted these lands be given over to the free labor of independent farmers and workers. Ultimately, this struggle began a chain of events that ignited tempers, sharpened regional differences, and changed public opinion. In short, they brought the nation to the very brink of war.

THE COMPROMISE OF 1850

When California's citizens applied for their territory's entrance into the Union as a free state, it set off a fierce debate between Northern and Southern legislators. The proslavery factions angrily insisted that at least a portion of it should be a slave state. Free-soilers just as angrily insisted that slavery had no business there.

Sensing that the Union was in peril, the venerable Whig leader (and Mary's childhood friend) Senator Henry Clay suggested a compromise. California would enter the Union as a free state, while the territories of Utah and New Mexico (which did not yet have enough American citizens to apply for statehood) would be created. This would allow the question of slavery in each to be determined by popular sovereignty. That is, each territory's inhabitants would decide whether their territory would be

Henry Clay proposes his famous compromise to members of the U.S. Senate.

admitted to the Union as a free state or a slave state, rather than Congress banning slavery in what would eventually become new states. In addition, the compromise would outlaw the buying and selling of slaves in the District of Columbia (although whites could still own slaves there). And for proslavery advocates it included the Fugitive Slave Act, giving Southerners the right to capture runaways in the North.

Despite bitter debate in Congress, the compromise eventually passed, and the nation breathed a sigh of relief. In Washington, crowds took to the streets to celebrate what one reveler called "this glorious day of salvation for our nation." And in Springfield, Abraham heard the news with pleasure. Like other Americans, he believed that all questions about slavery were finally "settled forever."

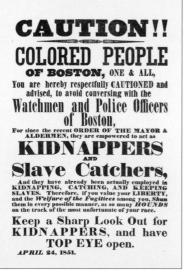

THE FUGITIVE SLAVE ACT

After passage of the Compromise of 1850, African Americans began to be hunted down in Northern cities. Almost overnight, antislavery sentiment grew. Northern newspapers attacked the "barbaric practice," while huge protest meetings were held in Chicago, Cleveland, and New York City. In Boston in 1851 a mob snatched a runaway slave from a U.S. marshal and sent him to safety in Canada. In Springfield, William Herndon—an ardent abolitionist—begged his senior partner to speak out. But Abraham refused. "Billy," he said, "you're too rampant and spontaneous." What Americans needed now, he added, was "reason—cold, calculating, unimpassioned—reason."

This broadside reveals Northern outrage over the Fugitive Slave Act. The reference to kidnapping comes from the fear that free blacks would be transported back into slavery under the law.

UNCLE TOM'S CABIN

In March 1852, Harriet Beecher Stowe published her novel *Uncle Tom's Cabin,* which dramatized the horror and brutality of slavery. An instant bestseller, the book sold 300,000 copies in nine months; by mid-1853, more than a million copies were in print. Stowe's novel brought the issue of slavery home to many who had never before given it much thought. Sickened by what they learned, many readers were shocked into a hatred for the institution, and Northern opinion began to galvanize against slavery. Later, when Abraham met Stowe, he was said to have called her the "little lady who made this big war," referring to the Civil War. But when the book was first published, he said nothing public about it.

An advertisement for Uncle Tom's Cabin

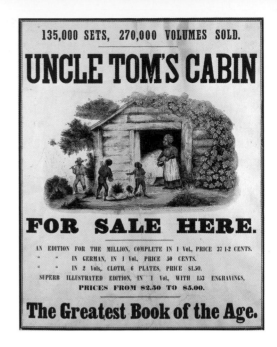

EVENTS IN SPRINGFIELD

THE EARLIEST KNOWN PHOTOGRAPH OF THE LINCOLNS' THIRD SON, WILLIAM WALLACE, AT AGE FOUR

In December 1850—the same year Clay proposed his great compromise—Mary bore her third son. She named him after the kind brother-in-law who had helped so much during Eddie's illness. The new baby was, said Mary, "a very beautiful boy with a most spiritual expression of face."

Willie, as he was promptly nicknamed, was sweet-tempered, bright, and highly sensitive to other people's feelings. From the moment of his birth, Abraham doted on him. And as the child grew, Abraham began to believe that Willie's mind was very like his own. Once, after proudly watching six-year-old Willie solve a difficult math problem, Abraham told a visitor, "I know every step of the process by which the boy arrived at [the] solution, as it is by just such slow methods I attain results."

Willie was also Mary's favorite. She couldn't help but notice his resemblance to her husband. Father and son had the same talents, the same interests. They even had the same mannerism of holding their head to one side when deep in thought. This striking likeness "formed a special bond between us," said Mary. She called Willie her "comfort." He called himself "Mother's boy."

But for all his sweetness, Willie was no goody-goody. He delighted in pranks and mischief. Once when he was four years old he escaped from his mother and the bathtub. Naked and dripping, he scampered out the door and down the street. His father, who happened to be on the porch, gleefully chased after him and caught him. Then, "chuckling with the fun of adventure," recalled one neighbor, "he mounted the boy on his shoulders and carried him back to his mother."

When Willie was eight, his father took him along on a train trip to Chicago. "This town is very beautiful," Willie wrote to a friend after they arrived. "Me and Father have a nice room to ourselves. . . . We have two little pitchers on a washstand. The smallest one for me, the largest one for Father. We have two little towels on top of both pitchers. The smallest one for me, the largest one for Father."

This trip would be the one and only time Willie would receive his father's undivided attention. Within a year, Abraham would win the Republican nomination for president. After that, said Willie, "everything changed."

PEEKING INTO A MARRIAGE

Abraham and Mary were as different in temperament as they were in physique. He was slow, moody, and given to bouts of melancholy and long periods of silence. She was lively, talkative, and temperamental, and she constantly needed the attention and admiration of others. These differences led to both fireworks and affection, as the following stories show.

+≈≈≈+

Once, as Abraham sat reading while Mary cooked dinner, she called out to him that the fire in the stove was about to expire. Absorbed in his newspaper, he didn't answer. Mary called again. He still didn't answer. So she called again . . . and again . . . and again. Finally, frustrated at being ignored, she grabbed a chunk of firewood and bopped him on the nose. She got his attention, and he wore a bandage for the next week.

+≈≈≈+

From the moment she said "I do," Mary set out to smooth Abraham's coarse country manners. She railed against her husband's habit of eating peas with his butter knife. She scolded when he chewed with his mouth open. And she raised "merry hell," said one neighbor, when he sat down to supper in his shirtsleeves. Once, he answered the door wearing his holey carpet slippers—the pair that exposed a big, bony toe. When the refined ladies on the front step finally recovered from their shock, they asked for his wife. Lincoln, in his homespun fashion, replied that "he'd trot the women out" immediately. This complete breach of manners so enraged Mary, she gave him a tongue-lashing right there in front of the guests.

+≈≈≈+

Mary did not allow anyone else to criticize her husband, whom, appropriately in those proper Victorian days, she called "Mr. Lincoln" in public. Once, when someone compared him unfavorably to another, handsomer politician, she bristled: "Mr. Lincoln may not be as handsome a figure . . . but the people are perhaps not aware that his heart is as large as his arms are long."

+≈≈≈+

Abraham did not allow anyone to criticize his wife, whom he called "Molly," "Mother," and occasionally "my child wife." When someone asked him why he put up with her temper tantrums, he tried to explain: "It does her lots of good, and it doesn't hurt me a bit."

+≈≈≈+

One day, Mary came home from shopping to discover that their children, Robert and Eddie, had made a mess in the parlor. She was scolding them when Abraham came in and intervened on the boys' behalf. Mary angrily turned on him, "but he only laughed," recalled a neighbor, "picked her up in his arms, and kissed the daylights out of her. And she clung to him like a girl."

One of the earliest photographs of the Lincolns' last child, Thomas

In the fall of 1852–just eighteen months after Willie's birth–the Lincolns discovered they were expecting again. They were thrilled, and earnestly hoped for a girl. But in May 1853 Mary gave birth to another boy, Thomas. When Lincoln saw the newborn with the unusually large head and thin body he laughingly called him a tadpole. The nickname "Tad" stuck for the rest of the boy's life.

Tad had a temperament like his mother's—he was volatile and impulsive, yet very affectionate. Tad was, remembered one old-timer, "completely engaging with his quaint little ways and fancies." Often, Tad would burst into a room where his parents were sitting. Throwing himself on them "like a small thunderbolt," he would give them a wild, fierce hug, then rush from the room before either grown-up could say a word.

Tad was handicapped by a speech impediment that made his words sound strange—breathy, nasal, almost another language. Sometimes only his parents could understand what he was saying, and other children picked on him. Tad's cousin John Grimsley remembered Tad once saying, "I love you, John, because you are nice to me and don't tease me."

Just seven years old when his father won the Republican nomination for president, Tad found all the hoopla exciting. When one Lincoln admirer sent the candidate a whistle, Tad claimed it as his own. Afterward, visitors to the Lincoln home found the little boy blowing blasts on his new toy, making ears ring and making conversation impossible. Between blasts, Tad hollered, "Hurrah for Old Abe!" His mother, complained one guest, "thought it adorable."

About the time Tad was born, the Dallmans, who lived down the street, also had a son. But Mrs. Dallman was too ill to nurse her newborn. Eager to help, the Lincolns came up with a plan. Mary would nurse their baby as well as Tad if Abraham would fetch the baby four times a day. Remembered Mrs. Dallman:

> *The tall, gaunt figure of Mr. Lincoln . . . knocked at my door, entered with a gentle step so as not to disturb me, and then gathered up the little mite of my newborn child into his big, brawny hands, formed like a basket for that purpose, and carried the infant across the street. . . . Soon he would return . . . with a tender expression of profound sympathy . . . as he [put] the little child in his crib.*

The Lincolns kept up this schedule for several weeks until Mrs. Dallman recovered.

PA

Abraham believed children should be hugged instead of spanked, praised instead of criticized, cherished instead of endured. "Mr. Lincoln," explained Mary, "was the kindest and most loving . . . father in the world. He gave us all unbounded liberty. He always said, 'It is my pleasure that my children are free, happy and unrestrained by parental tyranny. Love is the chain whereby to bind a child to its parents.' "

He was especially devoted to Willie and Tad, whom he called "the dear codgers." When he could, he helped with babysitting the two little boys—a practice so unusual that gossips called him "hen-pecked." When Willie and Tad were very small, he hauled them around in a little wagon, pulling it up and down Eighth Street, often while reading a book. One day, Tad tumbled out and lay squalling on the ground. Absorbed in his book, Abraham didn't notice. He was a whole block away before he heard Mary hollering for him to stop. Turning, he was surprised to see his wife holding the sobbing toddler.

The neighbors were appalled by the children's outspokenness, their rambunctiousness, their lack of respect for their elders. But no one was more candid about the "little devils" than William Herndon. On Sundays, Abraham often brought the boys to their law office. "Those children," Herndon recalled, "would take down the books—empty ash buckets—coal ashes—inkstands—papers—gold pens—letters etc. etc. into a pile and then dance on the

The only known photograph of Abraham with both Willie and Tad (on the fence), taken in 1860. There are no known photographs of Abraham with his son Robert.

pile. Lincoln would say nothing . . . so blinded to his children's faults. Had they shat in Lincoln's hat and rubbed it on his boots, he would have laughed and thought it smart."

Lincoln knew his child-rearing philosophies were unusual. In later years he told a friend, "We never controlled our children much."

By all accounts, Mary was a good mother. She constantly praised her "darling sons [who were] the noblest, purest, most talented [children] ever given to parents." Meanwhile, Springfield's citizens complained about "the Lincoln brats." "What those children needed was a real bottom burning," said one old-timer. But instead of spanking, Mary always "looked pleased as punch and abetted their mischief." In a time when parents believed in the adage "Spare the rod, spoil the child," Mary refused to raise a hand to her sons. And she refused to let anyone else do so, either. When Abraham tried to whack little Bob's bottom for some minor offense, Mary became hysterical and he stopped. Neither parent tried spanking again. Explained Mary, "[My sons] never needed a spanking, a gentle word was all sufficient for them."

Mary enjoyed dressing her children well, teaching them little verses, and training them in the manners and courtesies of cultured society. Recalled William Herndon, "It was Mrs. Lincoln's habit to dress up and trot out [the boys] and get them to monkey around—talk—dance—speak—quote poetry etc. Then she would become enthusiastic and eloquent over the children much to the annoyance of the visitor."

In later life, Mary admitted that her one parenting mistake was "in being too indulgent." If her boys wanted cookies for dinner, she baked them. If they cried for a new toy, she bought it. If they pleaded to keep a dog or a white rat or a talking crow for a pet, she let them. Once when Willie begged for a ninth-birthday party, she threw what she described as a "children's gala for fifty or sixty boys and girls," at a time when such parties for children were unheard of. The excessiveness of it shocked Springfield's mothers. Why would she do such a thing? they asked. Because she had promised, and "I feel it necessary to always keep one's word with a child," replied Mary.

Unlike most other mothers, Mary often played with her children. One day she heard a commotion outside

Mary Lincoln with Willie (holding his hat) and Tad (holding her hand) in 1860

and, running to the window, saw a medieval joust taking place. Bob and one of his playmates, using sharp-pointed fence railings for swords, were thrusting and parrying and shouting, "Take that!" and *"En garde."* Entering into the spirit of the game, Mary leaned out the window. "Gramercy, brave knights," she called out to them. "Pray be more merciful than you are brawny."

Of course, it wasn't all parties and games of "Let's pretend." High-strung, quick-tempered Mary sometimes found mothering her high-energy boys a nerve-racking ordeal. In fact, noted one historian, "she went to pieces at the slightest emergency in the family." Her neighbors were used to hearing her panicked cries for help. When Bobby was a toddler, recalled her next-door neighbor, she came running into the front yard "as usual, screaming 'Bobby will die!' Bobby will die!' " Apparently, she had caught the boy eating lime—a dry white powder used in privies during the nineteenth century to eliminate bacteria and odors. The neighbor calmly managed the situation. "[I] washed his mouth out," he said, "and that's all there was to it." Still, Mary always claimed that motherhood was her greatest joy, and that she had been "a happy, loving, laughing Mama."

Willie Lincoln will be pleased to see you, Wednesday Afternoon at 3 O'clock.

Tuesday Dec 22d.

An invitation written by Mary to Willie Lincoln's birthday party, December 22, 1859

THE KANSAS-NEBRASKA ACT

ON JANUARY 4, 1854, the Democratic senator from Illinois, Stephen A. Douglas, introduced a bill that would start Kansas and Nebraska on the road to statehood. He hoped to build a transcontinental railroad crossing through the Midwest that would boost Chicago's economy and encourage settlement on the Great Plains. But instead the bill caused a political whirlwind. Under the Missouri Compromise of 1820, the territories of Kansas and Nebraska had been declared off-limits to slavery. But under the new act, the future of slavery in those territories would be determined by popular sovereignty. Slavery now threatened to spread and establish itself permanently.

Lincoln was arguing a case when he heard that the bill had passed in Congress by a vote of 35 to 13. He was "thunderstruck and stunned." How would slavery ever die a "natural death" if it was allowed to spread? He was suddenly roused, he said, "as I had never been before." He began to neglect his law practice, traveling around the state to speak on behalf of anti-slavery Whig candidates and against Senator Douglas's policies. He told his audiences that slavery was a "monstrous injustice" and a "cancer" threatening to grow out of control "in a nation originally dedicated to the inalienable rights of man." If not stopped, he believed, slavery would eventually undermine the very foundations of democracy.

Still, while he opposed the *spread* of slavery, he admitted, "If all earthly power were given me, I would not know what to do, as to the existing institution."

This map, made just after passage of the Kansas-Nebraska Act, shows free states, slave states, and U.S. territorial expansion from 1819 to 1854.

LINCOLN WINS AN ELECTION . . .

Spurred by passage of the Kansas-Nebraska Act, Abraham returned full tilt to politics in the fall of 1854. He hoped to win a seat in the United States Senate. But before he could make his wishes widely known, some overenthusiastic Lincoln supporters published an ad in the *Illinois State Journal* declaring his candidacy for the state legislature. They did this without his knowledge, and at a time when he was out of town.

When Mary opened her newspaper on September 3, she was flabbergasted. Her husband wasn't running for state legislator! Rushing to the *Journal* office, she demanded that his name be withdrawn. She knew that if he was a legislator, he could not be elected to the Senate: at that time, senators were elected not by popular votes but by state legislatures. She also knew that the Illinois state legislature was about to replace an incumbent senator, James Shields. More than anything else, Mary wanted her husband to be that replacement.

Lincoln wanted it, too. But his friends in the Whig Party persuaded him to run for the state legislature instead, and in November he easily won a seat. Having just spent the summer traveling the state and making speeches, Abraham now believed he had enough support to make a successful grab at the still-open Senate seat. Only one thing stood in his way—the fact that he had been elected to the state legislature. What could he do? He declined to accept the seat he had just won.

Whigs across the state fumed. They believed he had put himself above the party. Said one Whig later, "[We were] down on Lincoln—hated him." A special election now had to be held to fill the empty seat in the legislature. Unable to find a worthy candidate on such short notice, the Whigs lost the seat to the Democrats. Opponents chuckled that the outcome was "the best Christmas joke of the season."

. . . THEN LOSES AN ELECTION.

On a snowy, cold day in January 1855, Mary Lincoln arrived early at the Illinois statehouse. After climbing the stairs to the gallery that overlooked the legislative chambers, she expectantly settled into a front-row seat. Today was the day the state legislature would elect a new senator, and Mary must have felt certain her husband would win. Hadn't she and Abraham measured his chances over the last few weeks, filling several notebooks with the name and vote of each legislator? And wasn't Abraham far ahead of his competitors? For weeks he had been calling in political favors amassed during his seventeen years of circuit riding. And even though many Whigs were still fuming over his resignation from the state legislature, they felt obliged to support him. More than a few Democrats also felt obliged to vote for him, as did a handful of third-party representatives.

In the chamber, the voting began. A candidate needed

A view of the legislative chambers and the gallery where Mary sat

fifty-one votes to win. On the first ballot Lincoln led with forty-seven votes; James Shields, the Democrat, had forty-one; and seventeen other votes were scattered among a handful of candidates. One of them, Lyman Trumbull, was the husband of Mary's friend and bridesmaid, Julia Trumbull. With only five votes, Julia's husband had absolutely no chance of winning.

Because no candidate had received the necessary votes the first time around, a second ballot was cast. To Mary's dismay, her husband's total went no higher. The legislators cast a third ballot . . . and a fourth . . . and a fifth! But not a single candidate received the required number of votes. By dinnertime, worried that the Democrat would win the seat, Lincoln threw his votes to the only other Whig candidate— Lyman Trumbull. Trumbull was promptly elected. "It was hard for the forty-seven to surrender to the five," Lincoln later explained, "but I could not . . . let the whole political result go to ruin on a point merely personal to myself." He was, however, "splendidly consoled" by the thought that the Democrats were "worse whipped than I."

Mary was furious. Why hadn't Trumbull thrown *his* votes to *her* husband—the candidate with the majority? It was, she believed, "cold, selfish treachery." That night, at a reception honoring the Trumbulls, Lincoln shook Lyman's hand. But Mary refused to even look at her old friend. Julia, she declared, was dead to her. Ever after, reported Julia, she "pretended not to see me."

Lyman Trumbull, the man who won the election and infuriated Mary

THE CRISIS GROWS...

By 1856, open warfare had broken out in Kansas. Both Northerners and Southerners recruited settlers to move into the territory. Each was determined to make Kansas free or slave. Clashes between the two groups led to violence. After proslavery groups rigged an election, free-staters responded by creating their own, unauthorized government. In retaliation, a proslavery posse sacked the town of Lawrence; in revenge, John Brown—a fanatic who saw himself as God's instrument to destroy slavery—murdered five proslavery settlers. Soon, the whole nation was talking about "Bleeding Kansas."

Lincoln did not condone this violence, even in the name of freedom. "Physical rebellions and bloody resistances," he said, were both immoral and illegal. Still, he gave an undisclosed amount of money to the "Freedom in Kansas" cause to stop the spread of slavery. He also urged the group to find "other more effective channels" of action—namely, politics.

This engraving from the New York Times *shows free-staters firing on a proslavery settlement near Leavenworth, Kansas.*

On the afternoon of May 22, 1856, the floor of the United States Senate became a combat zone. Charles Sumner of Massachusetts was delivering a passionate antislavery speech called "The Crime Against Kansas." The speech so enraged Preston Brooks—a congressman from South Carolina—that he savagely beat Senator Sumner into unconsciousness with a metal-topped cane. (It took three and a half years for Sumner to recover from the vicious attack, and ever after he walked with a limp.) The incident made both men heroes in their respective states. It also increased animosity between North and South. In Illinois, Abraham said

A nineteenth-century engraving of Representative Preston Brooks attacking Senator Charles Sumner on the Senate floor

nothing in public. In private he admitted that the attack deeply worried him. As he told Mary, it "symbolized the breakdown of reasoned discourse."

WHO'S IN?
THE REPUBLICANS!

Enraged over the Kansas-Nebraska Act, many Northerners vowed to put a stop to what they believed was the Southern threat to democracy. How? Well, they'd start by forming a new political party—the Republicans.

Forged just one month after the act's passage, the Republican Party was largely made up of former Whig members of the Know-Nothing Party (a fringe group that feared immigrants, especially the Roman Catholic Irish), as well as Northern Democrats who had deserted their Southern cousins over the slave issue. It quickly became the party of working white men who opposed the spread of slavery. This stand was based not on moral reasons but purely on economics. They did not want to compete against unpaid slave labor in lands opening up in the West.

Over the next two years, the party grew by leaps and bounds. By 1856, it was able to field its first presidential candidate, John C. Frémont. While Republicans did not win this election, they did carry all eleven Northern states. (They received less than 1 percent of the Southern vote.) For the first time, a purely Northern political party had pitted itself against supporters of slavery and achieved some success.

No wonder Southerners regarded the Republican Party with both hatred and fear.

WHO'S OUT?
THE WHIGS!

As the Republicans' star rose, the Whig Party's plummeted. Afraid to offend either its free-soil members in the North or its proslavery members in the South, Whig leaders chose to remain silent on slavery, clearly the most pressing issue facing America. And it was this silence that eventually destroyed the party. Formerly loyal Whig supporters began looking around for other political parties that addressed their concerns and represented their interests. Most found what they were looking for with the Republicans. While a few people still clung to the hope that the party could be revived, by 1856 the Whigs no longer mattered in national politics.

. . . AND THE LINCOLN HOME GROWS, TOO.

With money inherited from her father, Mary decided to expand her tiny house. Construction began in April 1856 and was finished that fall, while Abraham was away on the circuit. He returned to find himself the owner of a two-story upper-middle-class home tastefully painted chocolate brown with green shutters. Pretending bewilderment, he sauntered up to a neighbor. "Stranger," he joked, "do you know where Lincoln lives?" His humor was misunderstood, and the rumor spread that Mary had remodeled the house without her husband's approval. Of course Abraham knew about the project—he just didn't know how much it had cost. When he learned Mary had spent $1,300 (about $29,000 in today's dollars), he exploded. Mary's response? She continued to hide her spending from him, a habit that would eventually cause many problems.

The construction doubled the Lincolns' living space. Now there was a large sitting room where the parents could read and the children could play. There was a front parlor for receiving guests, which was connected by sliding doors to a back parlor used by Abraham as a library and study. Upstairs, Mary and Abraham had separate bedrooms—something all fashionable, well-to-do couples aspired to in the nineteenth century. Willie and Tad shared a second bedroom, leaving two other bedrooms open—one for Robert and one for guests.

Mary refurbished the house with bright carpets and

The house at Eighth and Jackson after its remodeling project (Abraham and Willie are standing inside the picket fence).

floral wallpaper. Said one visitor, "The air of quiet refinement pervaded the place. You would have known instantly that she who presided over that modest household was a true type of American lady."

This was exactly the image Mary wanted to project. She knew, even if her husband did not, that a man on the rise needed a proper home . . . and a proper wife to manage it.

FIDO

Sometime in the 1850s the Lincolns acquired a dog named Fido. They'd always had lots of pets. Unlike other Springfield mothers, Mary allowed all kinds of animals—turtles, mice, snakes—into the house. If the children "wanted a dog-cat-rat or the Devil," William Herndon muttered, "it was all right and well-treated—housed—petted—fed —fondled." Abraham loved animals, too. He doted on the horses that took him on those long, lonely journeys across the prairie. And as Mary once said, stray cats were his "hobby."

Where Fido came from and what year he actually took up residence with the Lincolns are unknown. We do know, however, that by 1857 Fido was a well-established and much beloved member of the family. A yellow mutt, he lived a carefree life. At night he lounged on the old horsehair sofa in the family's front parlor, and in the morning he trotted along behind Lincoln to the law office. If Fido was really lucky, they would stop in at Corneau and Diller's drugstore, where the dog might get a lick of his master's fruit-flavored soda water.

But in 1860, when Abraham was elected president, Fido's life changed. Fido couldn't come to Washington, Lincoln explained to his sons. A train filled to the brim, lurching and speeding along at thirty miles an hour, was no place for a dog. So Fido was given to Linden and Frank Roll, two of the Lincoln boys' favorite playmates, along with specific instructions. The dog, explained Tad, was never to be tied up alone in the backyard, or scolded for wet or muddy paws. He was to be let inside whenever he scratched on the door. And he absolutely had to be allowed in the dining room at suppertime because he was used to being given tastes by everyone around the table.

MARY LINCOLN, POLITICAL CONSULTANT

More than anything, Mary wanted recognition, distinction, and admiration. She yearned to "be somebody." To this end, she fought to make herself Abraham's most important political advisor. What could she give him? That "special intuition in which females are endowed," she said. She would be his "full-fledged, home-based counselor available for insightful judgments about the human motivations of political rivals, newspaper reporters and all those seeking favors from her husband."

Abraham always enlisted Mary's help with his speeches, reading them to her before he gave them. He would begin, "Mary, now listen to this." Afterward, she would offer comments, such as "Saying so-and-so would sound better." Mary knew a good speech when she heard it. And she knew how to improve a bad one.

Abraham often acted on Mary's advice. His male advisors, however, resented her intrusion. Behind Abraham's back they called his wife a "usurper" and a "meddling hag." For the sake of respectability, Mary's family always insisted she was simply "a domestic woman who loved her family above all." But Abraham knew different. His wife was a woman who loved politics.

THIS PENCIL DRAWING SHOWS LINCOLN ENERGETICALLY DELIVERING HIS FIRST GREAT REPUBLICAN SPEECH.

Just months after "buckling on the Republican armor," Lincoln traveled to Bloomington to help organize the Illinois Republican Party. While there, he gave what was acclaimed at the time as his greatest speech. Because he spoke without notes, there is no written record of what he said. Close to a thousand men sat in the audience, listening "as though transfixed. Reporters forgot to use the pencils in their hands." Even William Herndon, who always took notes when his legal partner spoke, was so moved he "threw pen and paper away and lived only in the inspiration of the hour." In his speech, recalled one reporter, Lincoln identified slavery as the cause of the nation's problems and pledged that he was "ready to fuse with anyone who would unite with him to oppose slave power." If the South didn't like this and threatened to secede, it should be told firmly that "the Union must be preserved!" He ended with a rousing shout: "Liberty and Union, now and forever, one and inseparable!" The speech, Herndon later wrote, not only was "full of fire and energy and force" but placed Lincoln at the head of his new political party. "If Mr. Lincoln was six feet, four inches tall usually, at Bloomington he stood seven feet."

A SHORT HISTORY OF SECESSION

Lincoln's Bloomington speech was not the first time a politician had brought up the subject of secession. States had been threatening to secede from the Union since America's beginning. The first time was in 1776, when the Continental Congress tried to tax states on a total population count that would include slaves. Furious, North Carolina threatened to secede. Slaves, they argued, could not be taxed "as people." Fearing separation, the Continental Congress gave in to North Carolina's demands. Ever after, when a state disagreed with the policies of the federal government, it waved the secession stick.

James Madison, one of the Constitution's framers, foresaw this. He repeatedly warned about "disunion" and begged to have a clause included in the Constitution prohibiting secession, but no one listened. Just twenty-five years later, New England—angry over the conduct of the War of 1812—threatened to secede from the Union if radical changes were not made to the Constitution.

But the most threats of secession came between the years 1819 and 1860. As the restriction of slavery became a significant goal in the free states, Southerners began to believe their way of life was under attack. Every time a state was admitted to the Union, tempers flared. Would it be a free state or a slave state? Again and again Southern states threatened to secede if slave states were prohibited. Only compromises like those made in 1820 and 1850 kept the secessionists at bay...at least for a while.

THE SUPREME COURT SHOCKS THE NATION . . .

In 1844 a slave named Dred Scott was taken by his master to the free state of Illinois and then to the free territory of Wisconsin. When he returned to the slave state of Missouri, two years later, he sued for his freedom, claiming that his lengthy presence in areas where there was no slavery had made him free. The case wound its way through the courts for eleven years, finally ending up before the U.S. Supreme Court, which ruled against Scott. Chief Justice Roger Taney declared that African Americans "were not intended to be included under the word 'citizens' in the Constitution" and

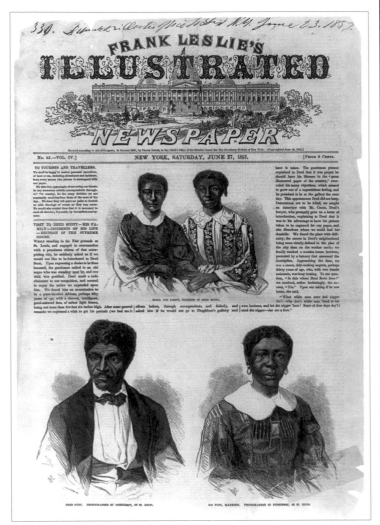

On June 27, 1857, Frank Leslie's Illustrated Newspaper *devoted its entire front page to Dred Scott, his family, and the Supreme Court's controversial decision.*

therefore could not claim any of the "rights and privileges [it] provides." Blacks, he determined, were property, and if a slave owner took his property into a territory where slavery did not exist, the law of the territory could not take it away from him. What this decision ultimately meant—incredibly—was that Congress had no power to prohibit slavery in the territories.

A storm of anger broke out in the North. "We are now one great homogeneous slave community," cried the *Cincinnati Daily Commercial.* The *Atlantic Journal* moaned, "Where will it end?"

. . . AND INFURIATES LINCOLN.

In Springfield, Lincoln took the Supreme Court to task. To make slavery "universal and eternal," Taney and the Court had "assailed and sneered at . . . , hawked at and torn" the Declaration of Independence. So badly had the chief justice misread the documents fundamental to American liberty that "the framers, if they could rise from their graves, would not at all recognize it." Deeply shaken by the decision, Lincoln believed it had struck "a deadly blow at our whole system of government."

"A HOUSE DIVIDED"

On a sweltering night in June 1858, Abraham stood before the twelve hundred delegates gathered at the state Republican convention in Springfield to accept his party's nomination for the U.S. Senate. He'd been thinking about his speech for weeks, scribbling thoughts and phrases on odd scraps of paper, then squirreling them away in his stovepipe hat. When it was finally written, he read it to a few political friends. They were not impressed. One advised him to cut the opening sentences because they "were too much ahead of the time." Another declared the speech "a damned fool utterance." Even William Herndon told his partner, "It is true, but is it wise or politic to say so?" Only Mary—who as a woman wasn't allowed to attend the smoke-filled convention—insisted he give the address as written. "It will make you president," she claimed.

Lincoln took her advice. He didn't change a word:

> *A house divided against itself cannot stand. . . . I believe this government cannot endure, permanently half slave and half free. . . . I do not expect the Union to be dissolved—I do not expect the house to fall—but I do expect it will cease to be divided. . . . It will become all one thing, or all the other.*

While most Republicans agreed with his sentiments, they thought Lincoln sounded too radical. They worried that Southerners would take it as "a pledge to make war on the institution in the States where [slavery] now exists." Controversial or not, listeners still leapt to their feet and cheered wildly.

Years later, Lincoln said, "If I had to draw a pen across my record, and erase my whole life from sight, and I had one . . . choice left as to what I should save from the wreck, I should choose that speech and leave it to the world unerased."

A BRILLIANT POLITICIAN

By 1858, leaders in Illinois generally agreed that Lincoln was an exceptional politician. Recalled one state legislator:

Mr. Lincoln manifested extraordinary abilities.... He did not follow the beaten track of other speakers and thinkers, but appeared to comprehend the whole situation of the subject, and take hold of its principles ... his memory was a great storehouse in which was stuffed away all the facts. Some were acquired by reading, but principally by observation; conversations with men, women and children, in their social and business relations; learning and weighing the motives that prompt each act in life. This supplied him with an inexhaustible fund of facts from which he would draw conclusions. He liked to illustrate every subject—however complicated—with anecdotes drawn from all classes of society. No one ever forgot—after hearing Mr. Lincoln tell a story—either the point of the story, the story itself, or ... the author.

A POLITICAL WIFE

Now when visitors came to the house at Eighth and Jackson, Mary sometimes leaned out the second-floor window and called down to ask if her husband was wanted for business or politics. Many folks in Springfield claimed the front door opened only to those who answered, "Politics."

AND THE CANDIDATES ARE . . .

THE DEMOCRAT

Name: Stephen A. Douglas
Nickname: The Little Giant
Age: 45
Height: 5' 4"

Description: Short, compact, and a seasoned campaigner, with "broad shoulders, a large, lion-like head and a deep, booming baritone voice. He [makes] an overall neat appearance, preferring to wear fine trousers and silk cravats . . . and he [partakes] of cigars and imported brandy."

Political Experience:
Attorney general of Illinois, 1834
Illinois state legislature, 1835
Illinois secretary of state, 1840
Illinois supreme court justice, 1841
United States House of Representatives, 1843-47
United States Senate, 1847-present

Political Position: Believes that each territory should decide whether it should be a free or a slave state.

THE REPUBLICAN

Name: Abraham Lincoln
Nickname: Long Abe or the Tall Sucker
Age: 49
Height: 6' 4"

Description: Tall, gaunt, and slightly bent, with "wiry, jet-black hair which [has] a way of getting up as far as possible in the world." He is often "clad in a rusty-black frock coat that should [be] longer, and black trousers that permit a very full view of his very large feet."

Political Experience:
Illinois state legislature, 1834-42
United States House of Representatives, 1847-1849

Political Position:
Opposes the extension of slavery into any of the territories.

THE GREAT DEBATES

One of the most famous face-offs in American history happened when Abraham Lincoln, Republican candidate for U.S. senator, challenged the incumbent Democratic senator, Stephen A. Douglas, to a series of seven debates. Those debates—which took place in seven Illinois towns between August and mid-October 1858—were not like modern televised debates. There was no panel of polite reporters asking pertinent questions. Instead, the two men slugged away at each other verbally. They questioned each other. They insulted each other. And they made clear where they stood on the issue of slavery.

The spectacle enthralled the thousands who flocked to each of the debates. They came not only to hear the candidates discuss their views but also to see "the best show going for a hundred miles around," recalled one old-timer. At every town, people cheered, waved flags, marched. There were bands, booming cannons, and even peddlers selling Lincoln and Douglas banners and ribbons.

Eventually, all the "fizzle-gigs and fireworks," as Lincoln called them, quieted, and the spectators settled down to listen. The candidates spoke on only one issue—slavery. Douglas tried to paint Lincoln as a fanatical abolitionist who wanted to "vote, and eat, and sleep, and marry with Negroes." Appealing to basic fears among white Americans, he conjured up the image of tens of thousands of freed slaves sweeping into Illinois and taking jobs and women from white men. "If you think the Negro ought to be on a social equality with your wives and daughters and ride in a carriage with your wife while you drive the team," Douglas told the crowds again and again, "then you should support Mr. Lincoln."

Lincoln denied these charges: "Mr. Douglas seems to believe that because I do not want a black woman for a slave, I must necessarily want her for a wife. I need not have her for either. I can just leave her alone." He insisted that he opposed the idea of blacks voting or serving on juries, and for the sake of winning the election, he even supported legislation that would keep freed slaves out of Illinois. But "the real issue," he claimed, "is one class that looks upon the institution of slavery as a wrong, [while] another does not look upon it as a wrong. That is the issue . . . the eternal struggle between right and wrong."

The debates became so heated that newspapers across the country began reporting on them. Calling them "the most interesting political battlegrounds in the Union," the *New York Times* sent reporters to Illinois. Reporters took down everything the candidates said, then telegraphed their stories back east to newspapers in Philadelphia, Boston, and New York. Once little known outside his home state, Abraham Lincoln and his position soon became familiar to people all over the country.

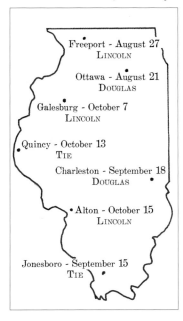

This map of Illinois shows the sites and dates of each of the debates, along with the name of the candidate who spectators believed made the better points or spoke more forcefully.

Freeport - August 27
LINCOLN

Ottawa - August 21
DOUGLAS

Galesburg - October 7
LINCOLN

Quincy - October 13
TIE

Charleston - September 18
DOUGLAS

Alton - October 15
LINCOLN

Jonesboro - September 15
TIE

Lincoln wrote this letter to Douglas agreeing to the debates' details.

A painting of Lincoln addressing a crowd in Charleston, Illinois, the site of the fourth debate. His opponent remains seated to the left. Behind them sit prominent members of the community.

ABSENT FROM ALL BUT ONE OF THE DEBATES, MARY STAYED HOME AND PASTED NEWSPAPER REPORTS LIKE THIS ONE INTO THE FAMILY SCRAPBOOK; LINCOLN WOULD LATER ADD THE ANNOTATIONS.

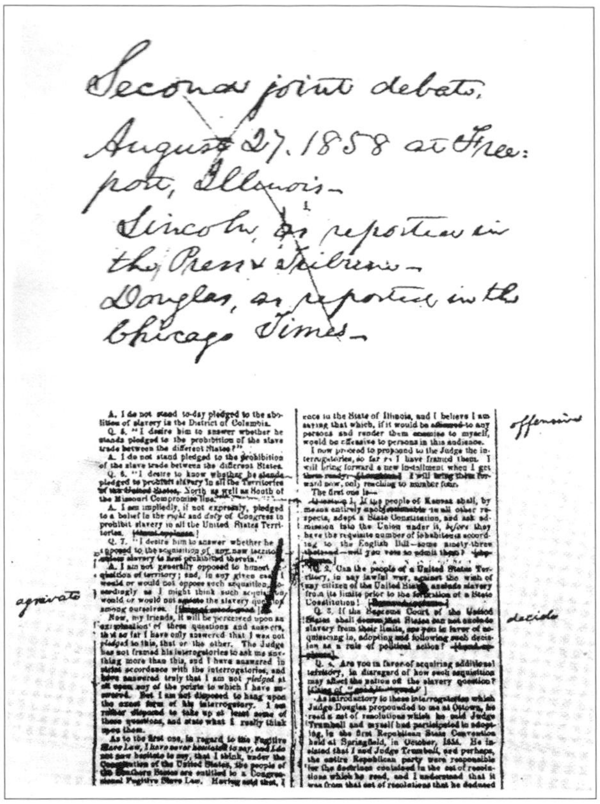

Mary would have loved traveling the state with her husband and sitting proudly beside him on the debate platform. But Lincoln insisted she stay home. He wanted to play up the marked differences between himself and Douglas. While Douglas traveled to the debate sites in a private railroad car, accompanied by his personal valet, an entourage of reporters, and his beautiful wife, who was once labeled the "Belle of Washington" by the *Chicago Tribune,* Lincoln came by ox-drawn cart, stagecoach, or, most often, train, where he always rode in a regular passenger car. Even though he was the most successful and prominent attorney in the state, Lincoln wanted the voters to see him as a common man with simple tastes. To have his elegantly dressed wife with her aristocratic bearing and fine manners standing at his side would spoil this carefully cultivated image. So Mary made the supreme sacrifice and followed news of the debates from Springfield, attending only the last one, held in Alton. To everyone who would listen she proudly declared that Douglas was "a very little giant" beside "my tall Kentuckian."

ELECTION RESULTS

In the nineteenth century, debates were held so that voters could understand the differences in both the candidates and their political parties. Thus informed, voters elected their state legislators, who in turn voted in the statehouse for the senatorial candidate of their party. When the returns came in for that election, in November 1858, the Republicans had not won enough seats in the legislature to send Lincoln to the Senate. Douglas was reelected.

How did Abraham feel?

"I feel like the Kentucky boy who stubbed his toe. I am too big to cry about it, but it hurts too awful bad to laugh."

How did Mary feel?

"One feels better after losing if one has had a brave, whole-hearted fight."

THE FIRST PAGE OF LINCOLN'S BIOGRAPHICAL SKETCH

On a December night in 1859, Abraham penned his life story. A year earlier, Jesse Fell, secretary of the Illinois Republican state committee, had asked for the details of his life because "people want to know more about the man who challenged Douglas." At first, Lincoln had shrugged off the suggestion. But as he began to seriously contemplate the presidency, he reconsidered. So he sat down and outlined his life on three pages. In an accompanying note, Abraham told Fell, "Herewith is a little sketch, not much of it, for the reason, I suppose, that there is not much of me."

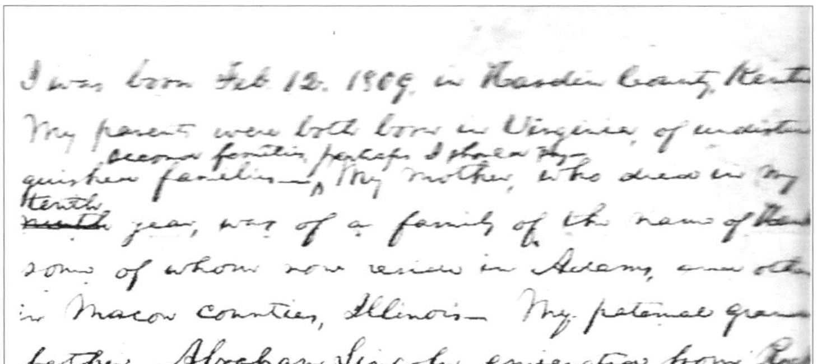

An especially handsome photograph of Lincoln taken just hours before he delivered his Cooper Union address. The photographer touched up the negative, eliminating the harsh lines in Lincoln's face and correcting his left eye, which roved upward.

Even though he lost the Senate election, Abraham had been thrust into the national spotlight by the debates. Suddenly, he was receiving invitations to speak all across the country (at least the Northern half). One of the most prestigious requests came from the Young Men's Central Republican Union, a group of important New York politicians who wanted Lincoln to speak at the lecture hall at Cooper Union, a new college in Manhattan.

Lincoln eagerly accepted. Knowing he would be speaking to sophisticated Easterners, he spent long hours writing his speech. He also ordered a new black suit.

On February 27, 1860, he appeared before a packed hall. Many of the fifteen hundred listeners expected something "weird, rough and uncultivated." After all, the man standing before them hardly fit their expectations of a polished politician. Noted one spectator, "the long, ungainly figure [with] the large feet; the clumsy hands . . . and the long, gaunt head capped by a shock of hair that seemed not to have been thoroughly brushed out made a [disconcerting] picture." Then he began to speak, and the audience forgot everything but his words. They were moved by his passionate plea to calmly consider all sides of the slavery issue. They applauded when he denounced the Southern belief that the

federal government had no authority to control the institution. And they were captivated by his dramatic ending: "Let us have faith that right makes might, and in that faith, let us, to the end, dare to do our duty as we understand it."

When Lincoln closed, the crowd went wild. Noah Brooks, a reporter for the *New York Tribune,* exclaimed, "He's the greatest man since St. Paul!" A Harvard student gushed, "It was the best speech I ever heard!" Newspapers from Rhode Island to Kansas published the speech in its entirety. And they began suggesting Lincoln as a possible presidential candidate.

Typically, Abraham remained modest about his achievement. The speech, he wrote Mary, "went off passably well."

SIDE TRIP

The day after the Cooper Union speech, Lincoln traveled to Robert's school in New Hampshire, Phillips Exeter Academy. One of the most exclusive and expensive schools on the East Coast, where powerful senators and wealthy plantation owners sent their boys, it was an unusual choice of school for a politician who wanted to be seen as "a man of the people." At some point, Abraham and Mary had decided that Robert should get the finest education money could buy—even if this didn't jibe with Lincoln's reputation as "a common man with simple tastes." So in the summer of 1859 they had shipped Robert off to New Hampshire, where he remained for a year before entering Harvard.

Lincoln was pleased to see his son and glad to chat with the boy's schoolmates. When one of them pulled out a banjo and played for their visitor, Lincoln said, "Robert, you ought to have one of those." His stiff, unmusical son was mortified. Robert's embarrassment continued into the next evening, when his father spoke before the school. Those students who hadn't already met Lincoln were astonished by the tall, awkward man. "Isn't it too bad Bob's father is so homely?" they whispered to one another. "Don't you feel sorry for him?" But within minutes, Lincoln "got hold of the audience and there was no more pity for Bob."

Suddenly proud of his father, Robert enjoyed the remainder of Abraham's visit. That night both of them slept in Robert's room. They went to church together the next morning, then strolled through the town before going out to dinner. For the first time, "my father centered his attention on me, and we were thrown into a new companionship," Robert later recalled. One historian claimed it was the "closest father and son would ever be."

HARPER'S WEEKLY PUBLISHED THIS ENGRAVING OF THE MEN MOST LIKELY TO WIN THE REPUBLICAN NOMINATION FOR PRESIDENT.

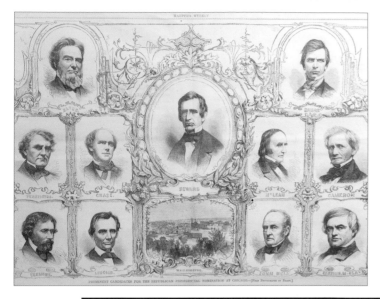

Even though his name was being mentioned as a possible candidate for president, Lincoln doubted his chances of winning. "What is the use of talking of me for the presidency," he asked Mary one night, "whilst there are such men as [William Henry] Seward [former governor of New York], and [Salmon P.] Chase [former governor of Ohio], and others who are much better known to the people?" Besides, he added, "I must say in all candor I do not think myself fit for the presidency."

"Oh," sniffed Mary, "how you underrate yourself. But you are the only person who does. . . . You've no equal in the United States."

Powerful Republicans shared Mary's sentiments. They began working for his nomination. And Abraham did not protest. "The taste *is* in my mouth a bit," he admitted.

"LINCOLN FOR PRESIDENT!"

In May 1860, the Republican Party met in Chicago. Three hundred and seventy-three delegates had come from the Northern and Western states to choose their candidate for president of the United States. Most expected William Seward, the powerful politician from New York, to win. But Abraham Lincoln, believing he had an outside chance, sent a team of his most enthusiastic supporters to the convention to work on his behalf. (In those days, it was considered improper for aspiring candidates to attend themselves.) His strategy was simple—to make himself the *second* choice of the delegates. Understanding that he was "new in the field" and not "the first choice of a very great many," he instructed his team to leave the delegates "in a mood to come to us, if they shall be compelled to give up their first love."

His team—led by his old friend from his circuit-riding days, Judge David Davis—did just that. They wined and dined delegates, promised government jobs in return for votes, and began a "Stop Seward" campaign, which appealed to those who did not want to cast their lot with the New Yorker. Recalled one of Lincoln's men, "It worked like a charm."

On the morning of May 19, voting began. The names of four men had been placed in nomination—William Seward of New York, Salmon P. Chase of Ohio, Edward Bates of Missouri, and Lincoln. Each was vying for the victory number—233 votes. At the end of the first ballot, the tally stood as follows: Seward, 173-1/2 votes; Lincoln, 102; Chase, 49; Bates, 48. Since no one candidate had won the necessary number of votes, the delegates tried again. This time Seward received 184-1/2 votes and Lincoln 181. Chase and Bates both lost votes, essentially removing them from the contest.

Tension rose in the convention hall as delegates voted a third time. When it was over, Lincoln was just one and a

The Republican convention hall is packed with spectators as delegates nominate their candidate.

half votes short of victory. "There was a pause," remembered one delegate. Then the head of the Ohio delegation, former congressman David Cartter (later Lincoln's minister to Bolivia), stood. "I arise, Mr. Chairman, to announce the change of four votes from Mr. Chase to Abraham Lincoln."

For a moment the convention hall fell silent. Then Lincoln supporters "rose to their feet applauding rapturously," recalled one eyewitness. "Waving their handkerchiefs . . . throwing their hats by thousands, cheering again and again."

Outside the convention hall, cannons fired and "between 20,000 and 30,000 [people] were yelling and shouting at once." Shouldering fence rails, symbolic of those that Lincoln had supposedly split, Republicans paraded through the streets shouting, "Lincoln for president! Lincoln for president!"

SPRINGFIELD CELEBRATES LINCOLN'S PRESIDENTIAL NOMINATION WITH A PARADE PAST HIS HOUSE.

Abraham—to the right of the front door in a white suit—towers above the crowd, while Tad and Willie watch excitedly from the second floor—the second window from the left—and an elegantly posed Mary looks out from the far left downstairs window.

A delegate wired the news of his nomination to Springfield: "Abe, we did it. Glory be to God!" Lincoln, who had been waiting for the news in the *Illinois Journal* office, turned to the cheering, shouting crowd that had suddenly formed around him. "Gentlemen," said the newly named candidate, with a twinkle in his eye, "there is a little woman at home who is probably more interested in this dispatch than I am; and if you will excuse me, I will take it up and let her see it."

Springfield reveled in its most prominent citizen's success. A victory parade featuring bands, floats, and ten thousand marchers carrying banners and broadsides took almost three hours to pass the Lincolns' house. At night there were bonfires and fireworks. There was even a rally at the fairgrounds, complete with tubfuls of lemonade and whole steers cooking in pits. "It is all terribly exciting," said Mary.

HANNIBAL HAMLIN, LINCOLN'S VICE PRESIDENTIAL RUNNING MATE

Lincoln wasn't the only man to be nominated at the Republican convention. Hannibal Hamlin, a prominent politician from Maine, was chosen to run as the vice presidential candidate. Lincoln had no say in the matter. In those days, presidential candidates did not choose their running mates; the party did. In fact, Lincoln and Hamlin did not even meet until three days *after* the election.

WHAT'S IN A NAME?

On the very day he was born, Abraham was given a nickname. "I commenced to callin' him 'Abe' the minute I laid eyes on him," recalled Dennis Hanks. The name stuck, even though he disliked it. It wasn't the only nickname Lincoln received—as an adult, he was given dozens of them. Some described his appearance: "Long Abe" and "The Tall Sucker," because he was so tall; "Old Abe," because of his deeply lined face. Others referred to his accomplishments: "Illinois Rail Splitter," the "Great Emancipator." His best-known nickname, "Honest Abe," stems from his days as a store clerk in New Salem: after realizing he had shortchanged one of his customers by a few cents, Abraham walked four miles to return the money. How did Lincoln feel about all these different names? "At least people are calling me something," he said.

As was the custom of the day, candidates seeking the presidency did not campaign. The office, it was believed, was a gift from the people. Instead, the candidates stayed home while other people campaigned on their behalf. So, from an office set aside for him in the state capitol, Lincoln read and answered mountains of mail, conducted delicate, long-distance negotiations with supporters, and clarified his position on national issues. More important, he met with the leading members of his party, who now traveled in a steady stream to Springfield to meet him. (By September there were as many as one hundred visitors a day.) Artists and photographers came to replicate his features; journalists came to talk with him, then sent their papers firsthand reports of the strange but compelling candidate; job seekers came looking for special favors. But Lincoln longed to join in the hurly-burly of the campaign—to take part in the huge rallies Republicans held in Northern cities, watch the parades, attend the picnics, and make a speech or two, rather than stay "shut up in Springfield."

THE PRESIDENTIAL ELECTION OF 1860

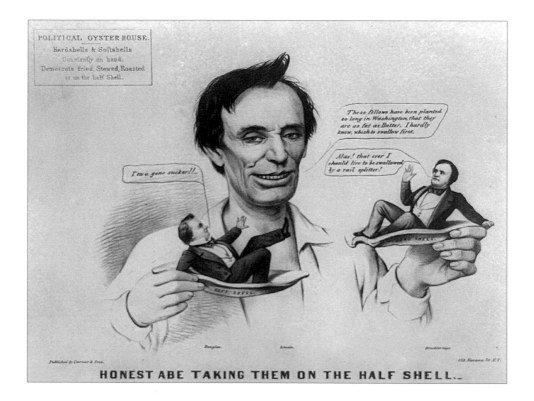

This political cartoon, called "Honest Abe Taking Them on the Half Shell," was published in newspapers across the North.

In 1860, Republicans classified Democrats as being either "hard-shell" (strongly proslavery) or "soft-shell" (moderate on the question). In this clever cartoon, an informally dressed Lincoln ponders which kind of Democrat to swallow first—soft-shelled Stephen Douglas (left) or hard-shelled John Breckinridge (right). Either way, the authors meant to show that Lincoln (grinning uncharacteristically) was bound to gobble up the election.

Stephen A. Douglas John C. Breckinridge Abraham Lincoln John Bell

STEPHEN A. DOUGLAS

Douglas finally received the Democratic Party's nomination in June 1860, but it hadn't been easy. In April of that year, the first Democratic convention had ended abruptly after fifty Southern delegates walked out in protest of the party's refusal to adopt a platform guaranteeing the constitutional rights of slave owners. A month later, the Democrats reconvened to try again. Still unable to reach a compromise, all 110 Southern delegates abandoned the party. The remaining delegates chose Douglas. But the senator from Illinois knew he couldn't win. The split in his party had made that impossible.

JOHN C. BRECKINRIDGE

Vice president of the United States and a cousin of Mary Lincoln, Breckinridge was nominated as a second Democratic candidate by the Southern delegates who had withdrawn from the earlier conventions. He represented slaveholding interests and was supported by all Democrats who were against

Douglas. Not optimistic about his chances, he said, "I trust I have the courage to lead a forlorn hope."

ABRAHAM LINCOLN

Lincoln, the Republican candidate, was not widely known outside his state. There was even some confusion about his name—"Is it 'Abraham,' or 'Abram'?" a *New York Times* reporter asked. Because the Democratic Party had split over the issue of slavery, however, Lincoln was almost certain to win. "Imagine," declared one politician, "a veritable unknown in the White House."

JOHN BELL

Bell was chosen by a handful of former Whigs in May 1860 to lead their newly formed Constitutional Union Party. The party, however, took few stands on the issues except to pledge to uphold the Constitution. Widely criticized as the candidate of the "Do Nothing" or "Old Man's" Party, Bell didn't stand a chance.

MARY LINCOLN: CELEBRITY

Her husband's nomination pushed Mary into the spotlight, too, as journalists flocked to the house at Eighth and Jackson to report on the candidate's home, his children, and especially his wife. Mary delighted in favorable press reports, like that of the *New York Tribune*, which called her "amicable and accomplished . . . vivacious and graceful . . . a sparkling talker." She spoke intelligently and candidly, and her knowledge of politics made good copy. So did the personal stories she often told. One reporter heard all about the election bet she had made with her neighbor Mrs. Bradford, who thought the Democrats would win. At stake was a pair of shoes. When Mary's story made headlines, some voters were appalled. Women gambling? How sinful!

So often did Mary spout off about certain Republicans and her husband's policies that reporters joked she was the candidate's "kitchen cabinet."

On October 15, 1860, eleven-year-old Grace Bedell wrote to Abraham promising to get her brothers to vote for him if he grew a beard. "You would look a great deal better for your face is so thin," she said. "All the ladies like whiskers and they would tease their husbands to vote for you and then you would be President."

Abraham wrote back, "Do you not think people would call it a piece of silly affectation if I were to begin it now?" Still, less than a month later he was seen with stubble sprouting from his chin.

Left, Abraham's reply to Grace Bedell. Above left, Abraham sports a small beard in November 1860. A reporter joked, "Old Abe is . . . puttin' on (h)airs!" A full-grown beard is in evidence by the time the photograph above right is taken on February 8, 1861.

Let the People Rejoice!

CAPITAL SHALL NOT OWN US!

LINCOLN ELECTED!

THE PEOPLE TRUE TO LIBERTY.
ILLINOIS REDEEMED!
SHE VOTES FOR LINCOLN.
She chooses Republican Legislature.
SHE REPUDIATES DOUGLAS.

GOD BLESS THE OLD KEYSTONE!!

GOD BLESS NEW YORK!

Lincoln carries all the Atlantic States but New Jersey.

AN AVALANCHE OF FREEMEN.

SHOUT BOYS SHOUT, VICTORY IS OURS, FREEDOM IS TRIUMPHANT.

NEWSPAPER HEADLINES PROCLAIM THE NEWS.

On Election Day, November 6, 1860, Mary awoke at daybreak. "You used to worry that I took politics too coolly," she wrote a friend later that day. "You would not do so, were you to see me now." Indeed, after bringing her husband his breakfast, she gave a light laugh and said, "It is well that the strain will soon be over. My hand is trembling so that I nearly spilled your coffee." After Lincoln went to his office in the state capitol, Mary could not sit still. She paced, scolded the boys, baked a cake, and paced some more.

Meanwhile, Lincoln and his fellow Republicans crowded into the capitol to hear the election returns relayed from the telegraph office. It was a long day. Not until two o'clock the next morning were results of the election known: Lincoln had received 1,865,593 votes and carried every Northern state. Douglas had 1,382,713 votes, and Breckinridge—the Southern Democrats' candidate—had 848,356, while Bell had received 592,906. The North had swept Lincoln into office. In the South his name hadn't even appeared on the ballot.

As soon as Abraham heard the news, he hurried home. "Mary!" he called out when he neared the house. "Mary! We are elected!"

THE CHARLESTON MERCURY EXTRA EDITION ANNOUNCING SOUTH CAROLINA'S SECESSION

Southern leaders had warned since Lincoln's nomination that they would not accept him as president. "Let the consequences be what they may," cried an Atlanta newspaper, "the south will never submit to such humiliation as the inauguration of Abraham Lincoln." In December—a month after the election and three months before Lincoln took office—angry delegates in South Carolina met to discuss the situation. They decided to secede from the Union with the expectation of eventually forming their own nation—a nation dedicated to preserving slavery. Within weeks, Mississippi, Florida, Alabama, Louisiana, Georgia, and Texas had followed suit.

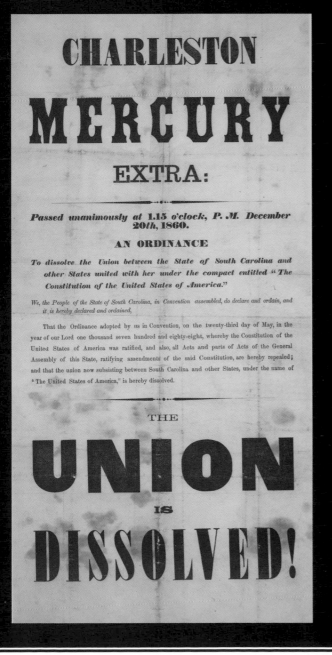

A COMMITMENT TO PRESERVING THE UNION

For Lincoln, the winter of 1860-1861 was one of frustration. Because he would not take office for another three months (at that time presidential inaugurations took place in March rather than January), he could only watch as the United States began to fall apart. He "practically pulled his hair out" when retiring president James Buchanan appeared before Congress to deplore secession but claim little could be done to stop it. And he closely followed events in Congress as it made last-minute efforts to save the Union. Both the Senate and the House established special committees to search for a satisfactory compromise. Their efforts eventually focused on two proposals: the creation of a constitutional amendment prohibiting future interference with slavery, and the equal division of all national territory between slave and free states.

These compromises might have been adopted had the president-elect endorsed them. But Lincoln refused to yield. He believed that the real purpose of the secessionists was not to leave the Union but to force the federal government to accept slavery in the new territories. "I will suffer death before I will consent to any compromise which looks like buying the privilege to take possession of this government to which we have a constitutional right." He went on to declare secession "the essence of anarchy," and claimed, "no state can, in any way lawfully, get out of the Union." He still hoped the situation could be peacefully resolved, but was prepared to fight if it couldn't. Lincoln's commitment to preserving the Union was absolute. "The concept of the Union," explained the historian David Herbert Donald, "older than the Constitution, deriving from the Declaration of Independence with its promise of liberty for all, had become the premise on which all his other political beliefs rested."

Still, members of his party in Congress pressured Lincoln to make some minor concessions that would give away nothing important but create the impression that he was willing to listen to Southern concerns. Again, Lincoln would not budge, refusing to consider any extension of slavery. Because of this, all hope for compromise was lost. "He was a terrible firm man when he put his foot down," Mary later said. "No man or woman could rule him after he had made up his mind."

MARY GOES SHOPPING.

In early January, while her husband worked on his inaugural address, Mary went shopping, suitably chaperoned by her brother-in-law Clark Smith (husband of her sister Ann, who had moved to Springfield in 1843). Knowing that Abraham would soon be drawing a salary of $25,000 a year (about $500,000 in today's dollars), she set about buying a whole new wardrobe from New York City's best stores. She intended to wear the finest clothes, not just because they befitted the wife of a president but also to prove to highbrow Washington society that she was no rough frontier woman. In New York City she discovered a dazzling array of fabrics, furs, jewels, and headdresses, the opulence of which she had never seen before. Fussed over by merchants who were only too eager to extend the president-elect's wife credit, she had so much fun, she decided to stay a few extra days. Too bad she forgot to tell her husband about her change in plans.

Back in Springfield, Lincoln missed his wife. For three nights in a row, the lonely president-elect trudged through ice and cold to meet the train from the East. But each time he was disappointed. Not until January 25 did Mary step from the train. Lincoln was "delighted," noted one reporter, while the happy shopper was in "excellent spirits."

◆ LINCOLN'S FAREWELL ADDRESS TO SPRINGFIELD ◆

On the rain-swept morning of February 11, 1861, Abraham stood on the train platform to say goodbye to his friends and neighbors. His eighteen-year-old son Robert, home from school, stood stiffly at his side.

Mary, eleven-year-old Willie, and eight-year-old Tad were not on the platform that day. Instead, they stood among the relatives who had come to see Lincoln and Robert off. Because of the many death threats on his life, the ghastly effigies sent through the mail, and the dark hints that he would not live to be inaugurated, Abraham had decided it was too dangerous for Mary and the little boys to leave with him. They would take a separate train and join him in Indianapolis. Together they'd complete the rest of the trip to Washington.

His voice trembling with emotion, Lincoln now addressed the throng of people:

My friends—No one, not in my situation, can appreciate my feeling of sadness at this parting. To this place, and the kindness of these people, I owe every thing. Here I have lived a quarter of a century, and have passed from a young to an old man. Here my children have been born, and one is buried. I now leave, not knowing when, or whether, ever I may return, with a task before me greater than that which rested upon Washington. Without the assistance of that Divine Being, who ever attended him, I cannot succeed. With that assistance I cannot fail. . . . Let us confidently hope that all will yet be well. To His care commending you, as I hope in your prayers you will commend me, I bid you an affectionate farewell.

CHAPTER FIVE

AND THE WAR CAME: WASHINGTON, 1861

In your hands, my dissatisfied fellow-countrymen and not in *mine*, is the momentous issue of civil war . . . with *you*, and not with *me*, is the solemn question of "shall it be peace, or a sword?"

—ABRAHAM LINCOLN IN THE DRAFT COPY OF HIS INAUGURAL ADDRESS, MARCH 1861

Washington . . . is perfectly charming.

—MARY LINCOLN IN A LETTER TO HANNAH SHEARER, MARCH 1861

PRESIDENTIAL TRAIN TRIP

The Lincolns took the long way to Washington. Slowly they toured the country—1,904 miles—from Springfield to Columbus to Pittsburgh and then to New York City. The purpose was to enable citizens to see the new president. Long before the presidential train rolled into any station, people lined the tracks, to get a glimpse of Lincoln . . . and his family.

At one stop, Lincoln had thrilled the crowd by bending over Mary so she could wrap his muffler more tightly around his throat. As he straightened, she kissed him and linked her arm in his. According to one reporter, everyone sighed. Only once had Mary refused to appear, even after crowds called her name. Abraham had shrugged off this behavior. "I have always found it difficult," he joked, "to make my wife do what she does not want to."

When the presidential train finally chugged into the station in Poughkeepsie, New York, a cry went up from those who had waited so long. "Where's the Missus? Where's Mrs. Abe? Give us the Old Lady and the Boys." Obligingly, Mary stepped to the rear of the train and waved. "Where are the children?" the crowd persisted. With his usual grace, Willie stepped out and bowed. But not Tad. He had been cooped up on this train for more than a week, and he was obviously tired of being stared at. Sticking out his tongue, he scrambled under his mother's voluminous skirts, and neither Mary nor Willie could haul him out. Finally, Mary laughed. So did the crowd. Then, with a shrill whistle and a huff of steam, the train moved on toward Washington.

Overnight, Mary and the boys had become public property. It was, she later wrote, both "an awful and a wonderful prominence."

This cartoon in a Baltimore newspaper ridicules Abraham's secret arrival in Washington.

On the night of February 22, 1861, a tall man disguised in a felt cap and an old overcoat slipped out of his Harrisburg, Pennsylvania, hotel room. Beside him lurked Ward Hill Lamon, friend and bodyguard. Making their way through the darkness, the two boarded a special train for Philadelphia. There they entered the sleeping car of yet another train headed to Baltimore. In a berth reserved for "an invalid passenger," the tall man slept while Lamon kept close watch. By morning, the train had reached Washington, D.C. Furtively, the two headed to the Willard Hotel, sneaking in through the ladies' entrance. They hurried to the registration desk, where president-elect Abraham Lincoln pulled off his disguise. He was checking in.

Why did Lincoln leave the presidential train to sneak into Washington by a separate route? Because Alan Pinkerton, head of the Pinkerton National Detective Agency, had heard whispers of a plot to assassinate Lincoln as his train passed through Baltimore and had persuaded him to do so. This pro-Southern city with a reputation for street violence had expressed a strong hatred for the president-elect.

Now, safely in Washington, Lamon rushed to the telegraph office and reported to Pinkerton: "PLUMS [meaning Abraham] ARRIVED HERE WITH NUTS [meaning Lamon] THIS MORNING. ALL RIGHT."

But such an unusual arrival did not escape gossip. Soon, newspapers picked up on the story, calling it "the flight of Abraham." Some reporters even questioned Lincoln's courage and wondered if this "nocturnal dodging and sneaking into the capital city . . . will be used to damage his moral position and throw ridicule on his administration."

Lincoln regretted his decision. As he told a friend, "I did not then, nor do I now believe I should have been assassinated . . . but I thought it wise to run no risk where no risk was necessary." Still, he knew he had damaged his image. He had wanted the public to see him as firm and resolved. Now, he said, he appeared "damned cowardly."

PRESIDENT OF THE CONFEDERATE STATES OF AMERICA

On the same morning that Abraham boarded the train bound for his inauguration, Jefferson Davis—a former United States senator from Mississippi—began his own journey. Leaving his family and slaves behind, he headed to Montgomery, Alabama, where delegates from the seceded states had gathered to form a new nation—the Confederate States of America. With Davis chosen as their president, all that remained was his inauguration.

Just five weeks earlier Davis had risen from his seat in the Senate to deliver an emotional farewell speech before resigning and heading south. "I am sure I feel no hostility to you, Senators from the North," he had begun. "I am sure there is not one of you, whatever sharp discussion there may have been between us, to whom I cannot say now, in the presence of my God, I wish you well." Still, Davis said that it was his strongly held belief that slaves were "inferior, fitted expressly for servitude" that left him with no choice but to lead the Southern cause. It was an honor he accepted out of duty. "Upon my weary heart was showered smiles and flowers," he later said, "but beyond them I saw troubles and thorns innumerable."

THIS 1861 VIEW OF WASHINGTON, LOOKING SOUTH TOWARD THE TREASURY BUILDING AND THE WHITE HOUSE, SHOWS COWS GRAZING IN A NEARBY FIELD.

Washington had changed in the thirteen years since the Lincolns had lived there. The last time Mary had gazed upon the Capitol, its dome had been made of wood. Now it was domeless, covered in scaffolding and awaiting a new, cast-iron dome. Several other government buildings–the Post Office, the Patent Office, the castle-like Smithsonian Institution–had just been completed. Still, only ten buildings, a few statues, and a half-built shaft honoring George Washington made up the federal city. Scoffed one Englishman, "To make a Washington street take one marble temple, a public office, a dozen good houses of brick and a dozen of wood and fill in with sheds and fields."

A SKETCH FROM HARPER'S WEEKLY SHOWS PRESIDENT-ELECT LINCOLN AND PRESIDENT BUCHANAN (TIPPING HIS HAT) EN ROUTE TO THE CAPITOL AND THE SWEARING-IN CEREMONY.

The weather on March 4, 1861, Inauguration Day, was like the mood of the nation–wavering between sunny and stormy. The city buzzed with rumors. At a nearby boardinghouse, a Southern sympathizer whispered, "Lincoln will . . . be shot before sundown." Meanwhile, in a brick row house just north of K Street (the unmarked boundary that separated the white neighborhoods from the black ones), Frederick Douglass–former slave, abolitionist, writer, and activist–expressed the cautious optimism felt by many African Americans: Mr. Lincoln was "one ray of hope."

At the White House, the city's mood made Lincoln nervous. He suggested Mary stay home. But Mary absolutely refused to miss out on this big day. After all, she considered it her big day, too.

Determined to protect the president-elect and his wife, the aging and infirm Winfield Scott, general in chief of the army, blocked off side streets and placed sharpshooters on the roofs of buildings lining Pennsylvania Avenue. For the first time in U.S. history a wooden barricade shielded the inaugural platform from the crowd, which numbered thirty thousand. But the general could not eliminate the air of menace that surrounded the Lincolns as their carriage rolled along the parade route to the Capitol. Many people shouted insults or shook their fists, and one spectator hollered, "There goes that Illinois ape. . . . But he will never come back alive."

At last they reached the Capitol and took their seats on the platform–Abraham in the front row, Mary directly behind him. Elizabeth Grimsley, a cousin, later recalled the "sea of upturned faces, representing every shade of feeling: hatred, discontent, anxiety and admiration." But all Mary could see was the back of her husband's head with "the dear familiar shagginess of his hair."

Finally, the president-elect stepped up to the platform railing. Adjusting his spectacles, he read his inaugural address. He had no intention of interfering with slavery in

the states where it already existed, he said again. But he spoke out against secession and affirmed that the government would "hold, occupy and possess" all its territories. In closing, he appealed to the South to reconsider its course because "we are not enemies, but friends. We must not be enemies."

When Lincoln finished, eighty-four-year-old Chief Justice Roger Taney tottered forward and administered the oath of office.

Abraham Lincoln had become the sixteenth president of the United States.

THE WHITE HOUSE IN 1861

"It's mine, my very own!" gushed Mary when she first crossed the White House threshold. But after she had inspected her new home from top to bottom, her joy turned to disappointment. The whole place, recalled White House secretary William Stoddard, "had the air of an old and unsuccessful hotel." It was believed that the White House belonged to the people; citizens had long been allowed to roam freely through the downstairs reception rooms. The house suffered from this open-door policy, as visitors often clipped tassels from curtains, cut strips from the carpet, and scraped away wallpaper as mementos. There were broken furniture, threadbare rugs, and curtains that Mary claimed looked "unchanged from George Washington's day." In the state dining room, she was dismayed to learn that the president of the United States could not serve more than ten guests with matching china. The only thing the mansion did have plenty of was "rats, mildew and foul smells," groaned Stoddard.

But the White House's disrepair gave Mary a grand opportunity. She had never intended to fade quietly into the Washington background like previous presidents' wives. No, she planned to become the first lady of the land, and she quickly decided to make refurbishing the White House her main project. She would, she pledged, transform the president's house into a symbol of power and refinement. She would turn it into a palace worthy of the leader of a great nation . . . and his wife.

THE NEW PRESIDENT

The country's most famous photographer, Mathew Brady, took this picture the very day Abraham arrived in Washington. Before the camera, Lincoln's expression always froze into a mask, all light vanishing from his face. Said his son Robert, "When an attempt was made to photograph father . . . he lapsed into a melancholy mood." This straight face was so familiar to the family that whenever he was in a bad mood Mary liked to tease him: "Mr. Lincoln, you look like you are having your picture taken."

. . . AND HIS WIFE

Eight months later, in November 1861, Mary had her picture taken by Mathew Brady. She chose to wear her most expensive and flattering dress but was disappointed by the photographic results. With its overabundance of velvet bows (sixty in all), countless black dots, and flowered bodice, the dress made her look shorter and plumper than she actually was. When she saw the portraits, she was appalled. She insisted Brady destroy all of them except this one, "standing with the back almost turned—showing only side face." Brady did not follow her directions. She was a celebrity, and he tucked the others away in his archives.

THIS MAP, CREATED IN 1861, SHOWS THE DIVISION OF LOYALTIES.

The Southern states of Virginia, North Carolina, Tennessee, and Arkansas seceded from the Union soon after Inauguration Day. In Kentucky and Missouri, however, popular sentiment was too divided for state governments to take decisive action. These slaveholding states teetered on the brink of secession but never toppled. Instead, they shakily remained in the Union, along with Maryland and Delaware.

THEIR FIRST DAY

WHAT TO DO ABOUT FORT SUMTER?

Major Robert Anderson, commander of the federal troops at Fort Sumter

On the morning after the inauguration, just hours into his new job, an urgent dispatch landed on the president's desk. "We are in desperate need of provisions," wrote Major Robert Anderson, commander of the federal troops at Fort Sumter, on March 4, 1861. "If we are not resupplied soon, we will have to surrender [to the Confederates]."

Years earlier, Fort Sumter—located at the entrance to Charleston harbor in South Carolina—had been built as part of the nation's coastal defense. The fort still flew the Union flag, even though South Carolina had seceded from the Union weeks earlier. At the time, the state's governor had demanded that the fort be given up to the South. But former president James Buchanan had ignored these demands, leaving the problem for Lincoln to solve.

It was a terrible quandary. If the new president reinforced the fort, he risked an armed attack and war—something he hoped to avoid. But if he evacuated the fort, he was already breaking his word: just the day before in his inaugural address he had pledged to defend *all* federal property—even property located in the South.

WHAT TO DO ABOUT A DRESSMAKER?

On the morning after the inauguration, Mary interviewed dressmakers. Choosing the right one was a critical decision; in Washington, association with a particular dressmaker could mean the difference between triumph and despair, praise and disdain. One distinguished lady claimed that the right dressmaker could "transform provincial newcomers, often overstocked with ill-made costumes and absurdly trimmed bonnets, into ladies of fashion!"

Last to be interviewed was Elizabeth Keckly, a former slave who had sewed for some of Washington's finest families. When Mary heard that Elizabeth had been dressmaker to Varina Davis (wife of Confederate president Jefferson Davis), she hired her on the spot. That very day Elizabeth left the White House carrying the fabric for the first of many dresses she would sew for Mary: a "bright rose-colored silk" that Mary wished to wear to the first reception of the Lincoln presidency.

Elizabeth Keckly, Mary's dressmaker

Choosing a cabinet—those seven men who would advise Lincoln on the issues of the day—was difficult. First, Lincoln believed, it had to have geographical balance; each section of the country, including the South, should be represented. Second, it had to have party balance, meaning it should include former Democrats in hopes of stitching together the various factions of the Republican Party. Third, it had to include some of the best political minds. After weeks of negotiations, deliberations, and considerations, the seven members of the President's cabinet finally emerged.

WILLIAM HENRY SEWARD, Lincoln's chief rival at the Republican convention in Chicago, reluctantly became his secretary of state. Believing Lincoln was an incompetent fool, Seward accepted the post to "save my freedom and my country." But slowly and inevitably, he came to appreciate Lincoln's sharp mind, peerless leadership skills, and political savvy. "He is," admitted Seward by the end of their first year together, "a chief executive in fact, as well as name." As for Lincoln, "his trust in Seward was so great that on subjects of gravest importance [he was the president's] only confidant and adviser."

SALMON P. CHASE, another of Lincoln's rivals for the Republican nomination, accepted the position of secretary of the treasury. While he would ably handle the complex and difficult task of financing what would soon become the Civil War, his desire for glory often put him at odds with the president, and his jealousy frequently got the better of him. "Chase resented the easygoing relationship Lincoln had with Seward," recalled one colleague. "The President often made impromptu visits to Seward's home to pass along gossip or share his most recent joke, but he never thought of dropping in on Chase." There was more to it. "Chase's discontent stemmed from the conviction that he was superior to Lincoln."

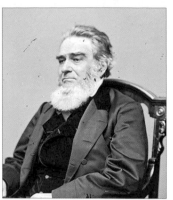

EDWARD BATES, yet another contender for president in 1860, took on the job of attorney general. "In times of such trouble and danger, I felt it my duty," he wrote in his diary. From the beginning, the relationship between Bates and Lincoln was friendly. While Bates's diary does display some frustration with Lincoln's loose management style—"no system, no unity, no accountability"—he admired the president's firm resolve to crush the Southern rebellion.

CALEB SMITH, a small-time politician from Indiana, received the job of secretary of the interior (overseeing conservation and development of natural resources) in return for having seconded Lincoln's nomination in Chicago. Smith, however, "had no aptitude for so serious a task as the administration of a great department," noted a fellow cabinet member. "He was a bungler." Luckily, Smith didn't stick around long. He resigned in December 1862 to become a U.S. district judge. He was replaced by John Palmer Usher of Indiana, who was later replaced by James Harlan of Iowa—Robert Todd Lincoln's future father-in-law.

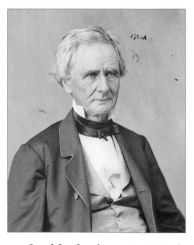

SIMON CAMERON had been promised a place in the cabinet in return for helping to switch his state's votes to Lincoln at the Chicago convention. Cameron wanted to be secretary of the treasury, but his reputation for swindling Native Americans, bribing public officials, and giving lucrative government contracts to friends kept him from the post. Instead, Lincoln offered him the position of secretary of war. It was a serious mistake. Charged with the important task of supplying the army with rifles, canons, horses, uniforms, food, and more, Cameron was "incapable either of organizing details, or conceiving and executing general plans." Even worse, he was dishonest. The war was less than two ☞

months old when accusations of corruption in the War Department began surfacing. Certain businessmen had made huge profits on contracts for rotten food, broken rifles, and blind horses. While Cameron did not pocket any of the money himself, his political cronies did. Vast amounts of money were wasted, and Union soldiers' lives had been jeopardized. Cameron had to go. In order to save the cabinet from scandal, Lincoln appointed him minister to Russia in January 1862 and replaced him with Edwin Stanton.

EDWIN STANTON, a brilliant land and patent

lawyer, made sweeping changes in the way the War Department was run. After Cameron's resignation, the place was "wholly and honestly devoted to the efficient running of the war," noted one clerk. Stanton managed this by shouting out orders and pounding on desks. "And if a subordinate made an error," remembered the clerk, "Stanton was for cutting off his head." But his ill-tempered behavior was outweighed by his honesty, loyalty, and capacity for hard work, and he and Lincoln eventually formed a close relationship. Lincoln liked nothing better than hanging around the War Department, reading telegrams from the front and discussing military strategy with "Old Mars," as he called Stanton. He admired Stanton and generally agreed with his decisions. Once, when he learned that the secretary of war had called him a "fool," Lincoln laughed. "Well, if Mr. Stanton said the President is a fool, it must be so, for the Secretary is generally right."

MONTGOMERY BLAIR, a lawyer from Maryland,

received the job of postmaster general. Blair was a "restless mischief-maker," wrote journalist Noah Brooks, "who was never so happy as when he was in hot water, or was making hot water for others." Lincoln included the temperamental lawyer because he needed a representative from the border states (those states between the North and the deep South). Blair's appointment would ensure support in both Maryland and Missouri (where Blair's brother, Frank, was a congressman). In spite of his volatile nature, Blair proved to be a valuable cabinet member. He modernized the postal system, recruiting more carriers, installing mailboxes on the street, instituting free delivery, and creating army post offices. This was especially important to soldiers who relied on letters from home to keep up morale. Sadly, all Blair's good work was eventually undone by his sharp tongue. He publicly bad-mouthed almost every cabinet member—Chase, Seward, Welles—and made political speeches in direct opposition to the administration's policies. He was, recalled Lincoln's secretary John Hay, "a most contentious man."

GIDEON WELLES, an editorial writer from

Connecticut, became secretary of the navy. When advisors wondered why he was fit for the job, Lincoln jokingly responded that Welles was from New England, "where there was so much shipping." In truth, Welles was an excellent choice. Conscientious and efficient, he accomplished an almost impossible task: building a navy nearly from scratch. When he took office there were only 76 vessels in the U.S. fleet. Four years later, there were 671. While Welles was a hard worker, he never did form a real friendship with the president; his personality was too stern and brusque. Still, he remained completely loyal to Lincoln and confined any complaints about the administration to his diary—a document that today is one of the most important historical documents about the war.

WHERE'S THE VICE PRESIDENT?

In those days the vice presidency was a powerless job, and soon after the inauguration Hannibal Hamlin was relegated to the background. Resenting his idleness, he spent most of his term in his home state of Maine, where—at the age of fifty-five—he enlisted in the coast guard, doubling as night watchman and cook.

MARY COMMENTS ON THE CABINET.

Believing she was a shrewder judge of character than Lincoln—"My husband places great faith in my knowledge of human nature"—Mary gave her opinion on everyone from military leaders to European royalty. But she was especially vocal about the cabinet, where, remarked one biographer, "she would have liked to sit." She rightly insisted that Secretary of the Treasury Chase was "only for Chase" and Secretary of War Cameron was "an utter thief." She claimed Attorney General Bates was "not to be trusted" and called Postmaster General Blair "a little firecracker."

But she saved her most heated words for Secretary of State Seward. "Father," she said to Abraham one night, "you will generally find it a safe rule to distrust a disappointed, ambitious politician [like Seward]. It makes me mad to see you sit still and let that hypocrite twine you around his finger as if you were a [piece] of thread."

But Lincoln refused to heed her advice. "If I listened to you," he finally replied, "I would soon be without a Cabinet."

The president thoroughly enjoyed the company of his two secretaries, John G. Nicolay and John Hay. Because the young men shared a bedroom in the White House, Abraham quickly formed the habit of dropping in on them at night to chat. Once, at midnight, he flung open their door and between snorts of laughter read them a funny poem. He was, John Hay noted in his diary, "utterly unconscious that he, with his short shirt hanging above his long legs and setting out behind him like the tail feathers of an enormous ostrich, was infinitely funnier than anything in the book he was laughing at."

"The boys," as Abraham's secretaries were called, had traveled from Springfield with the Lincoln family. John Nicolay had met Lincoln in the Illinois state capitol, where he'd been working as a clerk. Abraham had been so impressed by the serious, sensitive twenty-nine-year-old that he begged Nicolay to become his private secretary.

Nicolay, in turn, had begged Abraham to hire his friend John Hay as an assistant. Hay was, recalled one Washington observer, "smart, and he knew it; attractive to the ladies, and he knew it; witty, and he knew it." A graduate of Brown University, Hay had reluctantly returned to Springfield, where he halfheartedly began studying law. That was when the Lincolns swept him away to Washington. For this, the twenty-three-year-old was eternally grateful.

Absolutely devoted to Lincoln, "the boys" were convinced he would be remembered as a great president, and they promised to write a history someday. Behind his back they called him "the Ancient" (perhaps derived from "Old Abe") or "the Tycoon" (in reference to the all-powerful emperor of Japan). Abraham always called Nicolay by his last name and

Abraham and his secretaries John G. Nicolay (seated to Lincoln's right) and John Hay

treated him with great respect. But he called Hay "John" and treated him like a son.

In 1890, Nicolay and Hay published a ten-volume work on Abraham's presidency. Historians consider it one of the best works on the subject.

MARY VS. "THE BOYS"

Not long after moving into the White House, Mary learned—much to her dismay—that the president's secretaries were expected to make all arrangements for social functions. She put her foot down. Socializing and entertaining had always been *her* responsibility, and she stubbornly refused to give it up.

Nicolay and Hay just as stubbornly refused to give in to the First Lady's demands. When the Lincolns decided to give a dinner party for their political friends and supporters, John Nicolay, as was his duty, came up with a guest list. Mary looked it over. Not Salmon Chase, she declared. Didn't Nicolay know that the secretary of the treasury was her husband's secret political rival? Imperiously, she struck his name from the list.

Offended, Nicolay appealed to the president, who restored Chase's name. "There soon arose such a rampage as the White House has never seen," Nicolay reported. Mary—whom the secretary referred to as "her Satanic Majesty"—declared she would make all the arrangements herself.

But the task was too big. On the very afternoon of the party, she apologized to Nicolay and begged for his help. Wrote the secretary smugly, "I think she has felt happier since she cast out that devil of stubbornness."

Mary, however, got the last laugh. Nicolay spent the afternoon racing about to put the finishing touches on the dinner, only to discover at the last moment that *his* name had been struck from the guest list.

"She is, indeed," wrote John Hay, "a hellcat."

THIS WOOD ENGRAVING FROM HARPER'S WEEKLY SHOWS THE CONFEDERATE BOMBARDMENT OF FORT SUMTER.

For days after receiving Major Anderson's message about the need for provisions at Fort Sumter, Lincoln wrestled with the problem of whether to send supplies. The pressure of deciding became so great, Mary reported, that he "keeled over" and had to be put to bed with one of his rare migraines. At last, on April 8, he notified the government of South Carolina that Union ships were headed to the fort with food and other necessities but that neither soldiers nor ammunition would be sent. He hoped the Confederacy would see this as a peaceful expedition.

On April 12, Confederate cannons began firing on the fort. "The shells were bursting," recalled one Charleston citizen. "The roar of cannon—there it was—then a shell would light up the scene. . . . We watched and everybody wondered that Fort Sumter did not fire a shot."

Inside, federal soldiers scurried to defend themselves. But when they finally managed to return fire, their shots bounced harmlessly off the iron walls of a nearby Confederate fortress. And although the relief ships sent by Lincoln were beginning to arrive, the expedition was not prepared for this type of crisis. Instead, they dropped anchor and watched from a distance as the Confederacy pummeled the fort.

On the second day, the fort began to burn. The fort's commander, Major Anderson, ordered that the flag be lowered and a white bedsheet be raised in its place. Fort Sumter surrendered without any loss of men on April 13.

Even though there was no formal declaration, both sides recognized that war had begun—a war that would be the bloodiest in American history.

A WAR BY ANY OTHER NAME

The North and South not only disagreed on the causes of the war but had very different names for it. In the South, the conflict was known as the "War Between the States" or the "War of Northern Aggression." These terms reflected the South's belief that secession was their legal and legitimate right. They maintained that the North had no authority to send in federal troops or force them to remain in the Union.

The North, on the other hand, called the war the "Great Rebellion." This stemmed from Lincoln's steadfast refusal to acknowledge the conflict as a war between the governments of the United States and the Confederate States of America. To do so, he believed, would be the same as admitting that secession was constitutional. Instead, he maintained that what was really happening was a widespread Southern riot—one that he had to suppress by sending in federal troops. Though he sometimes called the conflict a "civil war," he usually called it a "rebellion"—a term he used more than four hundred times in his letters and speeches. In addition, he never once identified the enemy as the Confederate States of America. On the rare occasion when he was forced to refer to the Southern government, he called it "the so-called Confederate States of America."

On April 18, just four days after the surrender of Fort Sumter and one day after his home state of Virginia seceded, Colonel Robert E. Lee was invited to the home of Lincoln's good friend Francis Blair. Lee had served in the Mexican War, commanded a regiment in Texas, and held the position of superintendent of West Point. He was, according to General Winfield Scott, the "very best soldier I ever saw in the field." Desperately needing Lee's military expertise, Blair asked on Lincoln's behalf, "Will you take command of the Union army?"

"Mr. Blair," Lee politely replied, "I look upon secession as anarchy. If I owned [all the] slaves in the South, I would sacrifice them all to the Union; but how can I draw my sword upon Virginia, my native state?"

After two agonizing days of indecision, Lee finally resigned from the U.S. Army. "It would have come sooner," he said, "but for the struggle it cost me to separate myself from a service to which I have devoted all the best years of my life . . . and all the ability I possess."

Days later, Confederate president Jefferson Davis appointed Lee commander in chief of the Virginia forces. For the next several months, Lee oversaw coastal defenses and advised Davis on military strategy. In June 1862 he was appointed commander of all Confederate forces in the East (known as the Army of Northern Virginia). A brilliant tactician, Lee soon became the Union army's most formidable enemy.

GENERAL WINFIELD SCOTT

Seventy-five-year-old Winfield Scott had already served as the country's general in chief for two decades by the time the Civil War began. In 1861, the former hero of the War of 1812 and commander of the U.S. forces in the Mexican War weighed more than three hundred pounds and could no longer ride a horse. Because of his infirmities, he needed a field commander—someone who would carry out his orders on the battlefield. When Lee declined the position, the aging general was at a loss. Unsure of whom else to ask, Scott managed the war from Washington for the next six months.

A RECRUITING POSTER CALLS FOR VOLUNTEERS.

From the moment Fort Sumter surrendered, Lincoln was faced with the problem of raising an army. At that time, the entire U.S. Army had fewer than 16,000 men, most of them located west of the Mississippi River, where they guarded the frontier. Needing men quickly, Lincoln turned to the state militias, which were volunteer organizations. His first call was for 75,000 militiamen to serve for ninety days.

Immediately, Northern states began filling their quotas with eager volunteers. These men were young, itching for action, and, as one volunteer admitted, "wound up to the very pinnacle of patriotic fever." But it was soon apparent that 75,000 troops serving for a mere three months would not be enough. In July, Lincoln asked Congress to authorize recruitment of 400,000 more volunteers who would serve in the army for three years. For their commitment, they would receive anywhere from $25 to $100 for enlisting (called bounty money). Again, the quota was easily reached. Not only were volunteers lured by the money, but most doubted they would be in the army anywhere near that long.

Washington was in danger! Its neighbor Virginia had seceded, and now Maryland was threatening to do the same. Washingtonians shuddered at the thought. If Maryland—a state that surrounded the nation's capital—joined the Confederacy, Washington would be completely cut off from the rest of the country; the only route to the North passed through Baltimore. In addition, a steady stream of pro-Confederate soldiers and military officers had left for the South after the battle at Fort Sumter. Only a handful of recruits now guarded the White House. Urgently, the president put out a call for troops, and the Sixth Massachusetts Regiment responded. But as they passed through Baltimore, they were attacked by an angry secessionist mob. Four soldiers died. Dozens more were wounded.

Two days later, a committee from Baltimore descended on the president, demanding that he bring no more troops through their city. Lincoln exploded. He had to have troops to defend the capital, he declared, and they could only come through Baltimore. "Our men are not moles, and can't dig under the earth; they are not birds, and can't fly through the air. Go home and tell your people that if they will not attack us, we will not attack them."

They didn't listen. For nearly a week, Washington was under siege as Marylanders destroyed railroad bridges and cut telegraph lines. General Winfield Scott anticipated a Confederate assault from Virginia, with thousands of Southern sympathizers who lived in Washington aiding the attack. The capital—and the president—would fall into enemy hands.

In these dark and lonely hours, Lincoln paced the floor of his study and repeatedly looked out the window, searching the Potomac for a sign of ships bringing reinforcements. Every day there were rumors that additional troops, including the Seventh New York and a Rhode Island regiment, were on their way. "Why don't they come?" he cried in anguish. "Why don't they come?"

Miraculously, on April 25, the New Yorkers arrived. Finding an ingenious way to avoid Baltimore, their commander, Benjamin F. Butler, had ferried his men down the Chesapeake Bay to Annapolis, where they boarded trains bound for the capital. Within days, thousands of troops poured into Washington. They were greeted with jubilation as they marched with flying colors down Pennsylvania Avenue. Washington was safe.

But it was a changed city. Now soldiers slept in the White House's East Room, and rows of white tents lined the South Lawn. Wrote Mary glumly, "Thousands of soldiers are guarding us, and if there is safety in numbers, we have every reason to feel secure. And yet, it is all so gloomy. We can only hope for a quick peace."

THREE TALES ABOUT MARY
(AND ONE INTERESTING FACT) . . .

ON AN APRIL EVENING during one of the Marine Band concerts, Mary spied Mrs. Horatio Taft wearing a lovely bonnet trimmed with purple ribbons that tied under her chin. William, the fashionable French hatmaker both women frequented, had just trimmed Mary's new bonnet in the very same color. Too bad he had run out of purple ribbon before the job was finished.

Unhappily, Mary had been forced to settle for lavender chin ties. Now Mary stared intently at Mrs. Taft's bonnet for a few moments. Then she pulled her aside. As the president's wife, she insisted Mrs. Taft hand over those ribbons. What choice did the poor woman have? Angrily, she surrendered the ribbons. Wrote Mrs. Taft's teenage daughter, "This illustrates an outstanding characteristic of Mary Todd Lincoln—that she wanted what she wanted when she wanted it and no substitute!"

IN AUGUST, at her husband's request, Mary gave a small dinner party for Prince Jérôme Napoléon Bonaparte of France. Worried that France might come to the aid of the Confederacy, Lincoln was eager to meet and talk with the prince. Understanding the evening's importance, Mary insisted on doing everything herself—choosing the menu, supervising the cooking, arranging the flowers. She even made sure the Marine Band struck up the French national anthem when the prince arrived. It was an almost flawless evening, with one exception—the prince did not speak English. Without a translator, Lincoln had no way of communicating with his important guest. It was an awkward situation until Mary spoke up . . . in fluent French!

IN OCTOBER, Mary pleaded with her husband to pardon a twenty-one-year-old private from Vermont named William Scott who had fallen asleep during guard duty—an offense punishable by death. While Lincoln believed that the punishment was harsh, he also knew that his intervening could undermine military discipline. Mary, however, didn't care "a whit for discipline." The punishment was "unspeakable" and "immoral," she declared; "mercy, not stern justice, should be granted." When Lincoln hesitated, Mary—aware of Abraham's weakness for his sons—brought in a teary, sobbing Tad. "Think, father, if it was your own little boy who was just tired after fighting and marching all day," Tad cried.

Lincoln knew when he was beaten. The next day, he walked over to the War Department and issued a pardon. When asked his reason, Lincoln replied, "By request of the 'Lady President.' "

IN DECEMBER, the *Times* of London coined a new phrase to describe Mary—"First Lady of the land." The phrase stuck. Mary Lincoln became the first "First Lady."

. . . AND A CARTOON ABOUT ABRAHAM

GULLIVER ABE, IN THE WHITE HOUSE, ATTACKED BY THE LILLIPUTIAN OFFICE-SEEKERS.

*This cartoon, called "Gulliver Abe, in the White House, attacked by the Lilliputian office-seekers,"
shows just how overwhelmed the new president was.*

Every morning when the White House's north doors opened, people pushed and shoved their way inside. They were, recalled Senator William Pitt Fessenden, "an ill-bred, ravenous crowd," who badgered the doormen for drinks and directions to the water closet. What did they want? Government jobs—everything from ambassadorships to positions as lighthouse keepers.

At first, Lincoln tried to attend to the country's business while still interviewing everyone. His visiting hours began before breakfast and ended late at night. But he quickly realized he had little time left to eat or sleep. Something had to be done. Nicolay suggested the president's reception hours be limited to between ten and one each day. The idea worked. "At least," sighed Nicolay, "the bulk of the crowd is shut out in the afternoon."

Still, during his entire time in the White House, Lincoln "seldom if ever declined to receive any man or woman who came to the White House to see him." When one staff member wondered why, Lincoln replied, "They do not want much, and they get very little."

PRESIDENT LINCOLN TRAMPLES ON CIVIL LIBERTY.

On April 27, after Lincoln had been in office only a month, he sent General Scott a message. "You are engaged in repressing an insurrection against the laws of the United States. If at any point you find a resistance which renders it necessary to suspend the writ of habeas corpus for the public safety you . . . are authorized to suspend the writ." Basically, the writ of habeas corpus protects everyone from being arrested and held without reasonable charges. According to the United States Constitution, it can only be suspended in dire emergencies—"in cases of rebellion or invasion [when] the public safety may require it."

When Supreme Court Justice Roger Taney suggested that the president's action was unconstitutional, Lincoln replied that "such extreme tenderness of the citizens' liberty" could lead to the danger of allowing "the government itself to go to pieces, lest that one [civil liberty] be violated."

Over the next few years, Lincoln repeatedly suspended the writ of habeas corpus in places where secession talk was especially spiteful. And twice during the war he suspended the writ throughout the entire country. Roughly 10,000 to 20,000 United States citizens were imprisoned without ever being given a trial, most on suspicion of disloyal acts—spying, smuggling, blockade running, and carrying contraband goods. An additional 864 were truly political prisoners, jailed for expressing their beliefs.

MISCHIEF IN THE WHITE HOUSE

*Willie Lincoln in 1861. Tad Lincoln dressed as a soldier
and carrying his toy rifle in 1861.*

For eleven-year-old Willie and eight-year-old Tad, that first year at the White House was filled with **adventure, mischief, and fun,** as these stories show.

Full of ideas and schemes, Tad earned the nickname "Tyrant of the White House" after whittling the elegant rosewood furniture into designs he liked better, turning the hose on Secretary of War Edwin Stanton, and constantly interrupting important state meetings with three quick raps on the door followed by two short bangs. His father always let him in. "I promised never to go back on the code," Abraham explained to annoyed cabinet members.

Fascinated by money, Tad was not particular about how he got it. He once bet William Seward that the gentleman could not guess what new animal he and Willie had gotten. Seward guessed a rabbit. Tad shook his head, pocketed the man's quarter, and hurried away. Willie looked at the secretary of state, then remarked solemnly that it had indeed been a rabbit.

Of all Willie and Tad's pets, their favorites were two small goats, Nanko and Nanny. The goats had the run of the White House, tearing up the gardens and sleeping in the boys' beds. One time Tad harnessed Nanko to a kitchen chair and, using it like a sled, drove through the East Room. As elegantly dressed ladies shrieked and held up their hoopskirts, Tad hollered, "Get out of the way, there!" After circling the room once, he rode back out the door, leaving the ladies panting and swooning behind him. Sadly, the goats met a mysterious end. "Tell dear Tad poor 'Nanny Goat' is lost," Abraham wrote Mary while she vacationed with the boy in New York. "The day you left, Nanny was found resting herself, and chewing her little cud on the middle of Tad's bed. But now she's gone . . . and has not been heard of since. This is the last we know of poor 'Nanny.' "

*The letter Lincoln wrote to Tad about
Nanny Goat's disappearance*

One summer afternoon, a teenage friend of the Lincolns', Julia Taft (daughter of Mrs. Horatio Taft), arrived at the White House to discover that her younger brothers, Halsey (called Holly) and Bud, were performing a "circus" in the attic with the Lincoln boys. In her book *Tad Lincoln's Father,* she vividly described the chaos.

Tad flew out from behind the stage curtain—two sheets the boys had pinned together. "Come help, Julie," he cried. "We're having a circus and my face has got to be blacked up and Willie can't get his dress on and Bud's bonnet won't fit." He dragged the teenage girl backstage, where Willie was struggling into a very low-cut lilac silk gown belonging to his mother, while his friend Bud was ☞

Program of the "Circus," handwritten by Willie. Bud (right) and Holly (left) Taft, the Lincoln boys' best friends.

☞ trying to tie the laces of one of the First Lady's bonnets under his chin.

"Boys," cried Julia, "does the President know about this?"

Tad nodded. "Pa knows and he don't care, neither. He's coming up when those generals go away."

At that moment Willie handed Julia a bottle of perfume called Bloom of Youth.

"Put some of this on Bud and me," he said.

As Julia spritzed them, Tad burst into a popular song of the day—one that made fun of his father. "Old Abe Lincoln came out of the wilderness—"

"Tad," scolded Julia, "don't sing that. Suppose the President hears you?"

"I don't care if he does," answered Tad. "Anyway, I'm going to sing it in the show, see?" He showed Julia a copy of the "official program" made by Willie.

But before Julia could read it, the president arrived. "Well, here I am, come to the circus," he announced. "We're having a great time up here, eh?" Paying his five cents, he took the seat specially reserved for him. For the next half hour, along with a crowd of soldiers, sailors, gardeners, and servants, Lincoln "threw back his head and laughed heartily."

"What is that noise?" Mary cried one morning in September. "It sounds like someone banging on a drum."

"It is probably the 'dead march,'" replied Julia Taft. "I suppose the boys are again burying Jack."

Jack was Tad's doll. Dressed like a soldier, it was the focus of the boys' favorite game: court-martialing the doll, finding it guilty of sleeping on post, and sentencing it to be "shot at sunrise." Tad and his little brass cannon always did these duties. Then the other boys dug a grave and buried Jack with full military honors.

Now Mary leapt to her feet. "Oh no," she cried. "Go quick and tell them they must not dig holes among the roses."

But the White House gardener reached the little grave-diggers before Julia did. "Boys," he suggested, "why don't you get Jack pardoned?"

The idea was met with enthusiasm. "Come on," whooped Tad. "We'll get Pa to fix up a pardon."

Pounding up the stairs, the four boys flung themselves on the president. Tad explained what they wanted.

"Pardon for Jack, eh?" said Abraham, pretending to be serious. "You know, Tad, it's not usual to grant pardons without some sort of hearing. . . . Tell me why you think Jack should have a pardon."

"Well, you see, Pa," replied Tad, "most every day we try Jack for being a spy or a deserter or something, and then we shoot him and bury him, and Julie says it spoils his clothes, and [the gardener] says it digs up his flowers, so we thought we'd get you to fix up a pardon."

Abraham considered these words for a moment. Then he nodded gravely. "Yes, Tad, I think you've made a case. It's a good law that no man shall twice be put in jeopardy of his life for the same offense and you've already shot and buried Jack a dozen times. I guess he's entitled to a pardon." Turning around to his desk, he wrote something on a sheet of paper and handed it to Tad. It read:

> *The Doll Jack is pardoned*
> *by order of the President.*
>
> *Abraham Lincoln*

But poor Jack's pardon did not last long. In less than a week, the doll was found hanging from a tree in the garden—punishment for being a spy.

THE OTHER LINCOLN SON

Bob was away at Harvard during the Lincolns' first year in the White House, so he spent almost no time with his father. "Any great intimacy between us became impossible," Bob later wrote. "I scarcely had even ten minutes' quiet talk with him during his presidency, on account of his constant devotion to business." Still, Abraham was proud of his son. When Bob came home for Christmas that year, his father lovingly remarked, "Bob was such a little rascal, but now he is a very decent young man."

Robert Todd Lincoln in 1861

Just weeks after moving into the White House, Mary learned that every president since William Henry Harrison (1840) had received $20,000 from Congress (about $480,000 in today's dollars) to refurbish the White House. In the summer, she joyfully headed off to New York and Philadelphia, where she went on a breathless shopping spree. Merchants showed her the best and most expensive upholstery, carpeting, furniture. Never entirely rational when it came to spending, Mary bought everything. Her purchases included "one fine porcelain dining service of one hundred and ninety pieces," glassware, hand-painted wallpaper from Paris, custom-made carpeting from Brussels, chandeliers, silverware, rosewood furniture, a fancy carriage, books for the library, velvet hassocks, 320 "rare, exotic plants of varying types," and "French satin brocatelle curtains with tassels, fringes and lace."

In addition, she ordered the White House cleaned and painted, and she modernized it by adding gaslight and running water pumped up from the Potomac River. Soon the once-shabby executive mansion took on an air of elegant opulence.

When the bills came due in the fall, Mary was shocked to discover she had exceeded the $20,000 budget by almost $7,000. Too afraid to tell her husband, she turned to Benjamin French, commissioner of public buildings. It was French's job to supervise White House purchases and submit the bills to the Treasury Department for payment. On her behalf, French manipulated the budget, reassigning money to the White House account from other congressional projects. Soon money originally appropriated for curbs on Pennsylva-

nia Avenue or gaslights on Capitol Hill was diverted to pay for flocked wallpaper in the Green Room.

But it wasn't enough. Mary tried selling the secondhand White House furniture, but the broken antiques brought in little cash. She ordered the gardener to sell the manure from the White House stables at ten cents a wagonload, but the inflated price of her fertilizer resulted in more jokes than money. Finally, she fired the White House steward and oversaw the running of the household herself, pocketing the steward's salary to pay her bills. She also began padding the bills for household expenditures and presenting invoices for nonexistent purchases. Over the next several months, she collected for far more camellias, roses, lettuce, and strawberries than were ever planted in the White House garden.

But as the unpaid bills mounted and bill collectors began to hound her, Mary confessed to Abraham and begged him to ask Congress for an extra appropriation to cover her overrun.

Lincoln furiously refused. He would never ask Congress "for flub dubs for that damned old house," he fumed. It would "stink in the land to have it said that an appropriation of $20,000 had been overrun by the president when the poor freezing soldiers could not have blankets." He vowed to pay for Mary's purchases out of his own pocket.

"We cannot afford that," Mary wailed. She nagged her husband to change his mind.

Eventually, he did. In December he went to Congress, and it quietly passed a bill covering the entire cost of the White House's restoration.

An invoice for furnishings of the room known today as the Lincoln Bedroom, authorized and approved by Mrs. A. Lincoln

---

➤ WHERE ARE MARY'S FLUB DUBS NOW? ◄

Most of the furniture, china, and glassware Mary purchased is long gone. Because of a special clause in Congress's appropriation bill, "decayed furnishings" could be sold and the money used to buy replacements. During the nineteenth century, it was common for each new president to clean out the White House closets and cupboards. The contents were sold at auction. What does remain of the Lincoln furniture—an ornately carved bed, sofa, and matching chairs—can be seen in the Lincoln Bedroom at the White House. As for the Lincoln china, place settings are scattered throughout museums across the country, including the Smithsonian Institution.

On a scorching hot Sunday in July 1861, 30,000 Union troops under the command of General Irvin McDowell marched south toward Manassas, Virginia. With them came six U.S. senators, ten members of the House of Representatives, scores of newspaper reporters, and dozens of ladies with picnic baskets and opera glasses. Bursting with self-confidence, Northerners thought defeating the South would be a simple matter of attacking at Manassas, then moving on to take the Confederate capital of Richmond, Virginia, just sixty miles away. They sincerely believed this would be the one

This lithograph, made shortly after the first battle of Bull Run, shows the chaos and carnage of the event.

and only battle of the war, so they camped on a nearby hillside, nibbling on cold chicken and waiting for the action to begin.

Back in Washington, Lincoln waited, too. With members of his cabinet, he listened to the early reports. They were confusing. The two armies had met at a meandering creek called Bull Run. Each had advanced and retreated, advanced and retreated. It wasn't until six o'clock in the evening that Lincoln heard the news: the Union army had crumbled. Panic-stricken soldiers had fled back to Washington, only to find the roads blocked by terrified sightseers. People had pushed and shoved. Screams had filled the smoke-thick air. Artillery shells had rained down. And when it was all over, five thousand people lay dead.

As dawn broke, Lincoln watched from a White House window while mud-splattered, blood-streaked troops limped back into the capital through a dismal rain. It was clear the soldiers needed better training and leadership. Changes had to be made, and Lincoln was determined to make them.

LINCOLN'S "MEMORANDUM OF MILITARY POLICY"

Lincoln pondered the causes of the Union's defeat at Bull Run and determined that the attack had not been ill-advised. He knew his soldiers were raw and untrained. But so were the Confederate troops. A crushing Union victory could have ended the war.

Abraham had already heeded the advice of his general in chief, Winfield Scott, who months earlier had proposed that the North tightly blockade Southern ports, then move an army down the Mississippi River. Called the Anaconda Plan, its goal was to seal the Confederacy off from its supplies and eventually squeeze it into submission. But though Lincoln felt the Anaconda Plan would eventually work, he also believed it would move too slowly. He wanted his commanders to take the offensive. And so he made a list of nine military objectives he thought were keys to the Union's success. This list included improving and strengthening the existing blockade, calling up even more troops for longer enlistments, and most importantly, finding a commanding officer who could whip the band of ragtag recruits into a well-trained army.

Until Bull Run, Lincoln had clung to the hope that an all-out war might be avoided. But no longer. Now, Seward would recall, the "concentration and intensity of his mind [were] on the single object of crushing the rebellion."

Believing that General George McClellan was just the fighting general he needed, Lincoln summoned him to take charge of the Union forces around Washington in July 1861. At thirty-four, "Little Mac," as his men called him, had studied at West Point and served in the Mexican War. Handsome, with flashing blue eyes and reddish brown hair, he gave the impression of strength and vigor. He believed himself to be a military genius, and at first everyone in Washington agreed. "He looks as if he ought to have courage," remarked one senator, "and I think [he] is altogether more than an ordinary man."

McClellan also gave the impression that he was eager to move boldly against the South, but in reality he was reluctant to fight. So he claimed that his new army, known as the Army of the Potomac, wasn't ready. He pleaded for more troops and begged for more time to train them. When the president agreed, McClellan sneered at his naiveté. "The President," he told his wife, "is an idiot."

On November 1, 1861, the elderly Winfield Scott resigned his position as general in chief. Lincoln promptly offered the job to McClellan, making him commander of the whole United States Army, not just the forces surrounding Washington. "The supreme command of the Army will entail a vast labor upon you," Lincoln warned him.

"I can do it all," replied Little Mac.

By the end of November, McClellan had still not launched a campaign. But his promotion emboldened him to speak freely about Lincoln and his cabinet members. The president was "nothing more than a well-meaning baboon," while William Henry Seward was "a meddling, officious, incompetent little puppy," Edward Bates "a fool," and Gideon Welles "an old woman."

COMMANDER IN CHIEF?

By December, Lincoln was so desperate for action, he began to think of leading one of the armies into battle himself. After all, the Constitution made him commander in chief. Borrowing several books on the military from the Library of Congress, he began studying, and at times convinced himself he could do a better job than McClellan. But in the end, he knew he wasn't a military man and that "all this was pure fantasy" to help him escape from the real problem: McClellan would not budge. "What shall I do?" he asked Gideon Welles.

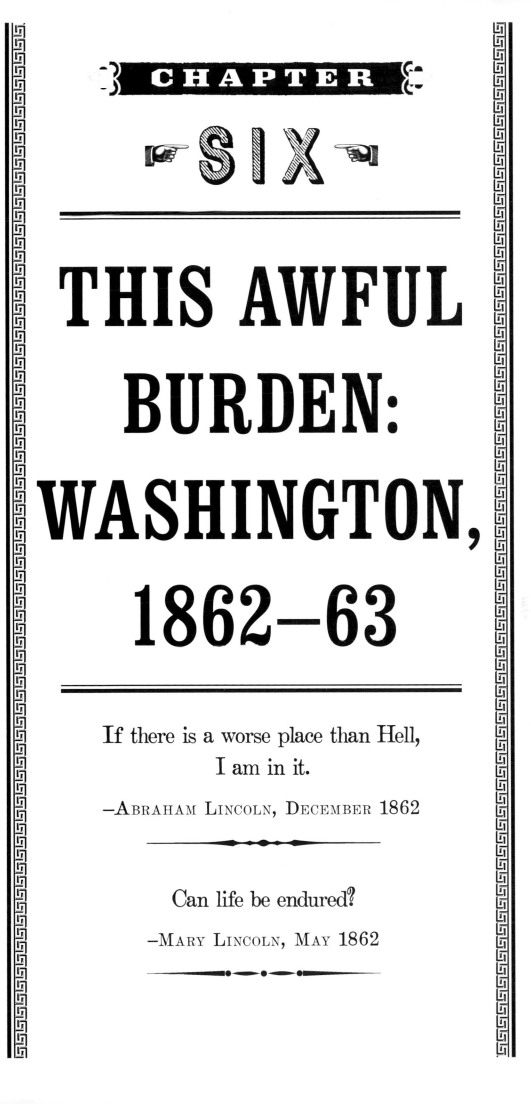

CHAPTER

SIX

THIS AWFUL BURDEN: WASHINGTON, 1862–63

If there is a worse place than Hell,
I am in it.

—ABRAHAM LINCOLN, DECEMBER 1862

Can life be endured?

—MARY LINCOLN, MAY 1862

THE LINCOLNS' WHITE HOUSE RECEPTION, FEBRUARY 5, 1862

Early in January, Mary decided to throw a lavish party to show off her White House improvements. By the end of the month, she had sent out five hundred invitations. "Half the city," wrote John Nicolay, "is jubilant about being invited. The other half is furious (much to the hostess' delight) at being left out." A few declined the invitation. Wrote one indignant senator, "Are the President and Mrs. Lincoln aware that there is a civil war?"

Despite criticism, Mary went ahead and hired the most expensive caterer in the country, ordered champagne and other wine from New York, and dressed her servants in new mulberry-colored uniforms to match her new mulberry-edged china. At nine o'clock on the appointed evening, Mary's guests began arriving. Greeted by the president (who wore a new swallowtail coat) and the First Lady (who shimmered in a white silk gown), they filed into the East Room.

There they were treated to the Marine Band playing a sprightly new piece, "The Mary Lincoln Polka," written especially for the evening. Finally, after an embarrassing delay when no one could find the key to the dining room, the doors swung open to reveal a feast of oysters, turkey, beef, quail, partridge, duck, and various cakes, ices, and fruits. There was even an immense cake shaped like Fort Sumter. It was, declared the *Washington Star,* "the most superb affair of its kind ever seen."

The party—which cost the Lincolns $1,000 out of their own pockets—should have been the high point of Mary's career as First Lady. But it wasn't. Upstairs Willie Lincoln was running a high fever. Instead of enjoying Mary's triumph, both parents spent much of the evening sitting beside their son's bed. As the strains of music and laughter drifted up the stairs, they watched, worried, and prayed.

ONE OF THE LAST PHOTOGRAPHS TAKEN OF WILLIE (STANDING) SHOWS HIM WITH TAD LINCOLN AND LOCKWOOD TODD, A NEPHEW OF MARY'S.

Willie's health did not improve. Day after day he "grew weaker and more shadow-like" as his body was ravaged by high fever, vomiting, exhaustion, and delirium. It is believed he had caught typhoid fever due to the unsanitary conditions in Washington, D.C. A week later, Tad fell sick, too.

After sitting up with his ailing children night after night, Abraham could hardly keep up with his work. He stumbled through his days, sick with worry. Mary refused to leave her sons' sides. For hours at a time she bathed their hot faces with cool water, spooned broth between their chapped lips, and sang them lullabies. "All that human skill could do was done for our sainted boys," she later wrote.

On February 20, eleven-year-old Willie Lincoln died. Overwhelmed with sorrow, Abraham appeared in his office, where John Nicolay was lying on the couch. "Well, Nicolay," he said, "my boy is gone—he is actually gone!" Then he burst into tears.

Meanwhile, Mary was wild with grief. As Elizabeth Keckly recalled, "The pale face of her dead boy threw her into convulsions." She screamed. She wailed. She sobbed hysterically. "Please, Ma," Tad cried weakly from his sickbed, "don't cry so, please!" But Mary couldn't control herself. She took to her bed, where, between these spasms, she lay stunned.

Four days later, Willie earned the sad honor of being the only child ever to have a funeral at the White House. Mourners—many of them the same people who had been present just two weeks earlier at Mary's grand ball—packed the East Room. Dr. Phineas Gurley read from the Scriptures. A prayer was said and a hymn was sung. Then the funeral procession wound its way to the Georgetown Cemetery with Abraham and Robert sharing the first carriage. Absent were Tad, who was slowly beginning to recover, and Mary, who was too grief-stricken to attend. "He was too good for this earth," said Lincoln as the little casket was placed in the tomb. "I know he is much better off in heaven, but then we loved him so. It is hard, hard to have him die."

A FATHER'S SORROW

One week after Willie's death—a Thursday—and for several Thursdays afterward, Abraham closed himself up in the Green Room to pace and sob. Gossips claimed he was so desperate to gaze upon his son again that he had been back to Willie's tomb twice to have the coffin opened. "That blow overwhelmed me," Lincoln later admitted. "It showed me my weakness as I never felt it before."

He eased his sorrow by keeping cherished mementos of his son close by. He placed a photograph of Willie on his office mantelpiece so he could show it to visitors and tell them stories about him. He showed people the scrapbooks Willie had kept. And he claimed that he often had conversations with "my lost boy in . . . my dreams." All this was vitally important to Lincoln because he believed the dead lived on only in the memories of the living.

A MOTHER'S SORROW

Mary stayed in bed for three weeks after Willie's death. "The mere mention of his name would . . . move her to tears," recalled Elizabeth Keckly. Mary couldn't look at Willie's photographs. She got rid of all his toys and clothes. And she banned the Taft boys from ever playing in the White House again because she couldn't bear the sight of them.

When she finally did rise from bed, she plunged deeply into mourning—the nineteenth-century practice of showing outwardly through clothing and actions that one has had a death in the family. She wore a dress "so dark that even gas lights could not lighten her appearance," recalled one friend, and her crepe bonnet was so heavily veiled, she couldn't turn her head. "Always, she must look forward: nothing must distract her from her misery." She bought mourning jewelry—black onyx cameos, bracelets, earrings—and used writing paper with the thickest borders of black.

She believed God had struck Willie down as punishment for her pride and extravagance. "I had become so wrapped in the world, so devoted to our political advancement that I thought of little else."

THIS PHOTOPRINT, MADE AFTER WILLIE'S DEATH, SHOWS WHAT TAD ONCE CALLED "JUST PA AND ME."

While Willie's body rested in the White House's Green Room and Mary lay sobbing in bed, eight-year-old Tad still "tossed with typhoid." Several times each night, the little boy would wake up and call for his father. "The moment [the president] heard Taddie's voice, he was at his side, unmindful of the picture he presented in his dressing gown and slippers," Tad's nurse recalled.

By April, Tad was out of bed and refusing to be away from his father. When Pa went to the War Department, so did Tad. When Pa visited troops in Maryland, so did Tad. And when Pa worked in his office, so did Tad. Recalled one visitor, "Tad was always present—and I must say, somewhat troublesome—always laughing when the adults laughed, asking questions, and squeezing between when the military maps were studied." When Abraham finished his day's work, he usually found his son asleep on the floor next to his desk. Picking him up gently, he would carry him off to the bed they had shared since Willie's death. (Because of Victorian conventions, Mary had her own room next door.) "When this is over," Lincoln said, "I tell my boy Tad that we will go back to the farm. . . . I tell him I will buy a mule and a pony and he shall have a little garden in a field all his own."

GHOSTS IN THE WHITE HOUSE?

An engraving from Frank Leslie's Illustrated Newspaper *shows a typical séance of the nineteenth century—much like the ones in which Mary participated.*

Mary longed to see Willie. She longed to stroke his hair, kiss his cheek, hear his laughter. "Oh, it is too terrible that I shall never see my sweet boy again," she wailed.

Soon after Willie's death, Elizabeth Keckly told Mary about Nettie Colburn, the spiritualist medium who claimed she could transmit messages from the dead.

During the Civil War, spiritualism—the belief that spirits of the dead can communicate with the living through a mysterious person called a medium—became very popular in the United States. Through crystal balls, tarot cards, and séances, Americans desperately tried to contact their dead fathers, husbands, and sons. Mediums could be found in every major city, where, for a few dollars, they stood ready to console parents and wives.

Throughout the spring of 1862, Mary's black carriage was often seen outside Nettie Colburn's home in Georgetown. Here the medium darkened the parlor, then arranged her clients in a circle with their hands on the table so they could communicate with those invisible beings who, intoned Colburn, "surround us like a great cloud." Sometimes Colburn was herself during the séance. Other times a spirit named "Pinkie" took control of her body. Either way, Mary claimed the spiritualist "made wonderful revelations to [her] about her son Willie, and also about things on earth," recalled one family friend.

Sometimes the medium came to the First Lady. As many as eight séances were actually held in the White House, and Abraham even attended one of them. After an hour of mysterious rappings and eerily flickering gaslights, the president said, "I have seen strange things, but nothing convinces me . . . that there is anything very heavenly about all this."

Mary, however, fervently believed in the spirit world. "Willie lives," she told her half sister Emilie. "He comes to me every night and stands at the foot of the bed with the same sweet adorable smile he always has had. He does not come alone. Little Eddie is sometimes with him."

LINCOLN'S GENERAL WAR ORDER NO. 1

By 1862, the Army of the Potomac had not advanced an inch. "Do not allow military matters to give you one moment's trouble," General McClellan wrote to Lincoln in early January. "Nothing shall be left undone in the pursuit of victory." Then the general promptly took to his bed, claiming he had a bad case of typhoid.

Lincoln didn't believe him. Convinced the general was using his illness as an excuse to do nothing, the president lost his patience. On January 27, he issued his General War Order No. 1, directing McClellan to advance into Virginia and seize the town of Manassas on or before February 22.

Upon receiving the order, McClellan sprang from his bed. He wrote Lincoln a twenty-two-page letter detailing his objections to the order. The Confederates, he claimed, had more men, stronger fortifications, and dozens of cannons trained on the Union army. He couldn't possibly lead his men into such a perilous situation. They simply weren't ready.

Meanwhile, anticipating an attack, the Confederates withdrew from their fortifications at Manassas. After hearing reports of their fallback, McClellan finally decided to break camp. Leading his entire army—all 112,000 men—he headed to Manassas to see what was happening. By the time they arrived, the Confederates were long gone. And it was clear from what they left behind that their army had numbered less than 50,000—about half of what McClellan had estimated. More embarrassing, the defenses that the general had claimed were so formidable were nothing more than logs painted to look like cannons. Little Mac had been duped! Wrote John Hay, "The entire country gave a giant horselaugh."

McCLELLAN VS. LEE

McClellan's Goal: To ferry his men to Fort Monroe on the James River Peninsula, then attack Richmond from the southeast.
Lee's Goal: To push back the Union army and defend Richmond.

The Battle: On April 4, McClellan's troops arrive at Fort Monroe. Immediately, 112,000 men, 1,200 wagons and ambulances, 300 pieces of artillery, tons of ammunition, and 15,000 horses begin slogging through Virginia's rain-soaked countryside. Arriving at Yorktown, twenty-five miles from Richmond, McClellan orders his army to dig in. Even though he outnumbers the Confederates by as much as three times, he insists that he cannot advance because he does not have enough men. Instead, he orders his men to begin building gun emplacements.

Meanwhile, the Confederates—on Lee's advice—use this time to reinforce Richmond.

An impatient Lincoln telegraphs from Washington: "I think you had better break the enemies' line . . . at once!"

Furious, McClellan writes to his wife: "I was tempted to reply that he had better come and do it himself."

Little Mac lets an entire month slip by before moving to attack. But by this time, not only have the Confederates fortified Richmond, but the troops protecting Yorktown have abandoned it, leaving McClellan empty-handed.

The Union army trudges on.

Confederate fortifications at Yorktown were reinforced with bales of cotton.

By May 3, it is within five miles of Richmond. But as usual, Little Mac does not advance. The weather is impossible, he complains to Lincoln: rain makes bogs of roads and repeatedly washes out bridges. When Lincoln observes that the weather does little to restrict the Confederates, McClellan replies, "Have no fear. Lee is too cautious and weak to worry about."

Little does McClellan know that Lee has formulated a plan to drive the Union troops back. On June 25, his army rips into the federals, resulting in a series of hard-fought skirmishes called the Seven Days' Battles (June 25 to July 1).

The Outcome: Lee wins. He forces McClellan to retreat down the peninsula, where he takes refuge at Fort Monroe. This victory makes Lee a hero to Southerners, and his soldiers begin developing an almost mythical belief in him as their leader.

As for the Army of the Potomac, it is back where it started. Weeks later, horses, wagons, and ammunition are loaded onto steamers for the humiliating ride back to Washington. It will take nearly three years for the Union forces to come as close to Richmond as they have been that May and June of 1862.

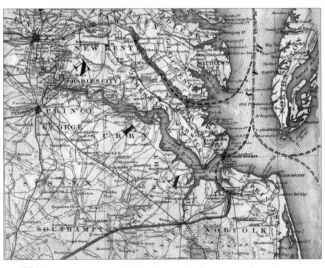

This map, made at the time of the campaign, shows the route of McClellan's army.

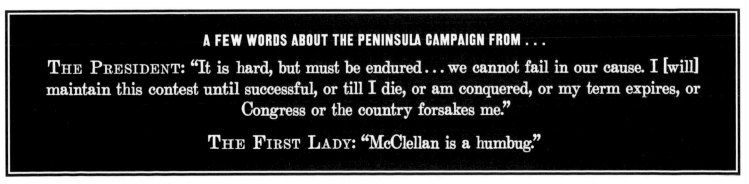

A FEW WORDS ABOUT THE PENINSULA CAMPAIGN FROM . . .

THE PRESIDENT: "It is hard, but must be endured . . . we cannot fail in our cause. I [will] maintain this contest until successful, or till I die, or am conquered, or my term expires, or Congress or the country forsakes me."

THE FIRST LADY: "McClellan is a humbug."

MARY'S GREATEST SOCIAL CAUSE—HELPING "CONTRABAND," LIKE THESE SLAVES IN WASHINGTON, D.C.

When the war began, many slaves took advantage of the turmoil to escape to the North. Others would be freed throughout the course of the war as Union armies captured territory. The government declared these captured and runaway slaves "contraband" (like animals, crops, and other Confederate property) and left them to fend for themselves. Flocking to the nation's capital, they came "with a great hope in their hearts and all their worldly goods on their backs. [But] the North is not warm and impulsive, [and their] appeals for help were answered by cold neglect," wrote Elizabeth Keckly.

By the summer of 1862, camps of former slaves had sprung up in alleys and on the outskirts of town. Living in shacks built from "tents, blankets, ends of plank, log and mud," they had little food or fresh water. The camps quickly became breeding grounds for typhoid, dysentery, and smallpox. Soon rows of little wooden crosses marking graves circled each camp. Said Keckly, "The transition from slavery to freedom was too sudden . . . they were not prepared for the new life that opened before them."

These former slaves had entered a world in which they had no experience. Yankee notions of finding a job, working for wages, and earning money to buy food and clothing were new to them. Up to this point, all of their basic needs had been provided by the slave owners.

Deciding that something needed to be done, Keckly formed the Contraband Relief Association, whose purpose was to raise money for the purchase of clothing, bedding, and shoes. But she needed help. As an African American woman, she could not solicit prominent white citizens for funds. So she turned to Mary Lincoln.

Mary, who had been raised in a household where taking care of its slaves was an important responsibility, was sympathetic. Memories of her own mammy, Sally, may have also inspired her to help. More importantly, she considered Elizabeth Keckly one of her dearest friends. So she gave Elizabeth money. She wrote recommendation letters appealing to other white members of the community to help. She even made a habit of stopping at the "contraband" camp on Seventh Street to hand out blankets and fruit from the White House kitchen.

Her actions shocked Washington's elite. Why was the First Lady wasting time and money on ex-slaves? Why wasn't she more interested in the comfort of wounded soldiers? Gossips buzzed. But for the first and perhaps only time, Mary completely ignored her critics. She knew she was doing the right thing. She explained, "The cause of humanity requires it."

A painting of Abraham Lincoln writing the first draft of his Emancipation Proclamation

In early June, Lincoln borrowed a desk in the War Department and began working on a secret document. "[He] would look out the window for a while and then put his pen to paper," recalled one clerk. "He did not write much at once, but would study between times and when he had made up his mind he would put down a line or two then sit quiet for a few minutes." That first day, he filled less than a page. When he left, he asked Major Thomas Eckert to take charge of it and not to let anyone see it. And for the next few weeks, Lincoln revised and edited what he'd written. Only when he finished did he tell Eckert he'd been writing a document "giving freedom to slaves in the south."

Lincoln had not come to this decision easily. Earlier in the war he had promised to leave slavery alone in the South if it would rejoin the Union. He feared angering the large number of Northerners who were loyal to the Union but opposed emancipation. He worried, too, about the slave-owning border states of Kentucky, Missouri, Maryland, and Delaware. Would they secede if emancipation was proclaimed?

But abolitionists like Frederick Douglass were clamoring for emancipation. Even some of Lincoln's cabinet members encouraged it. They reminded him that freeing a military opponent's slaves was within the president's war powers.

Lincoln understood that emancipation would cripple the Confederacy's war effort. Slavery was an essential part of the Southern war machine; it freed white men to fight while keeping food and factory production going. Every slave who escaped or refused to work meant less production and fewer fighting men available for the Confederate armies. Additionally, escaped slaves, or those declared contraband, could enlist in the Union army. Advised the abolitionist senator Charles Sumner, "You need more men. . . . You need the slaves."

Lincoln finally agreed, declaring, "Slavery is the real issue that divides this nation . . . [therefore] emancipation is absolutely necessary to its preservation."

LINCOLN READS HIS DRAFT—KNOWN AS THE PRELIMINARY EMANCIPATION PROCLAMATION—TO THE CABINET.

Lincoln kept his document a secret for more than a month before revealing it to anyone. Then, on July 22, 1862, he called for a special cabinet meeting to be held at 10:00 a.m. With everyone gathered in his office, Lincoln pulled out two sheets of paper and announced that he wanted them to hear the preliminary draft of a proclamation freeing the slaves. He was not asking for their advice, he added. He was already "resolved upon this step." Still, he wanted to hear their thoughts. Putting on his glasses, he read what amounted to little more than a legal brief. It was "written in . . . the most dry routine style; not a word to evoke a generous thrill, not a word reflecting the warm and lofty . . . feelings of . . . the people," remarked a journalist who later saw the document. In it Lincoln made no mention of morality or the cruelty of slavery. His wording was simple and straightforward. And his purpose was obvious—to end slavery.

Cabinet members were startled by the president's daring move, but only Stanton and Bates felt the proclamation should be put into immediate effect. Welles worried that it might intensify Southern fighting, while Caleb Smith later told a friend he would "resign and go home" if Lincoln issued it. Chase recommended a slower, quieter approach: why not let Union generals proclaim emancipation every time they occupied Southern territory? Still, for all their concerns, most members felt bold action was necessary, and they prepared to stand behind the president. The only real objection came from Secretary of State William Seward. He feared that if the proclamation was issued when the war was going so badly, people might view it as "the last measure of an exhausted government, a cry for help."

Abraham nodded. "We mustn't issue it until after a victory," he said.

He filed the document away in his drawer.

And waited.

FREDERICK DOUGLASS

Frederick Douglass never knew his date of birth because no one had kept "any authentic record containing it." He never knew his mother because "we were separated when I was just an infant." Owned by a succession of cruel slaveholders, he was eventually sent to Baltimore as a companion to a white boy. There his kind mistress taught him to read. But when the master found out, he ordered the lessons stopped. Besides being against the law, the master pointed out, "it will make him . . . discontented and unhappy."

Having been exposed to a world he was forbidden to enter, young Frederick wished he were dead. "Anything," he later wrote, "to get rid of thinking." Still, he secretly taught himself to write, and continued to read anything he could lay his hands on. In 1838, at the age of twenty, he escaped from Baltimore disguised as a free black sailor and eventually made his way to Massachusetts. There he attended the Nantucket abolition convention, where he stood and delivered an unrehearsed speech that forever marked him as a commanding, compelling speaker. Soon he was speaking all over the North, and he quickly became a celebrity. The publication of his book *Narrative of the Life of Frederick Douglass, An American Slave,* published in 1845, added to his fame. By the time he began editing his own newspaper (called *Frederick Douglass' Paper*) in 1851, he had become one of the most influential—and radical—abolitionists in the country.

"What to the American slave is your Fourth of July?" he asked in an 1852 Independence Day speech. "I answer, a day that reveals to him . . . the gross injustice and cruelty to which he is a constant victim. . . . To him your celebration is a sham . . . a thin veil to cover up crimes which would disgrace a nation of savages."

When Lincoln was elected in 1861, Douglass's hopes soared. For the first time the country had elected a man who publicly opposed slavery. Douglass expected great things. But after he read Lincoln's inauguration address, his hopes plummeted. The new president claimed he didn't want to interfere with slavery in the South. Why not? Douglass demanded. In a searing editorial, he wrote, "Some thought we had in Mr. Lincoln the nerve and decision of [a great man]; but the result shows that we merely have a continuation of the weak . . . groveling before the foul curse of slavery."

For the next year and a half, Douglass did not let up. Through his speeches and newspaper articles, he repeatedly urged Lincoln to free slaves and recruit black soldiers. Douglass wanted to stop the Confederacy from using slaves to grow the food that fed the army. "The negro is the stomach of the rebellion," he wrote. "Every slave who escapes . . . is a loss to the rebellion and a gain to the Loyal Cause." He also believed that the quickest way for blacks to gain equal rights was to become Union soldiers. But as the president continued with policies aimed solely at preserving the Union, Douglass grew frustrated. By July 1862 he was calling the administration's slave policy "tardy, hesitating and vacillating" and accusing Lincoln of being "a genuine representative of American prejudice."

A SLY APPROACH TO EMANCIPATION

What Douglass didn't realize was that since the beginning of his presidency, Lincoln *had* been moving the country toward accepting the elimination of slavery. Knowing that most white Americans would never tolerate sweeping changes, Lincoln made them slowly—even slyly. During an address to Congress in 1861, he offhandedly referred to the thousands of confiscated slaves—those who had been temporarily seized by the Union troops as a consequence of war—as "thus liberated." It was a history-making announcement. Up until this point, confiscated slaves were considered property. As such, they would have been returned to their owners once the war ended. But with these two little words Lincoln freed thousands of slaves. Few people even noticed. Why not? Because he had cannily buried this change in his congressional address.

In August 1862, Lincoln wrote a letter to the *New York Tribune* hinting that emancipation might be coming. "My paramount object is to save the Union, and is not either to save or destroy slavery. If I could save the Union without freeing any slave, I would do it, and if I could save it by freeing all the slaves, I would do it; and if I could save it by freeing some and leaving others alone I would also do that." By claiming he would free the slaves only as a necessity for preserving the Union, Lincoln hoped to make the idea of emancipation more palatable to Northerners.

Little did America know that Lincoln's Emancipation Proclamation already lay hidden in his drawer.

McCLELLAN VS. LEE

Lee's Goal: To march his army into Maryland in hopes of convincing the state to join the Confederate cause. If this happens, Lee believes, the federal government will have no choice but to end the war. Additionally, marching into the unharvested Maryland countryside will provide new food for his hungry soldiers.
McClellan's Goal: To keep Lee's forces out of Maryland and crush the rebel army.

The Battle: On September 4, Lee's troops wade across the shallows of the Potomac River into Maryland. Two days later, they arrive in the town of Frederick. Here Lee reads a proclamation inviting people to join the Confederacy. But while the people are polite, they obviously have no sympathy for the Southern cause. This discovery forces Lee to reconsider his plans. He now sets his sights on Harrisburg, the capital of Pennsylvania as well as a railroad center for the Union. Capturing this city, he thinks, will surely force an end to the war. On September 12, his troops begin heading out. But an unforeseen event thwarts Lee's plans. A copy of his military strategy is discovered by a Union private at an abandoned Confederate campsite. McClellan—who until this point has been sitting unmoving in the summer sun—now

This photograph made at Antietam is believed to be the only actual battle picture ever taken during the Civil War. Because cameras needed long exposure time, action shots were almost impossible to capture.

knows all of Lee's moves. Breaking camp, he pursues Lee, and on September 16, the two armies meet at Antietam Creek near Sharpsburg, Maryland. For the next twelve hours, they pound away at each other.

The Outcome: McClellan wins, but it is a grim victory. Antietam will become the bloodiest single-day battle in American history, with 12,401 Union and 10,318 Confederate soldiers killed. The loss of life shocks both sides. Lee's entire army is almost cut off from retreat across the Potomac and is nearly captured by the stronger Union force. But McClellan once again decides to play it safe. Instead of pursuing Lee's bedraggled army, he strikes camp and telegraphs the president with news of "a complete success." Lee's army seizes its opportunity and escapes back into Virginia, intact, to fight another day.

LINCOLN VISITING GENERAL McCLELLAN AT HIS CAMP OUTSIDE ANTIETAM

Noting that the battle-worn Confederates could be crushed, Lincoln arrived at the Army of the Potomac's headquarters to personally urge McClellan to cross into Virginia and take the fight to Lee's army. For the next two days, he warned the general about his "over-cautiousness" and ordered him to take the offensive. By the end of his visit, Lincoln believed he had secured Little Mac's promise to attack. But almost from the minute Lincoln returned to Washington, McClellan began telegraphing with reasons he could not advance: lack of supplies, lack of shoes, tired horses.

Lincoln's temper flashed. "Will you pardon me for asking what the horses of your army have done . . . that fatigue anything?" he asked. But he didn't wait for an answer. On November 5 he relieved McClellan of his command. The general, explained the president, has "a case of the slows."

GENERAL AMBROSE BURNSIDE

McClellan's replacement was Ambrose Burnside, a graduate of West Point who had served in Mexico. Best known for the muttonchop whiskers he wore on the sides of his face (nowadays called "sideburns" in his honor), Burnside was under no illusions about his military talent. A reluctant commander, he twice refused Lincoln's offer because he did not feel adequate to the job. "I am not fit to command an entire army," he explained. But Lincoln swept the general's worries aside. Burnside had a reputation as a fighting general, and that was exactly what the president needed.

While many Americans cheered Lincoln's document, it was far from popular. Many Northerners, including thousands of soldiers, believed they were fighting because of loyalty and patriotism. They did not want to lay down their lives for the freedom of blacks. "There are some who say they will desert before dying for Negroes," wrote one soldier. Across the country, newspapers blasted the president. The *New York World* declared Lincoln a "radical fanatic," while the *New York Evening Express* called the Emancipation Proclamation "an act of Revolution." One newspaper in Baltimore published a savage political cartoon showing Lincoln "doing the devil's work–writing the Emancipation Proclamation." In it the devil is shown holding the president's inkstand, while a figure of Liberty wears a baboon head, and a vulture holds back the curtain. The bats outside the window add to the theme of evil, as do the gargoyles on the table and chair.

ONE GOOD RESULT OF ANTIETAM

Two months after he presented it to his cabinet, Lincoln's Emancipation Proclamation still lay hidden in his desk drawer. Every now and then, he took it out and, as he remembered, "added or changed a line, touching it up here or there, anxiously watching the progress of events." He needed a victory. Any victory. When he heard about McClellan's minor success at Antietam, he decided it was good enough. Bringing the document out of hiding, he recalled that he "fixed it up a little" over the weekend, then called his cabinet together on September 22 to hear it one more time.

The next day the proclamation was released to the press. Across the North, opponents of slavery celebrated. They sang songs, waved flags, and paraded in the streets. In New York, Frederick Douglass expressed happiness but reminded his readers that the document was "but a first step." Lincoln himself remained solemn. "I can only trust in God I have made no mistake," he told a crowd who had jubilantly gathered at the White House. "It is now for the country and the world to pass judgment on it. . . . I will say no more upon the subject."

The preliminary Emancipation Proclamation

BURNSIDE VS. LEE

Burnside's Goal: To capture Richmond by way of Fredericksburg, a strategically important city on the Rappahannock River.
Lee's Goal: To defend Fredericksburg and repulse the Union attack.

The Battle: On December 13, Burnside launches his 115,000 troops against Lee's 78,000 men. Though outnumbered, Lee's men are strategically positioned around Fredericksburg. Wave after wave of Union soldiers are cut down by Confederates who shoot at them from their unassailable fortifications, while fires set in the brush kill the wounded who cannot escape. This slaughter continues until night brings an end to the butchery.

The Outcome: Lee wins, and a weeping Burnside orders his beaten army to retreat. He has lost 7,000 men in less than a day, causing Northern morale to plummet to an all-time low. A month later, the humiliated general resigns.

A handful of wounded soldiers at Fredericksburg

AN AWFUL BURDEN

For three days after the Battle of Fredericksburg, Abraham sat on the front porch of the White House and watched the wagons roll by with the dead. He was, recalled John Hay, "wrung by the bitterest anguish," weighed down by the "awful burden" of presiding over a nation tearing itself apart. He worried constantly, and often looked "weary, care-worn and troubled." At times "he felt almost ready to hang himself," Attorney General Bates reported Lincoln to have said.

But while Lincoln wrestled with his guilt and regret, he also pushed for a more ruthless prosecution of the war. "Engage the enemy," he repeatedly commanded. "Pursue them," "defeat them," "force a surrender." "Let us die to make men free."

DISAPPEARING ACT

By the end of 1862, Lincoln had almost disappeared as a husband. Distracted and exhausted by the war, he had little time left for his wife. Often alone, Mary wrote to a friend: "I consider myself fortunate if at eleven o'clock, I once more find myself in my pleasant room and very especially, if my tired and weary husband is waiting there to receive me."

The first page of the final version of the Emancipation Proclamation, as well as the fifth (and last) page, showing Lincoln's signature. His signature put the document into effect.

On January 1, 1863, the Lincolns held their customary New Year's Day reception. Abraham shook hands for two hours, then quietly slipped upstairs, where a final copy of the proclamation awaited his signature. "I never in my life felt more certain that I was doing right than I do in signing this paper," he told the cabinet members who had gathered to watch. Still, his arm was so stiff and numb from all the handshaking that he worried about controlling his pen. "Now this signature is one that will be closely examined," he said, "and if they find my hand trembled, they will say 'he had some [doubts].' But anyway, it is going to be done!" Usually, he signed his documents "A. Lincoln," but this time he carefully wrote his full name. "If my name ever goes into history," he said, "it will be for this act."

WHOM DID THE EMANCIPATION PROCLAMATION FREE?

No one, actually. Lincoln's proclamation read:

> *That on the first day of January, in the year of our Lord one thousand eight hundred and sixty-three, all persons held as slaves within any State or designated part of a State . . . in rebellion against the United States, shall be then, thenceforward, and forever free.*

In other words, it freed only those slaves in the Confederate states—and since the federal government had no control in those rebellious areas, it could not enforce the document. Complained the *New York World*, "[The president] has proclaimed emancipation only where he has no power to execute it!"

Meanwhile, the Emancipation Proclamation did *not* free any slaves in the Union—and there were many. The border states that had remained in the Union (Kentucky, Delaware, Maryland, Missouri) were slave states, but Lincoln did not want to risk losing their loyalty by freeing their slaves. He feared that such a move would push them into the Confederacy. So he wrote the document with no mention of these slaves. He also chose to overlook Southern areas that had come under the North's control since the war began, such as Tennessee and parts of Virginia and Louisiana. Remarked 👉

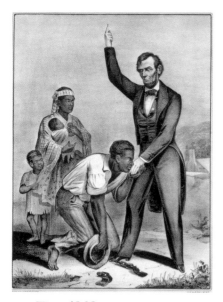

This 1863 lithograph was a sentimental tribute to Lincoln—the man who broke the slaves' shackles.

Secretary of State Seward, "We show our sympathy with slavery by emancipating slaves where we cannot reach them, and holding them in bondage where we can set them free."

It was, indeed, a puzzling and ambiguous document. But its achievement was symbolic and very important. As historian Doris Kearns Goodwin wrote, "It changed forever the relationship between the national government and slavery." No longer would the government protect slavery. From here on, it would work to secure people's freedom. Cheered the *Boston Daily Evening Transcript,* "Whatever [flaws] it may have, slavery from this hour ceases to be a political power in this country . . . such a righteous revolution as it inaugurates never goes backward."

A GRUDGING GOOD WORD

Even Lincoln's political enemies grudgingly admitted admiration for the Emancipation Proclamation. Wrote one Ohio congressman: "Strange phenomenon in the world's history when a second-rate Illinois lawyer is the instrument to utter words that shall form an epoch memorable in all future ages."

MARY AND EMANCIPATION

Rumor had it that Mary, "coming from an old slave family," would try to prevent her husband from signing the Emancipation Proclamation by persuading him to "give the slaveholders one more chance." This gossip not only hurt Mary "to the quick," but was completely untrue. Noted the antislavery journalist Jane Grey Swisshelm, "[Mrs. Lincoln] is more radically opposed to slavery than her husband, and had urged him to Emancipation as a matter of right, long before he saw it as a matter of necessity." By 1862, Mary believed "the oppressed colored race" should be not only freed but also granted equal rights under the law. "Negroes," she said, "are as capable as white men." This was a radical idea for the 1860s, especially from the daughter of a Kentucky slave owner. But over the years she had become an ardent abolitionist. There were many reasons for this—her husband's progressively stronger views on the subject; her own kindness and sense of justice; her friendship with Elizabeth Keckly, which had revived girlhood memories of the brutalities of the slave system; and her admiration for Senator Charles Sumner, the leading abolitionist in Congress. Recalled Mary's niece, "She could talk by the hour of schemes for the betterment of the Negro, [and] she would get quite breathless with interest and excitement."

THE PRESIDENT . . .

When Abraham arrived at Mathew Brady's photography studio in April 1863, the photographer's assistant, Thomas Le Mere, told him there was a "considerable call" for a full-length photograph of him. "Can it be taken with a single negative?" joked Abraham. He explained how he had seen a very wide landscape photograph that was actually a carefully joined series of photographs. "I thought perhaps this method might be necessary for my full-length landscape."

Le Mere assured him one negative would be enough. The result was this portrait showing all six feet four inches of a fit, trim, and surprisingly youthful-looking president.

Mary in mourning clothes

. . . AND THE FIRST LADY

Around the beginning of 1863, Mary sat for a new portrait at Mathew Brady's studio. This time she didn't concern herself with gowns and glittering jewelry. In just one year her life had turned as somber as the mourning clothes she now wore.

GENERAL JOSEPH HOOKER

In January 1863 Lincoln replaced the bumbling Burnside with Joseph Hooker. An ambitious man who had served in the Mexican War, Hooker once told the president, "It is neither vanity nor boasting in me to declare that I am a damned sight better general than any you have on the field." Hooker immediately began making plans to fight the rebels. "May God have mercy on General Lee," he declared, "for I will have none."

MANPOWER

AFRICAN AMERICAN MEN, SUCH AS THESE FROM THE 107TH U.S. COLORED INFANTRY, ENLISTED IN THE FIGHT.

Although many African Americans had longed to join the war effort earlier, they were prohibited from enlisting by a federal law dating back to 1792. But with Lincoln's Emancipation Proclamation, the door to military service was flung open. Over the next two years approximately 180,000 black men enlisted.

As soldiers, they faced more than the hardships of war; they faced racial prejudice. They were assigned menial chores such as cooking and caring for mules and horses. Additionally, they received lower pay—$10 a month compared to the $13 a month white soldiers received. And they confronted a much greater threat if captured by the Confederate army. Recalled one rebel soldier at the Battle of Fort Pillow in Tennessee, "I saw 25 Negroes shot down. . . . They had surrendered, and were begging for mercy. . . . The commanding officer ordered his men to 'kill the last God damned one of them.' "

In spite of their many hardships, African Americans served the Union bravely. Said Frederick Douglass, "Once let the black man get upon his person the brass letters 'U.S.,' let him get an eagle on his button, a musket on his shoulder, and bullets in his pocket, and there is no power on earth . . . which can deny that he has earned the right of citizenship in the United States."

A CIVIL WAR DRAFT NOTICE RECEIVED BY A PENNSYLVANIA FARMER

With the war grinding on, Lincoln needed still more men. But once-eager Northerners now felt angry and disillusioned about the war. Volunteering almost completely stopped. Desperate for soldiers, the president instituted a draft on March 3, which required all males between the ages of twenty and forty-five to serve. But it provided a loophole for wealthy men. Draftees could escape military service by paying the government a fee of $300 (equal to a worker's annual wage) or hiring a substitute—that is, paying someone to take their place. As a result, many called the Civil War a "rich man's war, but a poor man's fight."

FORM 39.

Provost Marshal's Office,
9th District, State of Pennsylvania
June 2, 1864

To Washington Denny
Lower Columbia.

SIR:

You are hereby notified that you were, on the 2d day of June, 1864, legally drafted in the service of the United States for the period of Three Years, in accordance with the provisions of the act of Congress, "for enrolling and calling out the national forces, and for other purposes," approved March 3, 1863. You will accordingly report, on or before the 22nd day of June 1864 at the place of rendezvous, in Lancaster Pa., or be deemed a deserter, and be subject to the penalty prescribed therefor by the Rules and Articles of War.

Transportation will be furnished you on presenting this notification at the station nearest your place of residence.

Capt. Provost Marshal,
9th Dist. of Pennsylvania

LAUGHING LINCOLN

Despite all his troubles, Lincoln still enjoyed telling a funny story. The president was "so funny he could make a cat laugh," claimed one senator. Lincoln said humor helped him cope with the stress of a nation at war with itself. "I laugh," he once explained, "because I must not cry." But his stories also conveyed practical wisdom that his listeners could remember and repeat. Below is just a sampling of his humor.

When Abraham replaced Secretary of War Simon Cameron, some senators demanded that the president fire all his other cabinet members, too. This put Abraham in mind of a story about a farmer who had seven skunks in his barnyard. "He took aim," the president told them, "blazed away, killed one, and it raised such a fearful smell that he concluded it was best to let the other six go."

Once, when accused by political foes of being two-faced, Lincoln replied, "If I had two faces, would I be wearing this one?"

While in the White House, Abraham penned a review for a badly written book authored by an old friend from Illinois. He wrote, "People who like this sort of thing will find this the sort of thing they like."

Since a Native American named Laughing Water had been introduced to Lincoln as Minihaha, when he met Crying Water he said, "I suppose your name is Miniboohoo?"

When Reverend Phineas Gurley, pastor of the Presbyterian church in Washington, asked Lincoln the best way to tell a funny story, the president replied: "There are two ways of relating a story. If you have a [good listener] who has the time, and is inclined to listen, lengthen it out, pour it out slowly as if from a jug. If you have a poor listener, hasten it, shorten it, shoot it out of a pop gun."

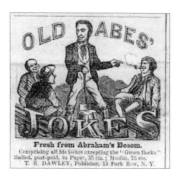

AN 1864 NEWSPAPER AD FOR OLD ABES' JOKES

Lincoln never claimed to be the author of the stories he told. "I don't make [them] mine by telling them," he said. But this didn't stop publishers from issuing books such as *Old Abes' Jokes* or *The Humors of Old Abe*, which claimed to be a collection of his stories. Thus Abraham Lincoln became the first president to inspire a presidential joke book.

General and Mrs. Tom Thumb, who visited the White House right after their wedding

On February 13, a three-foot man dressed in a miniature wedding suit and an even smaller woman, looking lovely in a white satin wedding dress, arrived at the White House. They were Charles and Lavinia Stratton, better known as General and Mrs. Tom Thumb—favorite exhibits of the showman P. T. Barnum. Accounts of their wedding just three days earlier had seized the imagination of the country and crowded news of the war off the front pages of many newspapers. When Mary had learned that the couple was traveling to Washington, she had quickly put together an evening reception. As the tiny couple was presented to the president, he had to bend "down and down and down to take their little hands in his great palm," recalled one guest. Then, said Lavinia Stratton, "the President led us to the sofa." Abraham lifted Tom and placed him on it, while Mary did the same for Lavinia. Tad could only stare. Finally, he said, "Mother, if you were a little woman like Mrs. Stratton you would look just like her." Everyone laughed, including Mary.

While Lincoln no longer sought his wife's political advice, he still turned to her for escape from his job's pressures. Often wandering into her room, the president liked nothing better than to slip off his shoes and stretch out on her couch. Sometimes he napped for a few minutes, but usually he spent those spare moments talking with his wife. Giving him a cup of tea, Mary always listened intently as he described his day or "recited some poem until [he was] recalled to the cares of state by the messenger." Mary's secretary, William Stoddard, remembered that Lincoln "at all times kept his wife in close touch with what he was doing, how he felt, and what was happening on the field of battle." Sadly, these conversations have all been lost to history, except for this brief glimpse recorded by Elizabeth Keckly.

One day in 1863, Lincoln appeared before his wife looking like "a complete picture of dejection." When Mary asked where he'd been, he answered, "The War Department."

Was there any news? his wife asked.

"Yes, plenty of news, but no good news," he replied. "It is dark, dark everywhere." Then, reaching for a Bible, he began to read. At the end of fifteen minutes, the "dejected look was gone, and [his] countenance was lighted up with resolution and hope."

MARY'S BLUE ROOM SALON

After Willie's death, Mary formed a circle of friends she called "my beau monde friends of the Blue Room." It was a very select group. You were admitted, recollected one member, only "if you could talk of love, law, literature and war, could describe the rulers and thinkers of the time, could gossip of courts and cabinets, of the boudoir and salon, of commerce and the church, of Dickens and Thackeray."

In the evenings, while Abraham worked upstairs, Mary's friends gathered in the Blue Room. Among them were such distinguished persons as the abolitionist senator Charles Sumner and Nathaniel Willis, editor of the *Home Journal,* as well as notorious callers like the spy Henry Wikoff and Union general Dan Sickles, who had shot and killed his wife's lover but had gotten off on a plea of temporary insanity.

Mary adored her beau monde friends and considered their gatherings *très chic*. But she soon learned that Wikoff was only pretending to be her friend. In truth, he was working for the *New York Herald.* When the *Herald* printed excerpts from one of the president's speeches before he gave it, the

White House had Wikoff arrested. He confessed to getting close to the First Lady just to steal "inside" information. Mary was devastated, and Abraham was furious. He tried to discourage the Blue Room salons. Still, they continued until Mary left the White House—a little group, recalled one cabinet member, of "affable, insinuating, and pleasant persons . . . although not particularly reliable."

HOOKER VS. LEE

Hooker's Goal: To cross the Rappahannock River, draw the rebels away from the unassailable fortifications at Fredericksburg, and engage them in battle. Once they were defeated, Richmond would be won easily.

Lee's Goal: To repel the Union Army and deliver a fatal defeat.

Union troops in the trenches at Chancellorsville

The Battle: On April 27, 70,000 Union soldiers cross the river. Their presence is detected by Confederate cavalry, who immediately inform Lee. Although conventional military wisdom dictates that the outnumbered Army of Virginia retreat south and escape Hooker's trap, Lee boldly opts to meet the federals head-on. He marches his 42,000 troops west toward the advancing Union army. But when they arrive in the town of Chancellorsville, Lee realizes with dismay that Hooker's army has taken up strong positions around the town, which will make it difficult to defeat. Then around midnight a Confederate scout brings astounding information. Hooker's right rear flank is "in the air"—that is, it has no fortifications. Lee seizes his chance. In a daring maneuver, he attacks the Union army from the rear. For the next five days the armies engage in fierce fighting, but Lee now has the advantage, and Hooker never regains it. Hooker's second in command claims he was "outgeneraled."

The Outcome: Lee wins again, and future historians will consider the battle his most brilliant victory. Hooker loses 17,000 men and is forced to retreat to his original position across the river. Upon hearing of the defeat, Lincoln cries, "My God! My God! What will the country say?"

GENERAL GEORGE MEADE

On June 28, Lincoln replaced Hooker with General George Meade. Nicknamed "Old Snapping Turtle" because of his reputation for hanging on to the enemy, Meade was a graduate of West Point and a veteran of the Mexican War. One of the most experienced corps commanders in the Army of the Potomac, having served in every major engagement since Bull Run in 1861, he had the respect of his men but not their affection. "He is not charismatic," reported one soldier. Instead, he "looks like a good sort of family doctor." Sadly, Meade did not have time to establish a relationship with his troops. From the moment he took command, his hands were full—Lee was headed for Pennsylvania.

ANDERSON COTTAGE, WHERE THE LINCOLN FAMILY STAYED TO ESCAPE WASHINGTON'S HEAT

Every summer the Lincolns packed up their clothes, toys, and furniture and moved to Anderson Cottage. Located just three miles from Washington on the grounds of the Soldiers' Home (a residence for disabled veterans), the place was cooler and less formal than the White House. It was also near enough for Lincoln to ride to the office every day, but far enough from town to discourage most White House callers. Here Abraham could let down his guard, toss his suit coat over the back of the sofa, and pad around in his house slippers. He and Tad went fishing in the nearby pond and climbed the tall copper beech tree that grew just behind the cottage. Because their place was so close to Fort Stevens—one of the fortifications surrounding Washington—they often shared meals and stories with the soldiers.

Mary whiled away the summer days, too. On evenings when her husband was kept late in town, she sewed, read, or played cards with Tad. She especially liked to sit on the porch long after dark. With her son snuggled beside her, she pointed out Venus and the Big Dipper. "It's odd," she said one night. "I don't think I've ever noticed the stars before in Washington."

"Maybe they've just come from Springfield to visit us," replied Tad.

Here Mary no longer awoke each morning with a "sense of misery." She admitted to a friend, "How I dearly loved the Soldiers' Home."

ACCIDENT OR ASSASSINATION ATTEMPT?

On July 2, the sweltering heat gave way to cool breezes. At the Soldiers' Home, Mary decided to make a trip into town. But as her carriage rolled along the shaded avenue, the horses suddenly reared, then plunged into a reckless gallop. Mary was flung from the carriage and struck her head on a sharp rock. Although the wound bled heavily, she seemed only slightly injured.

But days later, the wound became infected, and Mary fell dangerously ill. For the next two weeks she languished in bed, suffering from high fevers and splitting headaches. Sometimes she experienced periods of blindness. Other times she hallucinated. Thinking his wife was dying, Abraham sent a telegram to Robert, who was visiting friends in New York City, urging him to hurry home. By the time Bob arrived three days later, however, his mother was already on the mend.

While Mary convalesced, Pinkerton detectives discovered that the bolts on the driver's seat had been unscrewed, probably by someone hoping to hurt the president. Lincoln, who received dozens of threatening letters each month, was angry that Mary had been hurt. He ordered an investigation, but the culprit was never found.

MEADE VS. LEE

Meade's Goal: To force Lee's army out of Pennsylvania.
Lee's Goal: To cross the Susquehanna River at Harrisburg, Pennsylvania, and march on Philadelphia with hopes of taking that city and ending the war.

The Battle: On June 28, Lee crosses into Pennsylvania. Meade gives chase, forcing Lee's troops to change direction. The result is a chance meeting between the two armies at the crossroads town of Gettysburg in the south-central part of the state. Eighty thousand Union soldiers and 70,000 rebels will fight for three desperate days–July 1 to 3, 1863–in the largest battle ever fought in America.

"The [bullets] were whizzing so fast," a rebel later reports, "that it looked like a man could hold out a hat and catch it full." Meanwhile, a private from Massachusetts recalls the sound of battle: "The hoarse and indistinguishable orders of commanding officers, the screaming and bursting of shells, canisters and shrapnel, as they tore through the struggling mass of humanity, the death screams of wounded animals, the groans of their human companions, wounded and dying and trampled underfoot by hurrying batteries . . . a perfect hell on earth, never perhaps to be equaled, certainly not to be surpassed, nor ever to be forgotten in a man's lifetime."

The Outcome: On the third day, Confederate troops finally retreat after losing a third of their soldiers. "It was all my fault," moans Robert E. Lee as his men stagger back toward Virginia. "All my fault."

In Washington, Lincoln soon learns of Lee's defeat. Immediately, he orders Meade to go after Lee and destroy his army once and for all. "Do not let the enemy escape," he wires. But Meade postpones an attack, and Lee's army slips safely into Virginia. When Lincoln hears what his general has done, he roars, "If I had gone up there, I could have whipped them myself."

ANGRY ABRAHAM

Lincoln's anger did not fade quickly. Weeks later he wrote a scathing letter to Meade: "My dear general, I do not believe you appreciate the magnitude of the misfortune involved in Lee's escape. He was within your easy grasp, and to have closed upon him would . . . have ended the war. As it is, the war will be prolonged indefinitely. . . . Your golden opportunity is gone, and I am distressed immeasurably because of it."

But he did not send this letter. The act of writing had purged his frustrations. He came to realize that he had been expecting too much of Old Snapping Turtle. After Gettysburg, the Union army was exhausted. They had suffered huge losses. And they were working with a brand-new commander. It was enough to have won the battle—at least for the moment.

Some of the heaviest fighting on the first day at Gettysburg occurred at Cemetery Hill, as sketched by Alfred Waud.

The aftermath of the battle: 32,000 Confederate and 23,000 Union soldiers dead

ULYSSES S. GRANT, COMMANDER OF THE UNION'S FORCES IN TENNESSEE AND NORTHERN MISSISSIPPI

Ulysses S. Grant had come a long way since graduating at the bottom of his class at West Point. Though he had served in the Mexican War, he had resigned from the army in disgrace after being charged with drunkenness. After that, he failed at everything he tried—banking, storekeeping, farming. Down and out, he was clerking in his father's tannery when the war broke out and "rescued" him. Given command of an unruly group of Illinois volunteers, Grant whipped them into shape, and by 1861 he had risen to the rank of brigadier general.

Grant fought hard and hated surrender. During one battle in Missouri in November 1861, his troops found themselves completely surrounded by the rebel army. Aides begged the general to surrender, but Grant refused. "We must cut our way out as we cut our way in," he declared. Eventually, his troops did break through the enemy's line, but in the process 4,000 Union soldiers died. "Senseless," cried Washington's leaders, "horrific." They demanded that the "butcher Grant" be removed. Replied Lincoln, "I can't spare this man—he fights." Grant continued to fight in Missouri, Tennessee, and Georgia. And by the summer of 1863, he was poised for one of the most important battles of his military career.

THE INTERIOR OF THE AMORY SQUARE HOSPITAL, ONE OF THE HOSPITALS MARY OFTEN VISITED

Washington was slowly filling with wounded and dying soldiers—as many as 50,000 in 1863. The freshly injured were driven by ambulance to one of the twenty hospitals that marked the city's landscape. Housed in whatever space was available—schools, hotels, churches—these hospitals were too ghastly for most Washington ladies to visit. Still, genteel, nervous Mary managed to endure the endless moaning and screaming, the smell of rotting flesh and unemptied bedpans, the sight of row after row of sick and wounded men. At least three times a week she brought flowers from the White House conservatory, delivered meals to beds, spoon-fed those unable to feed themselves, and wrote letters such as this one:

> *I am sitting by the side of your soldier boy. He has been quite sick, but is getting well. He tells me to say that he is all right.*
>
> *With respect for the mother of a young soldier,*
>
> *Mrs. Abraham Lincoln*

TWO GREAT BATTLES

The battles of Gettysburg and Vicksburg—both fought during the summer of 1863, with Union victories declared on the same day—were the turning point of the war.

GRANT VS. PEMBERTON

Grant's Goal: To seize control of Vicksburg, a town in Mississippi located at a strategic bend in the Mississippi River, thus controlling passage of the entire river. As commander of the Union's Army of the Tennessee, Grant knows this is important not only because the Mississippi serves as the major transportation route between Pittsburgh and New Orleans but also because Union control of the river (which runs right through the middle of the Confederacy) will split the rebellious states in two.

Pemberton's Goal: To hold off Grant's troops until reinforcements arrived. As lieutenant general of the Army of Vicksburg, Pemberton understands the city's vital importance.

The Battle: After fighting and winning a string of battles—at Port Gibson (May 1), Raymond (May 12), Jackson, the capital of Mississippi (May 14), Champion's Hill (May 16), and the Big Black River (May 17)—Grant is finally in position to take Vicksburg. But the city is heavily fortified. Besides lines of cannons and tall earthworks, the Confederates have dug a deep, wide trench all the way around the city. Behind these fortifications, 31,000 rebels watch and wait.

On May 22, the siege of Vicksburg begins. For the next forty-four days, Grant's 50,000 soldiers bombard the city. Citizens take shelter in the caves dug in the clay hills on which the city stands. Men, women, and children huddle in these cavelike dwellings, living on rats, mule meat, and rainwater as Union bombs

This lithograph of the siege of Vicksburg, published a few years after the event, is a bit too tidy, but it does show Vicksburg's fortifications and the siege lines surrounding it.

destroy their homes, schools, and churches. They hang on as long as they can, hoping for reinforcements. But it is bad timing. Lee has invaded Pennsylvania, and there are no soldiers to spare. Eventually, the Army of Vicksburg loses hope.

The Outcome: On the morning of July 4, Pemberton has a white flag raised. Vicksburg and the Mississippi River from Cairo, Illinois, to New Orleans are now in Union hands.

Lincoln receives the news on July 5, just hours after learning about the victory at Gettysburg. His face beaming, he flings his arms around Gideon Welles, secretary of the navy and bearer of the good news. "I cannot, in words, tell you my joy over this result," he cries. "It is great, Mr. Welles, it is great!"

A Vicksburg citizen stands before the entrance to his cave home.

A POEM BY THE PRESIDENT

After the victories at Vicksburg and Gettysburg, Abraham's spirits soared. He was in such a good mood, he felt inspired to write the following:

General Lee's Invasion of the North
Written by Himself

*In eighteen sixty three, with pomp,
and mighty swell,
Me and Jeff's Confederacy went
forth to sack Phil-del,
The Yankees they got arter us, and
give us particular hell,
And we skedaddled back again,
and didn't sack Phil-del.*

One of the five known handwritten drafts of Lincoln's speech. Lincoln gave this to his secretary John Nicolay. It is often called the "first draft" because it is believed to be the earliest copy that exists.

Ever since the victories at Gettysburg and Vicksburg, Abraham had been looking for an opportunity to express his thoughts on the significance of the war. He wanted to make some sort of statement explaining why fighting this war—with its enormous sacrifices—was worthwhile.

An opportunity arose in November. After the Battle of Gettysburg, a national cemetery had been created so that soldiers killed during the battle could be properly buried. While the president was invited to attend the dedication ceremony, he was not originally invited to speak. This honor was given to Edward Everett, one of the most noted orators of the day. But organizers of the event soon changed their minds and asked Abraham to make "a few appropriate remarks."

During the next few weeks, Abraham thought long and hard about what he wanted to say. When he finally began to write, the words flowed. Only toward the end of the address did he have trouble. He was still wrestling with it when he boarded the special train that would take him to Gettysburg.

On the morning of November 19, Abraham took his place on the speakers' platform. Everett spoke first—a blow-by-blow description of the battle that left "his audience in tears many times during his masterly effort," recalled one spectator. The speech lasted two hours.

Then it was Abraham's turn. After fitting his spectacles over his nose, and pulling a folded piece of paper from his pocket, he delivered these words:

Four score and seven years ago our fathers brought forth, upon this continent, a new nation, conceived in liberty, and dedicated to the proposition that "all men are created equal."

Now we are engaged in a great civil war, testing whether that nation, or any nation so conceived, and so dedicated, can long endure. We are met on a great battle field of that war. We have come to dedicate a portion of it, as a final resting place for those who died here, that the nation might live. This we may, in all propriety do. But, in a larger sense, we can not dedicate—we can not consecrate—we can not hallow, this ground —The brave men, living and dead, who struggled here, have hallowed it, far above our poor power to add or detract. The world will little note, nor long remember what we say here; while it can never forget what they did here.

It is rather for us, the living, we here be dedicated to the great task remaining before us—that, from these honored dead we take increased devotion to that cause for which they here, gave the last full measure of devotion—that we here highly resolve these dead shall not have died in vain; that the nation, shall have a new birth of freedom, and that government of the people, by the people, for the people, shall not perish from the earth.

He gave what most historians consider the single greatest speech in American history.

When he finished, the crowd was "so astonished . . . that it stood transfixed." The president took the audience's silence for disapproval. Finally, there came applause, and Abraham turned to his friend Ward Lamon. "That speech won't scour," he said. "It is a flat failure, and the people are disappointed."

But the response quickly made it clear that this speech *did* "scour." "The few words of the President were from the heart to the heart," praised the editor of *Harper's Weekly.* Added the *Chicago Tribune,* "the remarks by President Lincoln will live among the annals of man. . . ."

What had Abraham's speech done? In simple, eloquent language, it had presented a broader statement about the larger significance of the war. By invoking the Declaration of Independence, with its principles of liberty and equality, Lincoln was reshaping the aims of the war. No longer were soldiers fighting to preserve the Union alone. They were fighting for union and something even more precious—freedom.

Lincoln declared the last Thursday in November a national holiday–Thanksgiving. The idea for this had come from Sarah Josepha Hale, editor of *Godey's Lady's Book*. For more than thirty years, she had been writing to state and national officials, urging them to create a day of thanksgiving. "Would it not be a renewed pledge of love and loyalty to the Constitution of the United States?" she asked. But no one had taken her idea seriously until the Civil War began. Realizing that the nation needed a day to focus on its blessings, even in its darkest hours, Lincoln authorized the holiday that Americans have been celebrating ever since.

THE END OF A LONG YEAR

Alexander Todd, Mary's half brother, who was killed in a skirmish in Baton Rouge, Louisiana

David Todd, another half brother, who was killed in the Battle of Vicksburg

Emilie Todd Helm, Mary's half sister, in widow's weeds after the death of her husband

Ben Hardin Helm, Emilie's husband, who was killed in the Battle of Chickamauga

REBELS IN THE WHITE HOUSE

Mary's family was as divided as the country. When the war broke out, her brother George enlisted in the Confederate army, as did three half brothers and three half sisters' husbands. For months, tongues in Washington wagged about the First Lady's "rebel family." But that didn't stop Abraham from inviting them to visit. In December 1863, he asked Mary's half sister Emilie Helm to stay at the White House. Just months earlier, Emilie's husband, Confederate general Ben Hardin Helm, had been killed in the Battle of Chickamauga in Georgia. Hoping to ease her sorrow, as well as to provide his wife with some company, Abraham received the young widow "with the warmest affection." That first night at dinner, however, they carefully avoided any talk of the war. "It comes between us," Emilie admitted, "like a barrier of granite closing our lips."

The sisters managed to enjoy each other's company until the evening General Dan Sickles and Senator Ira Harris came to call. Mary invited Emilie to join them in the Blue Room, but no sooner had her sister sat down than Senator Harris said, "We whipped the rebels at Chattanooga, and I hear, madam, that the scoundrels ran like scared rabbits."

"It was the example," replied Emilie, "that you set them at Bull Run and Manassas."

Senator Harris sprang to his feet. "If I had twenty sons they would all be fighting the rebels," he hollered.

"And if I had twenty sons," retorted Emilie, "they should all be opposing yours!"

Furious, General Sickles and the senator stormed from the White House, but not before berating the president. "You should not have a rebel in your house," cried General Sickles.

Lincoln drew himself up. "My wife and I are in the habit of choosing our own guests," he said coldly. "We do not need from our friends either advice or assistance."

The nasty confrontation put an end to Emilie's visit. Over the Lincolns' protests, she decided to go home. "Oh, Emilie," Mary cried as she kissed her sister goodbye. "Will we ever awaken from this hideous nightmare?"

TAD'S CONFEDERATE COUSIN

Even children felt divided by the war. When Mary's half sister Emilie visited the White House, she brought along her five-year-old daughter, Katherine. One day Tad and Katherine were sitting on the floor, looking at the photographs in the Lincolns' album. Tad picked up a picture of his father. "This is the President," he said.

Katherine shook her head. "No, that is not the President," she said. "Mr. [Jefferson] Davis is the President." (Davis, of course, was president of the Confederacy.)

Tad turned an angry red. "Hurrah for Abe Lincoln!" he shouted.

"Hurrah for Jeff Davis!" Katherine shouted back.

Tad stuck out his tongue and raced to his father's office. Katherine ran after him.

"Pa," cried Tad, "Katherine says you're not the President. Tell her you're the President. Go on, tell her."

But Abraham just smiled. "Well, Tad," he said, "you know who your President is, and your cousin knows who her Uncle Lincoln is. Let us leave it at that." Then he pulled the children into his lap and tickled them.

LINCOLN'S PROCLAMATION OF AMNESTY AND RECONSTRUCTION

In December 1863, Abraham came down with a mild case of smallpox. Feverish and contagious, he spent the next three weeks in bed. But even then, he didn't rest. He used this quiet time to tackle the vexing problem of reconstruction—that is, how to return the Confederate states to the Union. After the victories at Vicksburg and Gettysburg, it seemed certain the Union would win the war, and Abraham wanted to lay out a plan that would bring the two halves of the nation back together again. He knew that Southerners would need to prove their loyalty to the Union. And he knew that Northerners would have to be satisfied enough by this proof to welcome them back.

To this end, Abraham wrote his Proclamation of Amnesty and Reconstruction. It stipulated that before the president would pardon any rebel or restore his rights of property, he must not only swear allegiance to the Union but also accept emancipation. Once the number of men taking the oath in each rebel state reached 10 percent (women could neither take the oath nor vote), they could "re-establish a state government" that would be recognized by the United States. (This was known as the "10 percent plan.")

Although the plan was fair and well balanced, many Northerners complained. They felt the president was being too lenient with the rebels. "They should pay for their disloyalty," declared one congressman. But Abraham wanted to concentrate on the future, to "bind up the nation's wounds." The only way to do this, he said, was to "let [the rebels] up easy."

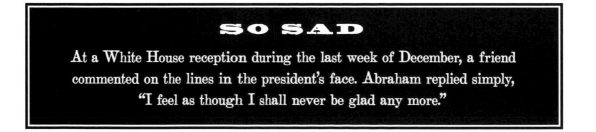

SO SAD

At a White House reception during the last week of December, a friend commented on the lines in the president's face. Abraham replied simply, "I feel as though I shall never be glad any more."

CHAPTER SEVEN

WITH CHARITY FOR ALL: WASHINGTON, 1864–65

Doesn't it seem strange . . . that I should be here? Doesn't it strike you as queer that I, who couldn't cut the head off a chicken, and who was sick at the sight of blood, should be cast into the middle of a great war, with blood flowing all about me?

—Abraham Lincoln to Representative
Daniel Voorhees, March 1864

I live in fear that the deep waters through which I've passed will overwhelm me.

—Mary Lincoln to Sally Orne, March 1864

THIS POLITICAL CARTOON SHOWS PRESIDENT LINCOLN MAKING A MEAL OUT OF THE SECRETARY OF THE TREASURY.

With the Republican convention fast approaching, Salmon P. Chase once again dreamed of the presidency. He'd never gotten over the fact that Abraham Lincoln, with his poor schooling and low breeding, had won the prize, while he—Ivy League educated—had been passed over. So when a group of friends offered to organize a movement on his behalf, he quickly agreed. Of course, his political maneuvering had to remain a secret. He didn't want people to think he was being disloyal to the president. So for the next several weeks, Chase pretended to be completely disinterested in the upcoming election while his friends worked at garnering political support.

Lincoln knew what his secretary of the treasury was up to, and it didn't worry him. He believed Chase's "mad dash for the presidency" would eventually result in a blunder. He sat back and waited.

In February 1864, Chase's election committee sent out a confidential circular, or pamphlet, to one hundred leading Republicans. Meant to mobilize support for Chase, the pamphlet claimed that "feebleness of will and want of intellectual grasp" were the real reasons the war continued, and warned that Lincoln's reelection would bankrupt the country and ruin the nation's reputation. At the end, the committee boldly announced that Salmon P. Chase had "more of the qualities needed in a President during the next four years

PLATE NO. 133 "Mike, Remove the Salmon," *Harper's Weekly*, July 16, 1864

than are combined in any other available candidate."

The election committee's confidential pamphlet got leaked to the press. Voters were shocked. Wrote one journalist, "It is so dastardly and mean . . . it dishonors Chase as a gentleman." Wrote another, "Chase is a traitor to the man who appointed him." In state after state, Republicans passed unanimous resolutions in favor of Lincoln's renomination.

Humiliated, Chase withdrew his candidacy on March 5. He expected to be dismissed from the cabinet as well. But Lincoln needed Chase. Despite his quarrelsome attitude, the secretary of the treasury had managed the exhausting job of financing the war with skill and imagination. So he continued in Lincoln's cabinet until June, when he and the president disagreed over hiring policies at the Treasury Department. Chase petulantly offered his resignation, and Lincoln accepted it. "You and I have reached a point of mutual embarrassment in our official relations," Lincoln explained.

It was the end of Chase's presidential dreams, but not of his political career. Six months later, Lincoln appointed him chief justice of the Supreme Court. When asked why, Abraham replied, "[Chase] and I have stood together in time of trial, and I should despise myself if I allowed personal differences to affect my judgment of his fitness for the office."

THIS HANDWRITTEN DOCUMENT SIGNED BY LINCOLN GAVE GRANT THE TITLE OF LIEUTENANT GENERAL.

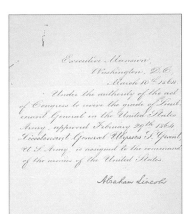

When the scraggly man in the battered uniform checked into Washington's fashionable Willard Hotel on March 8, the desk clerk almost turned him away. Then he read the man's signature in the register: U. S. Grant. The clerk rushed around the counter to pump the hand of the hero of Vicksburg. "It is an honor to have you here, sir," he gushed. "A true honor!"

Grant had been summoned to Washington to take command of *all* the nation's armies. Lincoln had even bestowed upon Grant the title of lieutenant general, a post not filled since George Washington held it. And all of Washington buzzed with excitement about that decision. "With Grant in command we are sure to catch the rebels," declared one newspaper.

The famous general arrived just in time for the president's weekly reception. Crossing the street to the White House, he made his way through a throng of people toward Lincoln. "Why, here is General Grant!" cried Abraham when he saw him. "This is a great pleasure, I assure you." It was obviously a great pleasure for the other guests, too. So many people pressed to greet him that Grant had to stand on a sofa to keep from being crushed by the adoring crowd. It was a full hour before the flushed and perspiring general could escape. Later he wrote, "That night Mr. Lincoln stated to me that he never professed to be a military man or to know how campaigns should be conducted. . . . All he ever wanted . . . was someone who would take responsibility and act." At last, Lincoln had that man.

GENERAL WILLIAM TECUMSEH SHERMAN ASTRIDE HIS HORSE, SAM

Born in Ohio, Sherman was named Tecumseh after the powerful Shawnee Indian chief. When neighbors said they thought the name was strange, Sherman's father replied, "Tecumseh was a great warrior." It was prophetic. The boy Tecumseh (who changed his first name to William after his father died) would grow up to attend West Point. After serving in the Mexican War, he retired to take up a series of jobs as a banker, a lawyer, and a real estate investor. But when the Civil War broke out, he reenlisted for service and was eventually given command of a division under Grant's generalship. It was the beginning of a fateful partnership. The two men not only liked and admired each other but worked together "like a well-oiled machine." When Grant was promoted to lead the Union armies, he gave Sherman command of the Army of the Tennessee. Together, these two fighting generals now turned toward winning the war.

THIS MAP CHARTS GRANT'S COURSE THROUGH VIRGINIA.

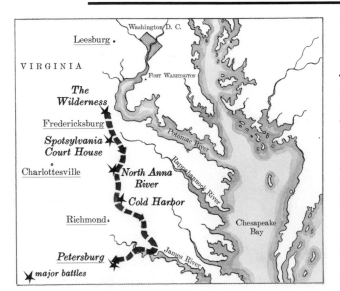

As soon as Grant assumed his position, he declared there would be "no more shilly-shallying," and planned a new strategy for the war. In the East, Grant would lead a drive against Lee's troops in Virginia, pushing toward the rebel capital, Richmond. In the West, he directed Union forces under General Sherman to advance from Tennessee to the South's crucial railroad center in Atlanta. Afterward, Sherman would head north toward Virginia, squeezing the Confederacy. "I will concentrate all the force possible against the Confederate armies," declared Grant.

Grant's plans thrilled Lincoln. "[He] is the first general I have had," the president cried. "You know how it has been with the rest. They wanted me to be the general. I am glad to find a man who can go ahead without me."

THIS 1864 ENGRAVING SHOWS CAPTAIN ROBERT TODD LINCOLN AND HIS FAMILY AT THE WHITE HOUSE.

After graduating from Harvard in the spring of 1864, Bob decided to join the army. "I am determined to see something of the war before it ends," he told his father.

The fact that his eldest son was not in uniform had long embarrassed Lincoln. Critics called Robert a "shirker" and a "coward." They criticized the president for sending other people's sons into harm's way but keeping his own boy safe. Lincoln had ignored these critics and blocked Bob from signing up, for Mary's sake, as she was terrified of losing still another

son. "Of course I know that Robert's desire to go into the army is manly and noble," she once wailed, "but oh! I am frightened he may never come back to us!"

Lincoln decided to write General Grant "as though I was not President, but only a friend," asking Grant to give his boy some "nominal rank" and allow him to "join your military family."

Grant immediately agreed. "I will be most happy to have him in my military family," he replied. Commissioned as a captain, Bob was stationed at Grant's headquarters in City Point, Virginia, seven miles from the fighting. Never exposed to danger, Robert Todd Lincoln had the job of escorting important visitors from place to place.

GRANT'S "ON TO RICHMOND" CAMPAIGN

A drawing by on-the-spot artist Alfred Waud showed the wounded escaping from the burning woods during the Battle of the Wilderness. Untold numbers perished in the flames started by artillery blasts.

THE BATTLE OF THE WILDERNESS

By the beginning of May 1864 (three years into the war), Grant was ready to lead his 115,000 men to Richmond. Plunging into the Wilderness, a thick maze of trees and undergrowth near Chancellorsville, Virginia, he hoped to take Lee by surprise. But the Confederates were waiting. For two days the armies went at it. Recalled Grant, "More desperate fighting has not been witnessed on the continent than the 5th and 6th of May." Grant lost 17,666 men to Lee's 7,500 and still could not turn Lee back. So Grant did what no other commander had done with the Army of the Potomac. Rather than retreating, resting, or waiting for reinforcements, he kept pushing south.

Lincoln wholeheartedly approved this action. For the first time, the Army of the Potomac was advancing—a strategy the president had been urging since the beginning of the war.

THE BATTLE OF SPOTSYLVANIA COURT HOUSE

Leaving the Wilderness, Grant marched his army all night to the vital crossroads at Spotsylvania Court House. But when he arrived on the morning of May 8, Lee was already there. For the next two weeks the armies battled, achieving nothing but death and destruction. By the fight's end, 30,000 men were wounded, killed, or reported missing—18,000 of whom were Union soldiers. In the White House, Lincoln paced. Recalled one visitor, "His long arms behind him, his dark features contracted with gloom, he moaned . . . , 'Is it ever to end?'"

COLD HARBOR

And still Grant kept pushing south. At four-thirty in the morning on June 8, he made a fateful assault on the Confederate entrenchment at Cold Harbor, Virginia. Within twenty minutes he lost 7,000 men. Recalled one Union soldier, "It was not war, it was murder." By noon, after two more failed assaults, Grant called off the attack. "I regret this assault more than any one I have ever ordered," he later said.

In the White House, Lincoln grieved. "Those poor fellows," he lamented. "This suffering, this loss of life."

A year later, remains of those who had died at Cold Harbor were still being buried.

THE SIEGE AT PETERSBURG

Realizing he could not take Richmond head-on, Grant tried a different tack. Slipping away from Cold Harbor, he marched his troops toward Petersburg. His hope was to cut the supply and communication lines that connected Richmond to the rest of the Confederacy. But he did not succeed. Even though only 2,000 men defended Petersburg, they miraculously managed to hold off Grant's army of 67,000 men until Lee arrived with reinforcements.

In the White House, Lincoln balled his fists. "Hold on with a bulldog grip," he wired Grant, "and chew and choke as much as possible."

Grant obeyed. He settled down to a siege of the city that would last an unimaginable nine months before Petersburg was finally taken.

The siege at Petersburg became one of spades and shovels as Union troops dug earthworks, then settled in. Occasionally the two armies shot at each other, occasionally there was a battle, but mostly they waited, wrote letters, played cards, and rested, like the Union soldiers in this photograph.

Confederate fortifications at Petersburg

MRS. LINCOLN ON GENERAL GRANT

Mary could not stand General Grant. "He is a butcher," she declared, "and is not fit to be at the head of an army."

"But he has been very successful in the field," argued Abraham.

"Yes," snorted Mary, "he generally manages to claim a victory, but such a victory! He loses two men to the enemy's one. He has . . . no regard for life. I could fight an army as well myself!"

"Well, Mother," Abraham replied lightly, "supposing we give you command of the army. No doubt you would do much better than any general that has been tried."

"No doubt I could," agreed Mary.

VICE PRESIDENTIAL CANDIDATE ANDREW JOHNSON

When the Republican party met in Baltimore to chose their candidates, Lincoln's nomination was already ensured. Observed journalist Noah Brooks, "The delegates have thought of no name but Lincoln's."

Not so when it came to choosing a vice presidential candidate. Although it was assumed Hannibal Hamlin would be renominated, some delegates began talking about nominating Andrew Johnson.

Johnson had the distinction of being the only Southern senator who had not joined the Confederacy when his state, Tennessee, seceded. This made him a good choice because it would help win votes for Lincoln in the border states and from some Democrats. But Johnson had some serious flaws, including a total inability to speak in public. Remarked one delegate, "His written speeches are fine, but when he opens his mouth, he either talks wild or is stricken dumb."

Concerned, John Nicolay wired the president from the convention in hopes of learning his preference. But Lincoln really didn't care who was chosen. Like most American presidents of the nineteenth century, he saw little of his second in command and never thought of giving him any important duties. "Wish not to interfere about vice-president," he wired back. "Cannot interfere about [party] platform. Convention must judge for itself."

The convention chose Johnson, not realizing they had just picked the next president of the United States.

RAID ON WASHINGTON

In June 1864, Robert E. Lee began to wonder who was protecting Washington. After all, most of the Army of the

Confederate General Jubal Early

Potomac was in Petersburg. Sensing an opportunity, he sent General Jubal Early and 15,000 soldiers north, hoping to catch the city unaware.

Swiftly, Early crossed the Potomac and marched toward Washington. By July 11, he had pushed aside the ill-trained unit of Union volunteers defending the nation's capital. Just miles from the city limit, his troops approached the feebly manned defenses of Fort Stevens (located on the grounds of the Soldiers' Home, where the Lincolns usually summered).

Union soldiers at the fort dug in. Knowing General Grant was rushing his highly trained Sixth Corps from Petersburg to Washington, they fought to hang on. For several days, the two armies skirmished. During that time, Abraham and Mary drove out to watch. One soldier reported seeing Mrs.

Union troops on the ramparts of Fort Stevens

Lincoln standing on the fort's parapet beside her husband as bullets flew around them. Another witness recalled how Lincoln, "with a long frock coat and plug hat," made a "very conspicuous figure." Cried one young officer, "Get down, you damn fool! Get down!"

On July 16, Early noticed "a cloud of dust from the direction of Washington" and knew the Sixth Corps had arrived. Realizing that he didn't have enough men to defeat the reinforced Union army, Early retreated as swiftly as he had come. He left behind an angry and frustrated citizenry, including the First Lady. Three days after the crisis, Secretary of War Stanton called on Mary. "Mrs. Lincoln," he said, "I intend to have a full-length portrait of you painted, standing on the ramparts of Ft. Stevens overlooking the fight."

"That is very well," retorted Mary, "but I can assure you of one thing, Mr. Secretary. If I had had a few *ladies* with me the Rebels would not have been permitted to get as close as they did!"

This map from a Confederate soldier's journal shows Jubal Early's plan of attack on Washington, D.C.

"The month of August does not open cheerfully," wrote journalist Noah Brooks. Jubal Early's raid on Washington had shaken the North's confidence. War-weary and disillusioned, the people were now "wild for peace." In an editorial, the *New York Tribune* urged Lincoln to end the war at any cost, and reminded him that "our bleeding, bankrupt, almost dying country . . . shudders at the prospect of fresh conscriptions, of further wholesale devastations, and of new rivers of human blood." But Lincoln refused to discuss peace unless the South promised to abandon slavery. His intractable position on the subject not only angered many Northerners but also caused his popularity to plummet.

By the end of August, most Republicans believed Lincoln would be defeated in the November election. "The tide is setting strongly against us," the chairman of the Republican Party warned the president. "Re-election seems an impossibility."

His message confirmed Lincoln's own pessimistic view of the situation. "You think I don't know I am going to be beaten," he said to a friend, *"but I do,* and unless some great change takes place, *badly beaten."*

A GREAT CHANGE

"ATLANTA IS OURS . . ."

A lithograph of Sherman's March to the Sea

While Grant's army hammered at the Confederates in Virginia, General Sherman's army of 100,000 had been fighting its way toward Atlanta, Georgia. On September 1, 1864, he occupied the city. The next day he sent Lincoln this message: "Atlanta is ours and fairly won."

Joyfully, the president proclaimed a day of thanksgiving and prayer for "the glorious achievement of the army under Major General Sherman."

But Sherman did not have time for prayer. His next move was to evacuate the city, because he planned to burn it. In desperation, Confederate general John Bell Hood wrote him: "In the name of God and humanity, I protest!" Sherman replied: "You might as well appeal against the thunderstorm as against the terrible hardships of war. They are inevitable, and the only way the people of Atlanta can hope once more to live in peace and quiet is to stop this war. . . . I want peace, and believe it can only be reached through Union and war."

On November 16, Sherman put Atlanta to the torch, then set out with 60,000 men on his famous "March to the Sea"—called so because he planned to march three hundred miles through the heartland of the Confederacy until he reached the Atlantic Ocean. Remarked Lincoln, "We all know where he went in at, but I can't tell you where he will come out."

. . . AND SO IS THE SHENANDOAH VALLEY

In retaliation for Early's raid, Grant sent 30,000 troops commanded by the brilliant young cavalry officer Philip Sheridan to Virginia's Shenandoah Valley. This part of the Confederacy was especially important because its rich farmland fed the rebel army. Sheridan's mission? "To make the valley a desert," ordered Grant. "All the provisions and stock should be removed and the people told to get out." By September, Sheridan began to "peel the land," as Grant had commanded. Jubal Early tried to stop him, and on the nineteenth, near Winchester, he almost succeeded. Only Sheridan's leadership saved the day. As the troops fell back and began to retreat, Sheridan galloped up and down the ranks, yelling, "Give 'em hell! Give 'em hell!" His men responded, recalled one soldier, and "went whirling back through Winchester."

General Philip Sheridan

The rebels were routed, and a month later Sheridan's army swept the last Confederates off the field and out of the valley.

Wired Abraham: "With great pleasure I tender you and your brave army the thanks of the nation, and my own admiration and gratitude for the month's operation in the Shenandoah Valley."

MOOD SWING

The fall of Atlanta, as well as news of Early's defeat, transformed the North's mood. Suddenly, Lincoln and the war were popular again. The president's secretary John Nicolay summed it up best: "Three weeks ago, our friends everywhere were despondent, almost to the point of giving up the contest in despair. Now they are hopeful, jubilant, hard at work and confident of success."

UNION AND LIBERTY!   AND   UNION AND SLAVERY!

This political broadside compared the platforms of Republican candidate Abraham Lincoln and Democratic candidate George McClellan. In the first scene, Abraham shakes the hand of a man wearing the square hat of a laborer while black and white children hurry from a schoolhouse flying an American flag. In the second scene, McClellan shakes the hand of Confederate president Jefferson Davis as a slave auction takes place behind them.

In August 1864, Democrats nominated George McClellan–Abraham's old adversary–as their presidential candidate. Running on a "peace at any price" platform, McClellan's party proposed an immediate cease-fire and a negotiated settlement with the Confederacy. It could not have been more different from the Republican platform–"no peace without union, and the abolishment of slavery." John S. Rock, an African American lawyer living in Massachusetts, summed up the differences this way: "There are but two parties in this country today. The one, headed by Lincoln, is for Freedom and the Republic; and the other, headed by McClellan, is for Despotism and Slavery."

WOODCUTS FROM AN ANTI-LINCOLN BIOGRAPHY, 1864

Lincoln was used to being attacked politically in newspapers and pamphlets. But as the election heated up, these attacks grew more and more venomous. One such pamphlet, a parody called the *Only Authentic Life of Abraham Lincoln Alias "Old Abe,"* made malicious fun of his life, ending with a description of Abraham's personal appearance and habits. "Mr. Lincoln stands six feet twelve in his socks, which he changes once every ten days. His anatomy is composed mostly of bones, and when walking he resembles the offspring of a happy marriage between a derrick and a windmill.... He brushes his hair sometimes and is said to wash. He can hardly be called handsome, though he is certainly much better looking since he had the smallpox. Mrs. Lincoln thinks well of him. He is 107 years old. Such is Abraham Lincoln."

MARY'S CAMPAIGN PLAN

Mary had a plan—a devious plan—to help her husband get reelected. "In a political canvass," she confided to Elizabeth Keckly early in 1864, "it is policy to cultivate *every* element of strength." The elements she had in mind? Unscrupulous politicians of questionable reputation—the type of men Abraham refused to deal with. "I will be clever to them until the election," Mary went on, "and then, if we remain at the White House, I will drop every one of them."

Elizabeth asked if the president approved of the plan.

"God no!" replied Mary. Her husband would never agree to such a thing, "so I keep him in the dark and will tell him of it when it is all over. He is too honest to take proper care of his own interests, so I feel it to be my duty to electioneer for him."

For the next several months, unbeknownst to her husband, Mary cultivated men like Abram Wakeman, an ambitious and well-connected New York lawyer who longed for a presidential appointment. Lincoln thought Wakeman was "insinuating and unreliable," and had no intention of giving him any job. So Wakeman cozied up to Mary in hopes that a friendship with the First Lady would win him influence. Mary let him fawn, all the while asking for favors: "Can you sway your friend, Mr. Bennett [editor of the *New York Herald*], to place a favorable notice of [Mr. Lincoln] in his newspaper?" And another time: "If anyone can deliver New York's bloc of voters, you can."

Her plan worked. Not only did these men—dozens of them—endorse the president's reelection, but most worked hard on his behalf, giving speeches, hosting rallies, and using their influence with other politicians to swing votes.

AN ABRAHAM LINCOLN CAMPAIGN BUTTON

As tradition dictated, Lincoln did not take part in any of the hundreds of parades and marches organized by the Republican Party on his behalf. He did not give any public speeches or interviews. But he was deeply involved in the campaign's behind-the-scenes management. Lincoln wooed the editor of the *New York Herald*, James Gordon Bennett, into an endorsement with a promise to explore the possibility of appointing him American ambassador to France. He sent his secretary John Nicolay out to Missouri to campaign. And he so enthusiastically encouraged soldiers in the field to vote that one friend said, "If it could be done in no other way, the President would take a carpetbag and go around and collect those votes himself." He even proclaimed Election Day a holiday in Washington so that federal employees would be sure to vote. "The President has done all he can," remarked cabinet member Gideon Welles. "Now we wait."

This cartoon title, "Long Abraham a Little Longer," happily announced Lincoln's reelection.

On Election Night—November 8, 1864—Abraham spent the evening waiting for returns in the telegraph office of the War Department. "Dispatches kept coming in all evening . . . showing a splendid triumph," remembered John Hay. The electorate had rallied behind the president, giving him almost half a million more votes than McClellan.

PREMONITION

The day after his reelection, Abraham called his journalist friend Noah Brooks into his office. With his victory celebration past, the president was now in a pensive mood. He told Brooks this story:

It was just after my election in 1860 . . . and looking in the [mirror] I saw myself reflected nearly at full length; but my face, I noticed, had two separate and distinct images . . . one of the faces was a little paler— say five shades—than the other. I got up, and the thing melted away, and I went off, and in the excitement of the hour forgot all about it—nearly, but not quite, for the thing would once in a while come up, and give me a little pang as if something uncomfortable had happened. I told my wife about it and she was somewhat worried. . . . She thought it was a "sign" that I was to be elected to a second term of office, and that the paleness of one of the faces was an omen that I should not see life through the last term.

THE MEASUREMENTS FOR ABRAHAM'S BEST PAIR OF BOOTS

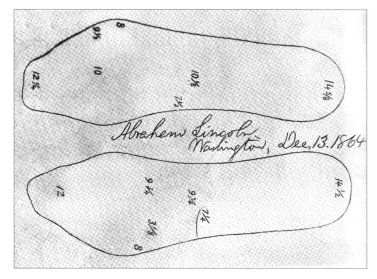

Abraham's size-fourteen feet always hurt—his shoes either pinched his heels or squashed his long toes. Because of this, he preferred to wear soft, low-cut slippers that made flip-flopping sounds when he walked. Sometimes he even wore those slippers when greeting guests—shockingly informal dress for a president. Then in 1864 he learned of a New York City shoemaker named Dr. Zacharie who made boots that neither pinched nor squeezed, simply by putting a lining of felt between the layers of leather. Eager to try them, Abraham stood on a sheet of butcher paper and marked the outlines of his feet. Then he sent both the paper and his order to the shoemaker. The result was a pair of boots so comfortable that Abraham felt compelled to write the shoemaker this testimonial to use in advertising:

Dr. Zacharie's boots operated on my feet with great success, and considerable addition to my comfort. —A. Lincoln.

HOME COOKIN'

Abraham's lack of appetite worried his wife, and she was constantly thinking up schemes to get him to eat. She had the cook bake his favorite cookies—gingerbread. She sent trays of sandwiches to his office. She even left a bowl of apples on his desk. But "he was often too busy or abstracted to touch it," she recalled. By 1864, he was so gaunt and hollow-eyed, she feared he would "keel over from malnourishment."

"Alice," she asked the cook one day, "do you know how to make a dish of fricasseed chicken and small biscuits with thick cream gravy poured over it, all on one platter?"

"I'll try," replied Alice.

While the cook labored over the meal, following Mary's recipe exactly, the First Lady set the table in the small dining room. Tonight, she had decided, it would just be family.

At dinnertime, Mary sent Tad to fetch his father. When Abraham entered the room and saw the homey food and atmosphere, he cried, "Oh, Mary, this is good. It seems like old times come back."

Through the closed door, Alice and the other servants could hear the president laughing. But was he eating?

The next morning, an excited Tad reported, "Pa ate three helpings and more gravy than me and Ma together!"

ONE OF ABRAHAM'S STOVEPIPE HATS

During his four years in the White House, Abraham owned several stovepipe hats. Some were lost. Some simply grew shabby. And one was absentmindedly left on a chair outside his office. When Abraham went to retrieve it, he found a very fat woman sitting there. She stood and bowed. Abraham bowed back. Then he walked behind the woman and picked up the remains of his hat. "Madam," he said, sadly shaking his head, "I could have told you that my hat wouldn't fit you before you tried it on."

STILL IN LOVE

Even after twenty-two years of marriage, Mary still adored her husband. In a letter to her friend Sally Orne, she expressed her deep feelings:

He [is] my lover—husband—father—ALL.

And at a White House reception in 1864, Abraham remarked to a bystander:

My wife is as handsome as when she was a girl and I, a poor nobody then, fell in love with her, and what's more, have never fallen out.

MRS. LINCOLN TRAVELS.

In an age when women traveled only with good explanation, and always with a chaperone, Mary preferred to have neither. "The President's wife wanders around . . . the watering places unprotected," grumbled one journalist. Traveling engaged her mind and eased her worries. Besides the shopping trips she took to New York, Boston, and Philadelphia each year, Mary also traveled for "pure pleasure." Below is just a sampling of the getaways she took during her years in the White House.

A beachside resort in New Jersey

In August 1861, Mary traveled by private railroad car to Long Beach, New Jersey, a resort town on the Atlantic coast. She hoped to rest but instead was met with a parade and a fancy-dress ball in her honor. She graciously put aside her desire for privacy and instead represented her husband at the events—a first for a president's wife. From there she traveled to upstate New York, stopping to take in the sights at Saratoga and Niagara Falls.

The Barnum Museum

In October 1862, Mary took Tad to New York City. They were gone nearly a month, visiting friends and enjoying the comforts of the city's best hotels. A highlight was their visit to P. T. Barnum's American Museum. For a twenty-five-cent fee they saw mastodon bones, an Egyptian mummy, and the famous Feejee mermaid (purported to be the remains of a real mermaid, it was really just a glued-together conglomeration of different animal parts). During their time away, Tad lost a tooth, which Mary mailed to her husband. They were gone so long that Abraham—who always let his wife decide when to return—wired: "I really wish to see you." Mother and son hurried home.

A hotel in New Hampshire, with Mount Washington in the distance

At the end of July 1863, after recovering from her carriage accident, Mary took the longest trip of her White House years (she was gone two months). Joined by her son Robert, she visited the White Mountains, where she shocked reporters by climbing Mount Washington . . . twice! Declared one shocked newspaperman, "Such female vigor!"

The Metropolitan Hotel, on the corner of Broadway and Prince Street in New York City

In April 1864, Mary and Tad returned to New York City for a brief visit—only five days. They stayed at the expensive Metropolitan Hotel, and Tad was fitted for two new suits while Mary relaxed. She needed the time away to restore her nerves, which had, as Abraham put it, "gone to pieces." From there she traveled on to Boston alone, sending Tad home. Two weeks later she traveled to Manchester, Vermont. There she stayed for a month in hopes, Abraham confided to a friend, that the rest would soothe her "wayward impulsive moods."

◆ THREATS ◆

May the hand of the devil strike you down before long—You are destroying the country. Damn you—every breath you take.

Abe you must die . . . you can choose your weapon: the cup, the knife, the bullet.

You have been weighed in the balance and found wanting. You shall be a dead man in six months.

Letters with passages like these had been arriving at the White House since Inauguration Day. Shoving them into a pigeonhole in his desk, Abraham once told a newspaper reporter, "I know I am in danger, but I am not going to worry over threats like these."

Because he believed democracy meant being available to the people, he refused most protective measures. "It would never do," he explained, "for a President to have guards with drawn sabers at his door, as if he fancied he were . . . an emperor." This attitude made him an easy target. Nearly every night, he strolled alone through the densely shaded White House grounds. He rode unguarded to and from the Soldiers' Home, as well as through the streets of Washington. And the only security he had at the White House was a plainclothes policeman who sat outside his private quarters.

One summer evening in August 1864, as he rode on horseback alone toward the Soldiers' Home at the end of a long day, someone fired a shot at him. The frightened horse raced for safety, taking the president along for the ride. The next morning soldiers found Lincoln's hat on the ground—a bullet hole through the crown.

Abraham made light of the incident for Mary's sake. Yes, there had been a shot, "but it must have been an accident, perhaps some hunter emptying his gun."

Mary wasn't fooled. "Mr. Lincoln's life is always so exposed," she told a friend. "No one knows what it is to live in constant dread of some fearful tragedy. . . . I have a presentiment that he will meet with a sudden and violent end."

A HOPEFUL ENDING TO A HARD YEAR

General Sherman sent this telegram to Lincoln.

After leaving Atlanta in smoldering ruins, Sherman had cut a 60-mile-wide, 250-mile-long path of destruction across the heart of the South. Believing it was better to destroy property than life, he burned houses, destroyed fields, and ran off livestock. At Savannah, Georgia, he mercilessly routed the small Confederate army there, then sent Lincoln a telegram, which was received at the White House on December 25. It read: "I beg to present you as a Christmas gift the city of Savannah."

Sherman remained there until February 1, then started on another march—this time toward South Carolina, the state where secession was born. "I almost tremble at her fate," the general wrote to a friend, "but feel that she deserves all that is in store for her."

THE PRESIDENT . . .

Although he was only fifty-six when this photograph was taken in 1865, people often noted how old Lincoln looked. Thirty-five pounds underweight, he was so weak he sometimes let his driver help him out of his carriage. When his old friend Joshua Speed visited the White House in March 1865, he was shocked to find Lincoln "so jaded and weary."

"I am a little alarmed about myself," admitted Abraham. "Just feel my hand."

It was "cold and clammy," Speed recalled. Lincoln's feet were cold, too—he propped them so close to the hearth his wool socks steamed.

"Poor Mr. Lincoln is looking so broken-hearted, so completely worn out I fear he will not get through the next four years," Mary confessed to a friend. Worried about his health, she urged him to keep a lighter schedule and encouraged him to take carriage rides, attend the theater, and get to bed earlier. But her efforts did little to curb his exhaustion.

"Nothing," he admitted to Noah Brooks, "touches the tired spot."

. . . AND THE FIRST LADY

This 1865 photograph shows forty-six-year-old Mary Lincoln dressed, as always, in expensive and stylish clothing. But while fashionable gowns helped disguise her increasingly plump figure, they could not cover a mental state that was growing more and more fragile. The once-dainty woman with the quicksilver temper had become riddled with fears and anxieties. She suffered from bouts of depression and often complained of back and eye trouble. She experienced frequent headaches, which she colorfully described as feeling like "an Indian is removing the bones of my face and pulling wires out of my eyes." Earlier that year, doctors had diagnosed her ailments as "nervous affliction" and prescribed weeks of bed rest. But Mary was too energetic for these rest cures and instead tried to find relief by shopping and traveling.

Sitting beside Vice President Andrew Johnson, Lincoln waits to make his second inaugural address.

March 4, 1865, dawned gray and drizzly. It had rained steadily for days, and Pennsylvania Avenue was a sea of mud measuring fifteen inches deep or more. Despite the miserable weather, a crowd began gathering in front of the Capitol hours before the inauguration. By the time the ceremony began at noon, people "were in a most wretched plight," recalled Noah Brooks. "Crinoline was smashed, and . . . velvet [and] lace were streaked with mud from end to end." Then Lincoln appeared on the platform. "Cheer upon cheer arose, bands blatted upon the air, and flags waved all over the scene," recalled one spectator.

The dignitaries took their seats—the president and vice president, leading senators, Supreme Court justices, and cabinet members in the first rows, family members directly behind. Mary, in her new velvet-trimmed dress and expensive point-lace shawl, took Tad's hand, not just to calm the wiggling boy but to warm his fingers. (He had left his new kid gloves at home.) On her other side, Robert sat tall and dignified.

Lincoln stepped forward. As he unrolled his inaug-ural address the sun suddenly "burst forth in . . . splendor," wrote Brooks, "and flooded the spectacle with glory and light." The president began by expressing his belief that the war was God's punishment "to both North and South for the offense of slavery." By apportioning responsibility equally to both sides, he hoped to make it easier for them to reconcile when the war ended.

Finally, he concluded his speech:

With malice toward none; with charity for all; with firmness in the right, as God gives us to see the right, let us strive on to finish the work we are in; to bind up the nation's wounds . . . to do all which may achieve and cherish a just, and a lasting peace, among ourselves, and with all nations.

Then, turning to Chief Justice Chase, Abraham laid his hand on the Bible and repeated the oath of office, ending with an emphatic "So help me God." Cannons boomed. The crowd cheered. And Abraham Lincoln began his second term as president.

Just weeks into his second term, Lincoln began making plans for life after his presidency. One afternoon in March 1865 he told Mary he wanted to take the whole family to Europe. After that, she recalled, "he intended to return and go to California over the Rocky Mountains and see the prospectors . . . digging gold." He no longer knew where they would make their home. While he had once talked about returning to Springfield and quietly practicing law, now he wasn't so sure. He thought less, he said, of settling and more of "roving and traveling."

THE THIRTEENTH AMENDMENT, SIGNED BY LINCOLN

The Emancipation Proclamation had freed only slaves living in rebel territory. Now the president wanted an amendment to the Constitution banning slavery forever from every part of the United States. In April 1864, the overwhelmingly Republican Senate had passed a resolution calling for that amendment. But the resolution still needed to garner the necessary two-thirds vote in the Democratic-controlled House of Representatives. Lincoln knew passage of the amendment was "only a question of time," but "how much better," he said, "if Democrats, as well as Republicans, could be brought to support its passage in a show of bi-partisan unity." Calling congressmen one by one into his office, he told them, "The passage of this amendment will clinch the whole subject. It will bring the war, I have no doubt, rapidly to a close." He also promised government jobs, granted special presidential favors, and made other secret deals. Grumbled one senator, "The greatest measure of the nineteenth century was passed by corruption, aided and abetted by the purest man in America."

On January 31, 1865, the House of Representatives passed the Thirteenth Amendment. Congressmen cheered. Spectators in the galleries applauded. The House, in honor of what it called "this great historic occasion," voted to take the rest of the day off. But first it sent the resolution to the president. He happily signed it the next day, even though constitutional amendments do not need presidential approval. "The greatest job is ended," he declared. "I . . . congratulate myself, the country, and the whole world upon this great moral victory."

That night, recalled a White House servant, Lincoln slept more soundly than he had in years.

Besides ending slavery and preserving the Union, Lincoln left a legacy of firsts. Here are just a few.

INCOME TAX

To help pay for the war, Abraham signed a bill in 1862 establishing the nation's first income tax—a tax on money earned by individuals. The tax was repealed ten years later, but in 1913 Congress made the income tax a permanent part of American life with passage of the Sixteenth Amendment.

TRANSCONTINENTAL MESSAGE

The first transcontinental telegraph system, invented by Samuel F. B. Morse, was completed in October 1861, just months after the start of the war. Before that, the fastest way to send a message across the country was on horseback via the Pony Express—a journey that took eleven days from St. Joseph, Missouri, to Sacramento, California. But now, an electric flow was simply sent through wires that had been stretched from coast to coast. This flow was broken by a switch—called a telegraph key—making a clicking sound. The long and short spaces between the clicks were decoded into letters from the alphabet, allowing people to communicate across the continent within a matter of hours—an incredible improvement that would make conducting the war easier. On October 24, Abraham received the first-ever transcontinental message. It was from the chief justice of California, assuring the president of California's loyalty to the Union.

HOMESTEAD ACT

For the first time, the U.S. government began giving away land. Abraham's signature on this 1862 act provided that any adult citizen (or person intending to become a citizen) who headed a family could qualify for a grant of 160 acres of public land. All that person had to do was pay a small registration fee and live on the land continuously for five years. This legislation greatly encouraged settlement and development of the Western territory. By the end of the Civil War, fifteen thousand homestead claims had been filed, and more followed in the postwar years—many by widowed women and recently freed blacks.

CONGRESSIONAL MEDAL OF HONOR

In December 1861 Abraham approved a bill authorizing the first congressional medal for the navy. Two months later, he signed a similar bill approving the army medal. Both are still given to honor heroic military actions. In March 1863, Secretary of War Stanton presented the first medals to six members of Andrews' Raiders, a group of Union spies who had worked behind enemy lines in Georgia. The first African American to receive the honor was William Carney, who kept the flag flying while under fire on the battlefields of South Carolina. And in 1866, Dr. Mary Walker—the first and only woman ever to receive the medal—was honored for her service as a Civil War surgeon.

TRANSCONTINENTAL RAILROAD

In 1862, Abraham signed a bill that chartered the first railroad to span the country from the Missouri River to San Francisco. Although it was to be built by private businessmen, the government not only provided rights of way (that is, permission to build on government-owned land) but also gave builders permission to use stone and timber from public lands. Within ten years, the vast country would be linked from the Atlantic to the Pacific.

"IN GOD WE TRUST"

In April 1864, Lincoln signed an act that would put "In God We Trust" on federal coins. The phrase first appeared on the 1864 two-cent coin. Today, these words still appear on all U.S. coins.

LINCOLN PENNY

Abraham became the first president to be featured on a U.S. coin. In 1909, his profile—taken from a photo made by Mathew Brady—was placed on the penny in celebration of the one hundredth anniversary of his birth.

A TELEGRAM FROM GENERAL GRANT INVITING LINCOLN TO VISIT CITY POINT, VIRGINIA

On March 20, 1865, General Grant invited the president to come down to his headquarters in City Point (located just four miles from Petersburg and nineteen miles from Richmond, where the war was being fought) for a visit. "I think," he said, "the rest would do you good." Lincoln readily accepted. Three days later—along with Mary and Tad—he boarded the *River Queen* and sailed down the Potomac.

MARY'S MELTDOWN

On March 26, the Lincolns decided to attend a grand review of Union troops. While Tad remained on board the *River Queen*, Lincoln rode out from City Point on horseback. Mary and Julia Grant followed in a carriage, which bumped slowly over the primitive road. Worried about missing the review, Mary grew increasingly angry and impatient. She hollered at the horses, the driver, even Mrs. Grant. At one point she tried to abandon the carriage and walk, but the mud was calf deep. By the time her carriage arrived, the review had already begun. Worse, General Ord's beautiful young wife was riding alongside Abraham in the place of honor that should have been her own. Mary erupted in an embarrassing tirade against Mrs. Ord, calling out such "vile names" that Mrs. Ord burst into tears and wheeled away. But Mary's anger wasn't spent. Clambering from the carriage, she yelled at her husband as everyone on the reviewing field watched. "Poor Mr. Lincoln," recalled one officer. "He pleaded with eyes and tone as she turned on him like a tigress, then he walked away hiding that noble, ugly face so

that we might not catch the full expression of its misery."

Mary continued her tirade that evening at dinner, berating the Grants and scolding her husband. Abraham bore her angry words with patience, knowing she would awaken in the morning feeling ashamed, apologetic, and mortified. On April 1, ill and embarrassed, Mary returned to Washington, leaving Tad with his father.

Mrs. Ord, the woman Mary insulted, photographed with her husband, General Edward O. C. Ord, and their daughter.

ANOTHER PREMONITION

While at City Point, Abraham had a dream. It began with

a death-like stillness. . . . Then I heard subdued sobs, as if a number of people were weeping. In my dream state I . . . wandered downstairs, [and] from room to room; no living person was in sight, but the same mournful sounds of distress met me as I passed along. I saw a light in all the rooms; every object was familiar to me; but where were all the people who were grieving as if their hearts would break? I was puzzled and alarmed. What could be the meaning of all this? I arrived at the East Room. . . . There I met a sickening surprise. Before me was a catafalque on which rested a corpse wrapped in funeral vestments. Around it were soldiers acting as guards; and there was a throng of people, gazing mournfully upon the corpse whose face was covered. "Who is dead in the White House?" I demanded. "The President," was the answer, "he was killed by an assassin."

When he told Mary about it, she was chilled. She believed in dreams and premonitions, and this one, she later wrote, left her in "terror from [that] time forth."

The day after Mary returned to Washington, Abraham stopped by Grant's telegraph hut and found three tiny kittens pitifully mewing by the door. Scooping up one of the cats, he asked it, "Where is your mother?"

"Their mother is dead," replied a soldier standing nearby.

The president continued petting the cat. "Then she can't grieve as a poor mother is grieving for a son lost in battle," he said. And picking up the other two kittens, he sat down with them in his lap. "Poor little creatures. Don't cry; you'll be taken good care of," he said, and looked up at Grant's chief of staff. "Colonel, I hope you will see that these poor, motherless waifs are given plenty of milk and love."

The colonel promised. "It was," he recalled, "quite a sight to see the President of the United States tenderly caressing three stray cats . . . and listening to them purring their gratitude."

BEHIND ENEMY LINES

General Lee had been able to hold back the Union forces for almost ten months at Petersburg, located twenty-three miles south of Richmond. But now his depleted forces were worn out and his supplies had dwindled to nothing. The best way to serve the Confederacy, he believed, was to abandon Petersburg, thus leaving Richmond open to Union capture. "While Richmond's fall will be a serious calamity," he told President Jefferson Davis, "once it happens I can prolong the war for two more years." He believed that if he just hung on, the Union would eventually tire of the war and negotiate a peace treaty favorable to the Confederacy (that is, one that would allow slavery to remain untouched in the South). Lee's first step was to retreat from Petersburg and march his troops south to join Confederate forces in the Carolinas. There the combined armies would focus on defeating the Union army under General Sherman.

On the morning of April 2, Jefferson Davis issued the first orders for the Confederate government's evacuation. "Quickly from mouth to mouth flew the sad tidings that Richmond's long and gallant resistance would be over," reported a correspondent for the *London Times.* Government offices began burning official documents. Carts and carriages thronged the roads as citizens fled. "Pale women and shoeless children struggled in the crowd," reported the *Richmond Examiner.* "Oaths and blasphemous shouts filled the air . . . disorder, pillage, shouts, and wild cries of distress made the event hideous." At 11:00 P.M., President Davis boarded a train that would take him to Danville, Virginia. He was, wrote the *Examiner,* a president "in exile."

Eight hours later, an unbroken line of Union soldiers marched into the capital as sullen residents watched. The only cheers came from Richmond's African Americans. But the war was not over. Lee had yet to be stopped.

AN ENGRAVING PUBLISHED IN HARPER'S WEEKLY SHOWS LINCOLN ENTERING RICHMOND.

On April 4, two days after Richmond's collapse, Abraham and Tad paid a visit to the capital of the Confederacy. Arriving without fanfare, the president was first recognized by some black laborers. Dropping their tools, they rushed forward, fell to their knees, and tried to kiss his feet. "Bless the Lord, there is the great Messiah! . . . Glory, Hallelujah!"

"Don't kneel to me," an embarrassed Lincoln told them. "That is not right."

But as he walked up Main Street, more and more African Americans surrounded him. They shouted, "Bless the Lord, Father Abraham has come!"

Finally, soldiers escorted him and Tad to the Confederate White House. Abraham sat down at Jefferson Davis's desk. "Thank God I have lived to see this," he said. "It seems to me I have been dreaming a horrid nightmare for four years, and now the nightmare is over."

A SOLDIER'S OBSERVATION

After two weeks at the front, Abraham returned home—not without seeming to absorb the horrors of the war into himself. Recalled his bodyguard, William Crook, "I witnessed his agony when the thunder of cannon told him that men were being cut down like grass. . . . I saw the anguish on his face when he came within sight of the poor, torn bodies of the dead and dying on the field of Petersburg. . . . I discerned his painful sympathy with the forlorn rebel prisoners, and his profound distress at the revelation of the devastation of a noble people in ruined Richmond." Lincoln appeared overwhelmed by "a sadness as indescribable as it was deep."

THE TERMS OF THE SURRENDER, HANDWRITTEN BY GENERAL GRANT

On April 8, Lee's starving, ragged army arrived at the small town of Appomattox Court-House, Virginia, one step ahead of the pursuing Union troops. Lee had hoped to reach Appomattox Station, where desperately needed supply trains awaited. But by the next morning Union soldiers had seized the supplies and surrounded Lee's army. "There is nothing left but to go see General Grant, and I would rather die a thousand deaths," Lee said. He sent Grant a note asking for an interview "with reference to the surrender of this army."

The two men met in a house owned by one of the town's citizens, Wilmer McLean. Thinking he would be arrested before day's end, Lee dressed in full uniform. "I must make my best appearance," he told an aide. Lee need not have bothered. In keeping with Lincoln's wishes to let the Confederates "up easy," Grant proposed lenient surrender terms. Confederate officers could return to their homes simply by promising never to take up arms against the Union again. He even let the rebels keep their horses so they could work their farms. After signing the surrender document, Lee mentioned that his men were starving. Grant immediately ordered rations for 25,000 men. "The war is over," Grant told his soldiers, "and the rebels are our countrymen again."

As Lee rode away from the McLean house, his men lined the road to cheer their leader. When their cheers brought tears to Lee's eyes, the men, too, began to weep. "I love you just as well as ever, General Lee," one soldier called.

The war was over.

Union soldiers standing outside the McLean house the day after the surrender

GLORIOUS NEWS!

On Sunday night, April 9, Lincoln's secretary of war, Edwin Stanton, burst into the White House waving a telegram from Grant. It read simply: "General Lee surrendered the Army of Northern Virginia this afternoon on terms proposed by myself."

Lincoln and Stanton flung their arms around each other; then Abraham hurried upstairs to tell Mary the glorious news. What the couple said to each other is not known, but the next day Mary wrote to a friend, "Mr. L— told me the news last night at ten o'clock... how I wished I could have sent the news to all our companions, knowing how much sweeter their dreams would have been."

THE FRONT PAGE OF THE NEW YORK TIMES ATTESTS TO THE NORTH'S JUBILATION.

At daylight the next morning—April 10—the firing of five hundred cannons spread the news throughout the nation's capital. The war was over! The union had been preserved! "The country seems delirious with joy," wrote journalist Noah Brooks. Added Secretary of the Navy Gideon Welles, "Guns are firing, bells ringing, flags flying, bands playing, men laughing, children cheering—all, all jubilant."

A crowd of several thousand gathered at the White House. They insisted on hearing a few celebratory words. But Lincoln—who did not plan on giving a formal address until the next evening—was not sure what to say. At that moment, Tad appeared at a second-story window, waving a captured Confederate flag. It gave the president an idea. Turning to the Marine Band, he asked them to play "Dixie," the unofficial Confederate anthem. "I have always thought 'Dixie' one of the best tunes I ever heard," he told the surprised crowd. "It is good to show the rebels that with us they will be free to hear it again."

Already, Abraham Lincoln was trying to bind up the nation's wounds.

JOYFUL WORDS FROM THE FIRST LADY

Like the rest of the country, Mary was giddy with happiness over the war's end. On April 10, she playfully wrote to Senator Sumner:

In honor of this great and glorious day . . . the gardener has sent up to my rooms an unusual supply of flowers, and I have concluded to exercise my rejoicing spirit . . . by having a bouquet left on your table. . . . If possible, this is a happier day than last Monday [the fall of Richmond]."

THE PRICE THEY PAID

	UNION	CONFEDERATE
Number of men who served	2,500,000–2,750,000	750,000–1,250,000
Number of men wounded who survived	275,175	102,703
Number of men who lost their lives	360,222	258,000
Civilians who lost their lives	None	50,000

Total cost of the war: $20 billion (approximately $250 billion in today's money), or five times the total expenditure of the federal government from its creation in 1788 to 1865.

Cemeteries sprang up all over the country as Americans buried their loved ones en masse. More Americans died in the Civil War than in all other wars in American history combined. Pictured here is a Confederate cemetery in Alexandria, Virginia.

Charleston, South Carolina, paid dearly for its secessionist beliefs and its firing on Fort Sumter. Union troops bombarded the once-beautiful city, leaving it like this.

After the war, many soldiers, like these photographed at a Confederate hospital, went home missing legs, arms, or feet. For decades to come, these disabled veterans would be a reminder of the terrible war.

In 1861, Richmond, Virginia, was the third-largest Southern city, with a population of 38,000. In 1865, the city (as seen in this photograph) was little more than rubble. Only a few thousand citizens remained.

LINCOLN'S LAST SPEECH

On the evening of April 11, Lincoln came to a second-story window on the north side of the White House with a roll of manuscript in his hands. With Mary watching from a nearby window and Tad kneeling at his father's feet to catch each page of the speech as his father dropped it, the president began: "Reuniting our country is fraught with great difficulty . . . and we differ among ourselves as to the mode and manner and means of reconstruction."

The crowd was puzzled. This wasn't the rousing victory speech they had expected. Instead, the president gave them a carefully reasoned discussion of his plans for reuniting the Union. Even more startling, he became the first president to publicly announce that he was in favor of African American suffrage, telling the crowd he favored giving the vote to some black men—"the very intelligent," he said, "and those who served our cause as soldiers."

In the crowd, a young actor and Confederate sympathizer named John Wilkes Booth was not happy with the president's words. "Lincoln's talking 'nigger citizenship,'" he snarled to a companion. "This will be the last speech he will ever make."

JOHN WILKES BOOTH

The younger brother of famed actor Edwin Booth, whose performances Abraham greatly admired, John Wilkes Booth was also a popular actor. Unlike his brother, who supported the Union, twenty-six-year-old John Wilkes was a passionate Southern sympathizer who considered slavery "one of the greatest blessings that God bestowed upon a favored nation."

At first, Booth planned to kidnap the president and take him behind Confederate lines, where he would be forced to negotiate. During the fall and winter of 1864-65, Booth recruited a band of conspirators to help him—six men and one woman living in Washington but loyal to the Southern cause. Although this group made big plans, they took very little action. Then the Confederacy collapsed, and Booth—seething—knew what he had to do. "By God," he told one of the conspirators, "I'll run [Lincoln] through."

Friday, April 14, began as a lovely spring day. Dogwoods bloomed and the scent of lilac hung in the air. As always, Abraham worked in his office for a while before breakfast. "His face that morning was more cheerful than I had seen it in a long time," remembered Elizabeth Keckly. "He beamed at everyone."

Lincoln enjoyed a leisurely breakfast with his family. Robert, who had been at Appomattox Court-House when Lee surrendered, was home, and this was the first chance father and son had had to speak. While Lincoln ate his simple breakfast–a single egg and a cup of coffee–Robert placed a portrait of General Lee on the table. Abraham studied it a moment. "It is a good face," he said. "It is the face of a noble, brave man. I am glad the war is over."

This photograph of the theater box taken the day after the murder shows how it was decorated.

Mary was eager to know if her husband wanted to attend the performance of *Our American Cousin* at Ford's Theater that evening. She hoped the Grants would accompany them. All the while, Tad prattled on about the play *he* was going to see–*Aladdin,* at Grover's Theater.

By 9:00 A.M., Lincoln was back in his office. He read dispatches from the now-quiet battle fronts and met with all the members of his cabinet except Seward, who was recovering from a carriage accident. "Didn't our chief look grand today?" Secretary of War Stanton remarked later. All agreed that Lincoln did indeed "look happier than at any other time."

After lunch, Abraham sent a messenger to Ford's Theater with the happy news that the Lincolns would be attending the performance that evening. Harry Ford–the theater owner's brother–was thrilled. Realizing that the president's appearance during the week of national victory was an honor, he set about decorating the box. He used a sofa, flags, a picture of Washington, and two stuffed chairs. At the last minute, he dragged an old rocker up from his office. He knew the president would enjoy it.

John Wilkes Booth learned of Lincoln's attendance when he went to collect his mail at the theater. Calling together two of his cronies–George Atzerodt and Lewis Paine–he devised a plan for simultaneous assassinations to be carried out that night. Atzerodt, he decided, would murder Vice President Andrew Johnson in his room at the Kirkwood Hotel, while Paine was assigned to kill Secretary of State William Seward in his Lafayette Square home. Booth would assassinate the president.

The actor made preparations that day. He rented a horse on which to make his escape. He wrote a letter to the *National Intelligencer* explaining his deed. And he stole into Ford's Theater, where he bored a peephole in the theater-box door. Through it, he had a deadeye view of the back of the president's rocking chair.

Meanwhile, the Lincolns were having trouble finding someone to attend the performance with them. They had invited twelve people. All had declined. Most were too busy, but others–such as the Grants– could not stand the idea of being confined in a theater box with Mary and her uncertain temper. Finally, the president and First Lady settled on Henry Reed Rathbone and Clara Harris, a young couple they were fond of.

That afternoon around four o'clock, Mary and Abraham took their usual carriage ride. Earlier he had written a little note to his wife, "playfully and tenderly worded," she confessed, "notifying the hour of the day he would drive with me." Mary had tucked the note away to treasure with others she'd been keeping, "dear, loving letters to me, many of them written . . . in the long ago and quite yellow with age."

Now, as their carriage rolled across the Potomac River into Virginia, where the war had ended and springtime begun, Mary said, "Dear husband, you almost startle me by your great cheerfulness."

"We must *both* be more cheerful in the future," replied Abraham. "Between the war and the loss of our darling Willie, we have both been very miserable." Recalled Mary, "His mind was fixed upon having some relaxation, and bent on [going to] the theater."

On their return, Lincoln saw a group of old friends, including Illinois governor Richard Oglesby, just leaving the White House. "Come back, boys, come back!" he hollered. The men stayed for some time. "Lincoln got to reading some humorous book," recalled Oglesby. "They kept sending for him to come to dinner. He promised each time to go, but kept reading. . . . Finally, he got a sort of peremptory order from the missus that he must come at once."

An engraving from Frank Leslie's Illustrated Newspaper *shows Booth firing the fateful shot.*

Afterward, the Lincolns prepared for the theater. Mary put on a small-patterned blue dress and her newest bonnet. Abraham brushed his hand through his mop of stubborn hair and picked up his silk hat. By the time they arrived at Ford's Theater the performance had already begun. As they entered, the orchestra interrupted the actors and played "Hail to the Chief." The audience cheered and waved. "The President," remembered one theatergoer, "stepped to the box-rail and acknowledged the applause with dignified bows and never-to-be-forgotten smiles." Then he settled into the rocking chair to enjoy the play—a pun-filled slapstick comedy.

Mary "seemed to take a great pleasure in witnessing his enjoyment," remembered a member of the orchestra. At one point, she nestled close to her husband's side and slipped her arm through his.

One of the biggest laughs in the play came during the third act. "Don't know the manners of good society, eh?" intoned the male lead. "Well, I guess I know enough to turn you inside out, old gal—you sockdologizing old mantrap."

Those were the last words Abraham heard. As the audience—including the president—laughed and clapped, John Wilkes Booth burst through the box door. With a derringer in one hand and a dagger in the other, he raised the gun at arm's length and shot Lincoln in the back of the head.

Everything in the box suddenly became a whirl of gunsmoke and confusion. Major Rathbone sprang forward to seize Booth. Dropping the gun, Booth slashed the major in the arm with his dagger, then leapt over the box railing to the stage below. As he fell, the spur of his boot caught in the American flag draped over the box and he landed badly. The actors onstage heard his leg snap. They rushed toward him, but Booth brandished his knife. *"Sic semper tyrannis,"* he shouted (Latin for "Thus it shall ever be for tyrants"). Then he was gone through the wings, hopping out the backstage door, knocking over the boy who was holding his waiting horse, and clattering down the alley into the night.

In the box, the force of the shot propelled Lincoln forward. At first Mary thought he was falling over the railing. Instinctively, she grabbed him and struggled to hold his large frame upright. Then she saw the blood . . . and she knew. Heartrendingly she shrieked, "They have shot the President! They have shot the President!"

In the audience, Dr. Charles Leale heard Mary's cries and raced for the box. He found Lincoln almost dead—his pulse weak and his breath coming in occasional snorting gasps.

"Oh, doctor," Mary gasped. "Is he dead? Do what you can for him. Oh, my dear husband! My dear husband!"

Dr. Leale knew the wound was fatal. Realizing the president could not be taken far, he enlisted the help of several men and moved him across the street to a boardinghouse. Carrying Lincoln's slack body into the shabby back bedroom, they arranged him diagonally on the bed, his head next to the door and his feet sticking out the opposite side.

Mary followed along, but in the darkness and confusion outside the theater, she got separated from the group. "Where is my husband?" she cried. "Where is my husband?"

Clara Harris found her. Tenderly, she led her across the street.

Once inside, Mary flung herself onto her husband and tried to revive him. "How can it be so? Do speak to me," she implored. She began kissing his face, until someone dragged her back into the front room.

There she spent the next nine hours, waiting for her husband to die. Most of the time she was alone, though

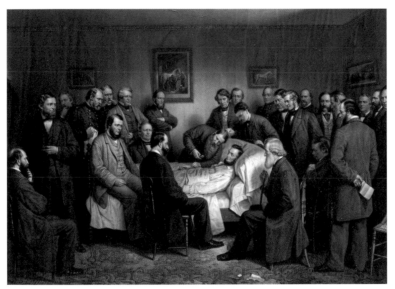

Probably the most accurate depiction of Lincoln's death scene; the artist made detailed sketches of the room a day or two after the president's death.

Robert Lincoln and Phineas Gurley (pastor of the Lincolns' church) occasionally sat with her. All the cabinet members except Seward (who had also been attacked that night) visited their fallen leader, as did senators, congressmen, and other officials. None of them comforted Mary. Every hour, she struggled to her feet and made her way to the increasingly crowded bedroom. Each time, she tried to kiss her husband awake, begging him to open his eyes and live. When this failed, she insisted someone fetch Tad from the White House. Always in the past, Abraham had responded to Tad. But the physicians decided this was not a wise idea. Once, when the president's breathing developed a frightening rattle, Mary let out a piercing cry and fainted. Growled Stanton, "Take that woman out and do not let her in again."

Mary saw Abraham for the last time in the early morning hours when, as one observer recalled, the light "was struggling with dim candles." During the night, his pillow had become blood-soaked and his face had grown swollen and discolored. Standing beside the bed, her face covered with tears, she sobbed, "Oh, my God, have I given my husband to die?"

At 7:22 on the morning of April 15, 1865, Abraham Lincoln took his last breath.

"Now he belongs to the ages," sobbed Stanton.

THE FINAL CONTENTS OF LINCOLN'S POCKETS

An anonymous mourner carefully emptied Abraham's pockets and found an ivory pocketknife, a linen handkerchief with "A. Lincoln" stitched in red, a brass sleeve button, a fancy watch fob, two pairs of spectacles (one of which he had mended with a bit of string), a tiny pencil, a leather wallet containing a Confederate five-dollar bill, and nine old newspaper clippings. A few gave news of the war, including one that detailed Sherman's march on Atlanta. There were also a newspaper article about declining morale among Confederate soldiers, a reprint of a letter from a disgruntled rebel asking to be "banished" to the North, and an account of a speech made by a Philadelphia minister praising Lincoln's greatness. One clipping quoted a British politician who, just before the 1864 election, wrote:

All those who believe that Slavery weakens America's power and tarnishes your good name throughout the world . . . are heartily longing for the reelection of Mr. Lincoln . . . they think they have observed in his career a grand simplicity of purpose and patriotism which knows no change and does not falter.

A few of the items taken from Lincoln's pockets at the time of his death, along with a newspaper announcing the assassination.

CHAPTER EIGHT

BLIND FROM WEEPING

No place is home for me.

—MARY LINCOLN IN A LETTER TO
ELIZABETH BLAIR LEE, AUGUST 25, 1865

MARY'S LOSS

As Robert Todd led his mother to the carriage that would take her to the White House, she looked back at the boardinghouse and cried, "That dreadful house! That dreadful house!" A few minutes later, an honor guard carried out her husband's body and placed it in a hearse. With measured tread, this desolate little group made its way toward Pennsylvania Avenue.

When they arrived, Mary Jane Welles (wife of cabinet member Gideon Welles) was waiting to help. Following the doctor's orders, she insisted that Mary get into bed. But as she led Mary into the room that adjoined her husband's, the bereaved woman drew back, crying, "Not there! Oh, not there!" So Mrs. Welles helped Mary to a bedroom with no special memories, one that had been fitted up for the president to do some writing. The shades were drawn, and Mary climbed into bed. Here she remained for the next five weeks, tossing and sobbing. Sometimes she was hysterical. Other times she was delirious. Claimed one official, "The sudden and awful death . . . somewhat unhinged her mind, for, at times she exhibited symptoms of madness."

"Alas," Mary moaned again and again, "all is over with me."

A PHOTOGRAPH OF TAD TAKEN JUST WEEKS AFTER HIS FATHER'S DEATH

When his mother arrived back at the White House, twelve-year-old Tad ran weeping to her and buried his face in the folds of her gown. But he was shooed away. His mother needed to get into bed, the doctor told him. Trailing her up the stairs, the boy watched her agonizing outbursts. Every once in a while he covered his ears and wailed, "Don't cry so, Mama. You will break my heart!"

Later that day, while being dressed by his nurse, he said, "Pa is dead. I can hardly believe that I shall never see him again. I must learn to take care of myself now." He looked thoughtful a moment, then added, "Yes, Pa is dead, and I am only Tad Lincoln now, little Tad like other little boys. I am not a President's son now."

This letter, written in shaky handwriting to Judge Davis, shows the tremendous strain Robert was under.

Overnight, twenty-two-year-old Robert became the head of the family. Having sobbed uncontrollably at his father's deathbed, he now pulled himself together. He wired Lincoln's old friend Judge Davis from Springfield to come and take charge of the family's financial affairs, notified family members of his father's death, and approved funeral plans. But even though Robert appeared clearheaded, he was drowning in grief. "In all my plans for the future," he wrote just twelve days after the assassination, "the chief object I had in mind was the [approval] of my Father, and now that he is gone . . . I feel utterly without spirit or courage."

AN ENGRAVING OF THE CATAFALQUE (OR "TEMPLE OF DEATH," AS NEWSPAPERS CALLED IT) THAT WAS BUILT IN THE EAST ROOM FOR LINCOLN'S COFFIN

The men of Abraham's administration were determined to give their fallen leader the biggest funeral in American history. Work started immediately. Acres of black crepe were draped across public buildings. President George Washington's hearse was pulled from storage and repaired. And an elaborate eleven-foot-high catafalque was built in the East Room. The sounds of the sawing and hammering "gave [Mary] spasms," recalled one friend, "and every nail that was driven seemed to her like a pistol shot."

People in charge tried to be considerate of Mary's feelings. On April 17, Lincoln's body was moved from an upstairs guest bedroom, where it had lain on a cooling board, to the East Room in preparation for the funeral. The men who carried his coffin took off their shoes and tiptoed past Mary's door; they didn't want the First Lady to have any hint of what was happening.

A PHOTOGRAPH OF LINCOLN IN HIS COFFIN

On Wednesday, April 19, Washington said good-bye to President Lincoln. During the funeral service, General Grant sat alone at the head of the coffin, while Robert—his face drawn and haggard—sat alone at the foot. (Spared the pain of being present, Tad remained upstairs.) Newly sworn-in President Andrew Johnson, along with all the cabinet members except Seward (who was still recovering from the attempt on his life), stood at the coffin's right. Six hundred other guests—family friends, politicians, and dignitaries—crammed into the room to listen to four ministers conduct the service. At the same time, twenty-five million citizens across the country were attending similar memorial services in their own churches. Mary, however, was not one of them. Too ill to attend, she stayed in bed with a pillow pressed over her head.

This photograph, taken during a pause in the marching, shows the funeral procession as it heads up Pennsylvania Avenue to the Capitol.

After the White House services, Lincoln's coffin was placed in a black-plumed hearse and escorted up Pennsylvania Avenue. Behind the hearse rode both Robert and Tad (who had insisted on taking part in the funeral procession), followed by wave after wave of blue-uniformed soldiers, dignitaries, government officials, and tens of thousands of civilian mourners. The African American citizens made one of the most impressive sights. Wearing high silk hats and white gloves, they held hands and walked in forty lines, straight across the avenue from curb to curb—four thousand of them!

Solemn and unforgettable, the procession moved toward the Capitol, where the coffin was placed in the rotunda. Here it was left under the watchful eyes of the honor guard until the next morning, when the doors were opened to the public. All day long, people filed past the open casket. "All were sad; many wept openly," remembered journalist Noah Brooks. And on people's faces he noted "a strange mixture of horror, fury, tenderness, and a stirring wonder brewing."

A PHOTOGRAPH OF LINCOLN'S FUNERAL TRAIN

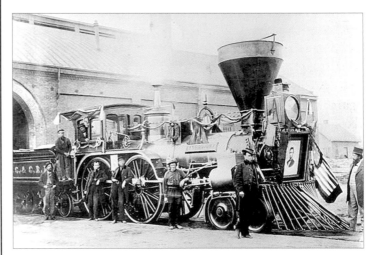

A week after the assassination, the president's body was placed in a black-draped funeral train. He was headed home to Springfield, but it was a long, circuitous ride. Over the next twenty days, the train stopped in eleven cities. In each, the coffin was reopened so thousands of Americans could view his remains.

Robert did not accompany his father's body. He stayed in Washington to look after his mother and Tad, as well as to deal with the family's legal and financial matters. But the president did not travel alone. Officials removed Willie's casket from its tomb and placed it in the railroad car beside Abraham's. Now father and son headed home.

Springfield's leaders desperately wanted Lincoln to be buried in their city. Within hours of the assassination, they sent a delegation to the White House begging Mary to allow this. But Mary felt torn. Having quarreled with most of her friends and family there, she never wanted to set foot in that small prairie town again. On the other hand, she remembered that her husband had once asked her to bury him "in some quiet place." Finally deciding on Oak Ridge Cemetery—a peaceful, shady burial ground two miles from Springfield—she directed city leaders to place his remains in the public tomb there until she could choose a beautiful spot for him.

Springfield's leaders ignored her wishes. Believing that their most famous citizen should be buried in the middle of the city, where all could pay homage, they bought an expensive plot of land at the intersection of two main streets. At additional expense, construction crews worked day and night to build a handsome monument in time for the funeral.

Six days before the event, Mary discovered what was happening in Springfield. Startled out of her depression, she fought Springfield's officials for her husband's body. If the city did not comply with her wishes, she threatened, "I shall have his precious remains placed in a vault in the National Capitol."

All Springfield fumed against Mary Lincoln. "The people are in a rage about it," wrote one citizen, "and all the hard stories that were ever told about her are told again. She has no friends here."

With Mary's threat hanging over them, city leaders sent carpenters out to Oak Ridge Cemetery, where they readied an already existing tomb for the final funeral on May 4—an event attended by close to ten thousand people. Other than Robert (who arrived in Springfield the morning of the funeral), the only other blood relative present was Lincoln's cousin John Hanks. He had come to represent old Sarah Bush Lincoln, the president's stepmother. Too weak to make the trip from her Goosenest Prairie cabin, she had cried when she learned of Abraham's murder. "I know'd they'd kill him," she sobbed. "I know'd it."

MARY LINCOLN IN MOURNING

The sophisticated woman who had once delighted in clever conversation, the theater, and high fashion was now completely gone. In her place sat an aging creature shrouded in black and drowning in fear and self-pity. When she wasn't weeping, recalled one of the widow's few visitors, she "was in a daze; it seemed almost a stupor. She hardly spoke: No one could get near enough to her grief to comfort her."

MARY'S ASSASSINATION THEORY

In late April, Mary called Secretary of War Stanton to her bedside and accused Andrew Johnson of killing her husband. "That inebriate had cognizance of my husband's death," she said. "He had an understanding with [Booth]. . . . As sure as you and I live, Johnson had some hand in this." It was a completely unfounded charge, and Stanton tried to lay out the facts for her, but no amount of evidence to the contrary could shake her belief. A year later, when Johnson visited Lincoln's grave in Springfield, Mary fumed. A cold-blooded murderer, she claimed, was "desecrating" her husband's grave.

THIS ENGRAVING, CREATED THREE DAYS AFTER BOOTH'S CAPTURE, SHOWS HIM BEING CORNERED AND SHOT IN A BURNING TOBACCO BARN.

While Mary Lincoln lay sobbing in bed and the nation mourned, federal soldiers searched for John Wilkes Booth. "[I have been] hunted like a dog through swamps and woods," Booth wrote in his diary six days after the murder. The actor, along with his friend David Herold, a feebleminded former drugstore clerk, had been hiding in the woods on the Maryland side of the Potomac. Booth was desperate to cross the river into Virginia but worried his leg wouldn't hold out. The leg—broken during Booth's leap from the theater box—had been set days earlier by an unsuspecting Dr. Samuel Mudd after the actor had suddenly shown up at his house just hours after the murder. Now it had "become terribly swollen and infected . . . all black and painful to the touch," he noted. But as patrols swarmed the area, Booth made the decision to go. On Friday night, April 21–the same day Lincoln's body left Washington–the two men attempted to row across the river. But the strong current swept them off course, and they took a full day to cross. Worse, the men were seen by many people as they stumbled across the countryside. By Tuesday, they had ended up in a tobacco barn in Caroline County.

Early Wednesday morning, Union soldiers surrounded the place. Their calls to surrender were answered by Herold, who appeared with his arms raised. But Booth stayed inside. Setting fire to the barn, the soldiers hoped to smoke him out. Then one infantryman, Boston Corbett, claimed to hear the voice of "Providence" telling him to shoot President Lincoln's murderer. Taking aim, he fired through a chink in the barn wall, striking Booth in the neck. As the fire raged, they dragged the mortally wounded actor into the open. "Tell Mother I die for my country," he whispered. Two and a half hours later, he was dead.

FROM LEFT: MARY SURRATT, LEWIS PAINE, DAVID HEROLD, AND GEORGE ATZERODT HANG FOR THEIR INVOLVEMENT IN ABRAHAM'S MURDER.

With Booth gone, the nation needed a new focus for its anger. A furious dragnet ordered by Secretary of War Stanton reeled in seven men and one woman—all friends of Booth accused of helping him kill the president. These accused were treated inhumanely. Fitted with arm and leg manacles, they were kept in tiny, dirty cells and forced to wear padded canvas head bags that lacked any openings except for a small eating hole. For weeks they lived under these conditions, disoriented and afraid.

After a military trial twelve weeks later, the court found them guilty one by one. David Herold, who had accompanied Booth to Virginia; Lewis Paine, who had attacked and almost killed Secretary of State Seward in his home the same night Lincoln was murdered; and George Atzerodt, the man who couldn't bring himself to murder Vice President Johnson at his hotel, were sentenced to death by hanging. Michael O'Laughlin and Samuel Arnold—unjustly accused of helping plan the murder—got life sentences at hard labor, as did Dr. Samuel Mudd. Edman Spangler, a stagehand at Ford's Theater, got six years for holding Booth's horse in the theater alley during the murder.

And then there was Mary Surratt. Owner of the boardinghouse where the men met, she was portrayed in court as "the incubator of the entire plot, and as guilty as Booth." Even though witnesses swore she knew nothing about the murder, the court sentenced her to death, too. On July 7, 1865, along with the three men, she was led onto the high scaffold and hanged. Wrote Orville Browning, Abraham's old friend from Illinois, "The execution of those people [was] . . . murder." But Browning was one of the few people who felt this way. Most Northerners' desire for retribution was now satisfied.

A TALE OF TOO MANY TRUNKS

"Packing afforded quite a relief from Mrs. Lincoln's all-consuming grief," Elizabeth Keckly later recalled. Into sixty-four trunks went everything Mary had brought from Springfield, as well as every personal item she had bought while living in Washington, from bonnets and dresses to jewelry and fans. She also put in nearly five years' worth of gifts given to her as First Lady—tablecloths, yards of imported lace, silverware, paintings, books. More than once Robert grew frustrated with his mother's obsessive attention to her trunks. He wished the trunks would catch fire and "burn all your plunder up." But Mary ignored him. She had, said a friend, "a passion for hoarding all things."

For the next seventeen years, these trunks (and more!) went wherever she did. One of her greatest joys was to rummage through their contents. "Every day, even when Aunt Mary was sick, she was able to be up all day bending over those trunks," recalled her great-niece Mary Edwards Brown.

The Hyde Park Hotel as it looked when the Lincolns lived there

GOODBYE, WASHINGTON.

On May 22, Mary Lincoln, shrouded in pitch-black mourning clothes, climbed into the carriage that would take her to the train depot. With her went a sorrowful entourage—Tad, Robert, and Elizabeth Keckly. Only a handful of people came to see her off. One of them, Building Commissioner Benjamin French, "felt really very sad," he wrote in his diary. "Although she has given a world of trouble, she is a most singular woman."

To Elizabeth Keckly, Mary's departure was "so unlike the day the body of the President was borne from the hall in grand and solemn state." Then, thousands had lined the route of the funeral procession. "Now, the wife of the President was leaving the White House, and there was scarcely a friend to tell her good-bye. . . . The silence was almost painful."

HELLO, CHICAGO.

After leaving the White House, Mary found the idea of returning to Springfield unbearable. "After the many years of happiness there with my idealized husband, to place me in that home deprived of his presence and the darling boy we lost in Washington, would not require a day for me to lose my entire reason," she explained. Instead, she went to Hyde Park, a resort community seven miles south of Chicago on Lake Michigan's shore.

Tad seemed happy there, swimming and building sand castles. Noted Elizabeth Keckly, who had traveled west with the family, "Tad was a child of sunshine . . . nothing seemed to dampen the ardor of his spirits."

Robert, however, was miserable. Every morning he commuted into Chicago to read law in a local office. Every evening he dragged himself back to the Hyde Park rooms where his mother and little brother depended on him for a strength he didn't always have. Said Robert to a friend, "I would almost as soon be dead, as to be compelled to remain in this dreary house."

He didn't remain long. When Mary and Tad moved to a Chicago boardinghouse just a few months later, Robert refused to join them. Using a portion of his inheritance, he rented his own apartment, escaping, he later said, "my mother's gloom."

LIZZY GOES HOME.

After the assassination, only Elizabeth Keckly could soothe Mary's grief. She slept in Mary's bedroom, encouraged her to eat, helped her to dress. "Lizzy," Mary said as Elizabeth bathed her temples their first night in Chicago, "you are my best and kindest friend, and I love you."

Mary wanted her friend to remain in Chicago permanently, but Elizabeth was eager to return to Washington. Not only had she neglected her dressmaking business since Lincoln's death, but she was worn out. "I had listened to Mrs. Lincoln sobbing for eight weeks," Elizabeth later wrote. So in mid-June, Elizabeth headed home. Once there, she promptly sent a bill to Congress for her services, and eventually received a check for $360: $35 a week for a total of six weeks as "first class nurse and attendant on Mrs. Lincoln"; $100 for "traveling and incidental expenses" for accompanying her to Chicago; and $50 for "mourning apparel."

After Lincoln's death, his old friend Judge Davis was given the job of "settling the Lincoln estate." For the next two and a half years he controlled the family's money while he collected outstanding salaries and fees, paid outstanding bills, liquidated assets, and sold property. In the meantime, he gave each family member a yearly allowance of $1,500 (about $19,000 in today's money) to live on. Mary raged against what she called "a pittance . . . a mere clerk's salary." How was she expected to live on such a small income? She couldn't buy a house, travel to Europe, or put Tad in a good school. "I could starve for all you care," she wrote Davis. At various times she begged, threatened, and demanded that he give her *all* the money her husband had left her. She couldn't wait until the estate was settled, she insisted. She needed her money *now.*

Davis refused. Mary's extravagance in Washington was common knowledge, and he feared she would foolishly spend it all. With prudence, he told her, she could manage on her income.

What Judge Davis didn't know was that Mary owed thousand of dollars to New York merchants, and they were demanding payment. So she determined to raise her own money. She wrote to wealthy acquaintants, begging for their financial aid: "With a stroke of the pen, you can prevent my future spent without a dime, forever a wanderer on the face of the earth." She negotiated her debt with her creditors: "I absolutely refuse to pay the full price of the silk moiré." And in September 1867, she traveled incognito to New York City, where, registering at a second-rate hotel, she signed the name "Mrs. Clarke of Chicago."

The next morning, Mrs. Clarke hurried to the brokerage firm of W. H. Brady & Company. There she handed over a diamond ring for appraisal. Curiously, the ring was inscribed with the name "Mary Lincoln." How had Mrs. Clarke come into possession of the former First Lady's jewelry? asked the broker. Lifting her black veil, Mary revealed herself. Her disguise had lasted only one day.

Why was Mary skulking around, pretending to be someone else? She had decided to sell some furs, gowns, shawls, jewelry—things she no longer wore because of her perpetual state of mourning—but hoped to keep their ownership a secret. After all, while she needed the money, she didn't need any more bad publicity.

As soon as the broker learned her true identity, he begged her to sell the items under her own name. Her celebrity, he promised, would increase the value of the items. Why, they might bring in as much as $100,000 (well over $1 million in today's money).

Mary quickly agreed. So in mid-October, Mr. Brady rented a space at 600 Broadway, placed ads in all the major newspapers, and put the former First Lady's wardrobe on display. Crowds came to stare and pick over her things. But no one came to buy. Especially humiliating was a small book placed by the door. In it, viewers were asked to pledge at least one dollar to help out Mrs. Lincoln. But those who signed it treated it like a joke, offering a dime, a penny, and "$75 from the 'Committee to Save Us from National Disgrace.'"

Mortified, Mary retreated to Chicago. But she could not escape the scandal. For weeks, every paper in the country had something to say about "Mrs. Lincoln's Second-Hand Clothing Sale." The *Springfield Journal* noted, "Mrs. Lincoln has been known to be deranged for years, and should be pitied for all her strange acts." And the *Chicago Tribune* predicted that "Mrs. L. will end her life in a lunatic asylum."

Mary fired off letter after letter explaining her action and denouncing her enemies to anyone who would listen. She resented "the people of this ungrateful country . . . [who] will neither do anything themselves [for me], nor allow me to improve my own conditions."

If only Mary had waited a few weeks, she might have avoided the scandal. A month after the rummage sale, Judge Davis finally "settled" the Lincoln estate. Mary's portion—$36,000, or about $450,000 in today's money—made her a wealthy woman. But the financial embarrassments of the past few years had left her fearful of poverty; she became manic on the subject of money.

This engraving published in Frank Leslie's Illustrated Newspaper *shows shoppers rifling through trunks at Mary's secondhand clothing sale.*

A black lace shawl from the sale. Viewers did not admire Mary's things. They claimed that the shawls were soiled and the gowns had perspiration stains.

WILLIAM HERNDON INVENTS A LOVE STORY.

On the night of November 16, 1866, Abraham's former law partner, William Herndon, strode to the podium to address a crowd gathered in Springfield's Old Capitol. For the past several months, he had been rummaging around in the president's past, interviewing Lincoln's New Salem neighbors, his Springfield associates, his childhood friends. Now the lawyer-turned-historian considered himself Lincoln's foremost biographer. And tonight he would reveal the secrets he had uncovered.

His lecture, oddly titled "A. Lincoln–Miss Ann Rutledge, New Salem, Pioneering, the Poem," created a sensation inside the statehouse. Lincoln had loved only one woman in his life, declared Herndon, "this beautiful, amiable and lovely girl of nineteen" named Ann Rutledge. But all too soon, his adored one died. "Lincoln's mind wandered from its throne, and when he recovered, he had lost the woman he should have married." The president's marriage to Mary Todd, he declared, "was a domestic hell. . . . For the last twenty-three years of his life, Mr. Lincoln had no joy." As evidence of the couple's misery, Herndon falsely claimed that his friend could never sign his letters "love" or "affectionately." Instead, he wrote "your friend," as he did on letters to political associates and clients.

The public believed this romantic story, ignoring the fact that Herndon had embellished most of it and imagined the rest. The *Chicago Tribune* quickly reprinted every word of the lecture, and the story spread like a prairie brush fire.

When Mary read the speech, she was devastated. "It was always music in both my ears," she once wrote, "when my husband told me that I was the only one he ever thought of, or cared for. It will solace me to the grave." Now it pained her to think that most of the world believed Abraham had loved someone else, and she was "nothing more than his misfortune."

An engraving of the author taken from Elizabeth Keckly's tell-all book <u>Behind the Scenes: Thirty Years a Slave and Four Years in the White House</u>

On the second floor of her Chicago boardinghouse, on a chilly May evening in 1868, Mary Lincoln sat reading a book. As she turned the pages she groaned or rubbed her forehead. Once she burst into tears and tossed the book aside. But after a few minutes, she picked it up again. The book was written by none other than Elizabeth Keckly.

Since their first meeting in 1861, Mary had trusted "dear Lizzy" with her greatest joys and darkest secrets. She'd given Elizabeth gifts, taken her along on trips, and sent her dozens of long, deeply personal letters. "She is," Mary had often said, "my best . . . friend."

Sometime in the fall of 1867, Elizabeth had found a publisher for a book she was writing–a tell-all about the Lincolns. Called *Behind the Scenes,* it appeared in bookstores in the spring of 1868 and was the first example of what has today become a popular form of literature: an employee's backstairs glimpse into the life of a public figure. In her book, Elizabeth freely discussed Mary's emotional and financial problems. She included private, overheard conversations between Mary and her husband. And she described some of the family's most personal moments–Willie's death, Tad's response to his father's assassination, Mary's health problems. Worse, all of Mary's heartfelt letters to Elizabeth were included in the book's appendix.

Although widely publicized, the book had little effect on public opinion and sold few copies. Why? Because it violated the Victorian codes of privacy and racial separation. Reviewers across the country condemned it as "illiterate, ungrammatical twaddle" and "the back-stairs gossip of Negro servant girls." And newspapers labeled Elizabeth "a traitorous eavesdropper," "ignorant and vulgar." (Nowadays, historians consider Keckly's book an accurate and important account of the Lincolns' time in the White House.)

Mary took no pleasure in the newspapers' defense. Her friendship with Elizabeth was over, and she felt humiliated and betrayed. Unable to hold up her head among her countrymen, Mary made plans to escape to Europe. She admitted, "I am now completely friendless."

ROBERT'S BRIDE, MARY HARLAN

On the evening of September 14, 1868, a trembling Mary Lincoln stepped from a train. Gripping fifteen-year-old Tad's hand, she steadied herself. She was here–*really here*–in the city where her husband had been murdered three and a half years earlier.

She hadn't wanted to come. "The terror of it . . . almost overpowers me," she wrote. But Robert was getting 🖜

married, and she was "exceedingly anxious to witness it, especially with a young lady who is so charming and whom I love so much." The young lady was Robert's long-time sweetheart, Mary Harlan, daughter of Iowa senator James Harlan. The ceremony was being held in the Harlan home on H Street.

But as her carriage wove through the city's all-too-familiar streets, Mary struggled to control her emotions. On the verge of a breakdown, she finally decided "not to look around me [so that] the feeling of being there did not oppress me so much."

Things were easier once she arrived at the Harlans' home. Attended by only close friends and family, the ceremony was small enough that Mary could relax. For a few hours she was able to enjoy the parlor, "elegantly decorated with blossoms," and the bride, in "a rich glowing veil of illusion." Beside her, the groom looked "the very personification of joy."

But Mary's nerves could only take so much. As soon as the wedding cake had been served, she escaped to her Baltimore hotel. The next day she fainted in its dining room, a result—she claimed—of "the after effects on my mind."

A PHOTOGRAPH OF FRANKFURT, GERMANY, TAKEN WHEN MARY AND TAD LIVED THERE

"To avoid persecution from the vampire press," Mary explained to a friend, "I have decided to flee to a land of strangers." The land Mary chose was Germany. She planned to settle Tad into a school in Frankfurt (Mary believed a German education was the best), then travel on to the spas at Wiesbaden and Marienbad (recommended by her doctor for her nerves and arthritis). But soon after setting foot in Frankfurt on October 6, 1868, she was charmed. Planning to stay only a week, she lived there for the next two years.

There was plenty to do. While Tad attended school, she went shopping and sightseeing, and even bumped into European royalty: "I came face-to-face with a Prussian princess who was selecting some gorgeous table covers. . . . Our eyes met. . . . We looked earnestly at each other. . . . Yet until I left the store I did not know who she was." No wonder Mary referred to the place as "dear, old Frankfurt."

A DIFFICULT DAUGHTER-IN-LAW

Mary's three grandchildren (from lower left), Jessie, Abraham II, and Mary Lincoln

In October 1869, while still living in Frankfurt, Mary received wonderful news—a baby girl had been born to Robert and his wife. And they had named the baby Mary, after both her mother and her grandmother. Joyously, the new grandmother set out to do some celebratory shopping. Soon, a tiny coral bracelet and "other choice little things" were on their way to Chicago.

Plenty of advice also arrived. "Don't mope around the house. Attend operas and concerts," Mary cautioned the new mother. And if Robert would not hire a nurse, Mary offered to pay for one. "If I was in Chicago, I would take young Miss Lincoln out for carriage rides, so her young mother can be as gay as a lark." Finally, Mary offered her daughter-in-law this important lesson learned in life: "Have fun; be happy. Trouble comes soon enough, my dear child."

But while her granddaughter was always in her thoughts, Mary did not hold the "blessed baby" until she returned from Europe in 1871. Then she set about spoiling her. Calling her "Little Mamie," Mary indulged the child with toys, sweets, and expensive clothes. Because of her granddaughter, Mary's grief receded. For the first time since her husband's death, she began enjoying life.

This happiness, however, was short-lived. Mary's domineering personality, endless advice, and sharp criticism angered Robert's wife. Soon the two Mrs. Lincolns were shouting and slamming doors. "My mother became violently angry over some trifle," recalled Robert. "She drove my servants out of the room with her insulting remarks concerning [my wife]." He felt he had no choice but to ban his mother from visiting his home.

The Robert Lincolns had two other children—Abraham, born in August 1873, and Jessie, born in November 1875. But because of the family's strained relationship, the children were never close to their paternal grandmother. Mary saw little Abraham only once, when she visited him as a newborn. And by the time Jessie was born, Mary and Robert were so estranged she never even met the child.

MARY'S PETITION TO CONGRESS ASKING FOR A WIDOW'S PENSION

Even while living in Frankfurt, Mary continued to obsess about money. When she learned that the U.S. Congress had begun doling out pensions to needy widows of soldiers who had died in battle or from war wounds, she wanted one, too. She believed that if anyone deserved one, she did. In January 1869 Congress received this pitiful and not entirely truthful letter:

Sir:

I herewith most respectfully present to the honorable House of Representatives an application for a pension. I am a widow of a President of the United States whose life was sacrificed in his country's service. That sad calamity has very greatly impaired my health, and by the advice of my physician I have come over to Germany to try the mineral waters. . . . But my financial means do not permit me to take advantage of the urgent advice given me nor can I live in a style becoming the widow of the Chief Magistrate of a great nation, although I live as economically as I properly can. In consideration of the great service my dearly beloved husband had rendered to the United States, and of the fearful loss I have sustained by his untimely death . . . I respectfully submit to your honorable body this petition. . . .

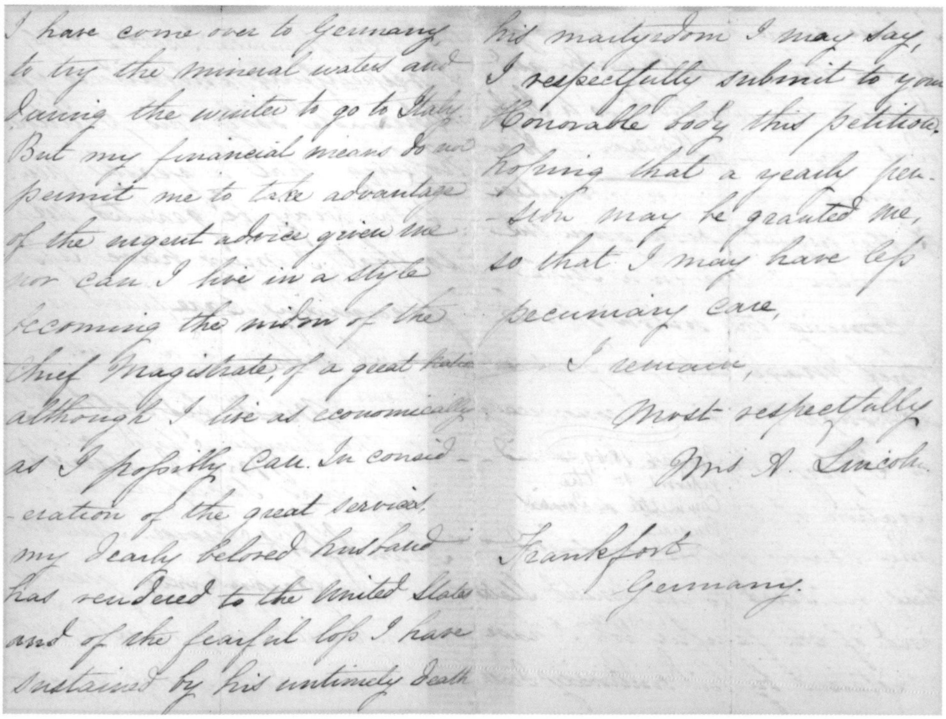

Mrs. A. Lincoln

When the letter was read aloud in Congress, it caused a heated debate. Senate members were particularly opposed to giving her a pension because her husband had not been killed on the battlefield. Others were simply opposed to giving Mary Lincoln a pension. "If the Senate wanted to exercise . . . charity," railed one member, "they should select a Martha Washington or a Dolley Madison or a proper object, not un-American, un-feminine Mary Lincoln." For days, these members publicly attacked Mary, calling her "harsh" and "indecent." They reminded their fellow members of the old-clothes scandal. And they dredged up rumors about her Confederate family and her Washington debts.

Finally, Mary's old friend Charles Sumner of Massachusetts stood. "Surely," he said, "the honorable members of the Senate must be weary of casting mud on the garments of the wife of Lincoln; those same garments on which one terrible night, a few years ago, gushed the blood and brains of Abraham Lincoln. She sat beside him in the theater and she received that pitiful, that holy deluge on her hands and skirts because she was the chosen companion of his heart. She loved him. I speak of that which I know. He had all her love and Lincoln loved, as only his mighty heart could love, Mary Lincoln. Let us vote."

Utter silence fell. No one shouted. The gavel didn't bang. Instead, the Senate voted. And when it was all over, Mary Lincoln became the first widow of a U.S. president to receive a pension. Congress awarded her $3,000 a year (about $42,000 in today's dollars).

When Mary heard the news, she was disappointed. She had hoped to receive twice that much; she believed it was her due. Still, she told herself to be happy and allow "not a muttering word . . . as to the amount."

To the Honorable Speaker of the
House of Representatives.

Sir:

I herewith most respec-
-tfully present to the Honorable
House of Representatives an
application for a pension.
I am a widow of a President
of the United States, whose
life was sacrificed in his
Country's Service. That sad
Calamity has very greatly
impaired my health, and
by the advice of my physician

I have come over to Germany
to try the mineral waters and
during the winter to go to Italy.
But my financial means do not
permit me to take advantage
of the urgent advice given me
nor can I live in a style
becoming the widow of the
Chief Magistrate, of a great nation
although I live as economically
as I possibly can. In consid-
-eration of the great service
my dearly beloved husband
has rendered to the United States
and of the fearful loss I have
sustained by his untimely death

his martyrdom I may say,
I respectfully submit to your
Honorable body this petition
hoping that a yearly pen-
-sion may be granted me,
so that I may have less
pecuniary care,
I remain,
Most respectfully
Mrs A. Lincoln

Frankfort
Germany.

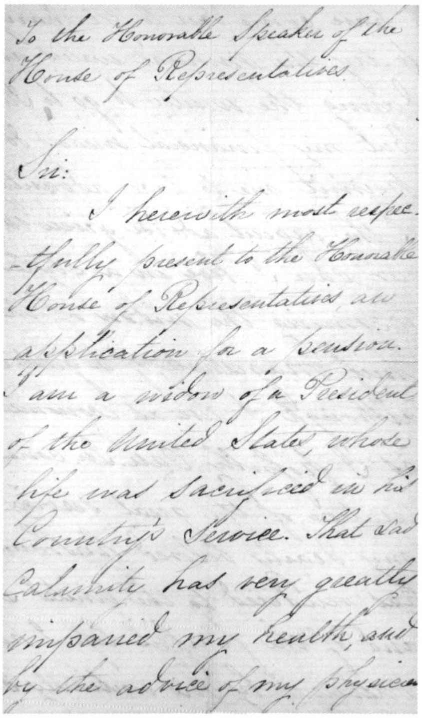

A PHOTOGRAPH OF TAD, AGE FIFTEEN, TAKEN WHILE HE AND MARY LIVED IN FRANKFURT

After his father's death, Tad became his mother's nurse, companion, and reason for living. "Taddie is my bright little comfort," Mary once told a friend. Gone was the playful, mischievous "tyrant of the White House." In his place was a solemn teenager who focused on two things—caring for his troubled mother and studying.

When the Lincolns had moved to Chicago in 1865, Tad had not been able to read or write. His parents had hired a tutor while living in the White House, but the boy hated schoolwork. "Let him run," his father said. "There's time enough for him to learn his letters and get pokey." After Lincoln's death, Robert had urged his mother to send Tad to a good boarding school. But Mary said no: "It is impossible for me to separate myself from him." Instead she enrolled him at the Chicago Academy, a coeducational day school, where he studied hard. Soon he could read as well as the other students. But he didn't make many friends. Instead of attending dances or sledding parties, he hurried home every afternoon to be with his mother.

Things didn't change much when they traveled to Germany in 1868. Mary enrolled Tad in Dr. Hohagen's boarding school but quickly came to dislike the place. Its "air of restraint," as she put it, repelled her. So did the bare dormitories with "the little white beds, where the boys sleep so far from their loving Mothers." Mary got special permission for Tad to eat at her hotel every evening and stay over anytime he wanted. "[Tad's] presence has become so necessary, even to my life," she admitted to her daughter-in-law.

In 1871, the Lincolns returned to the United States. Mary might have settled permanently in Frankfurt, but Tad was "almost wild to see Robert," Mary confessed. "So with trembling voice and aching heart I have consented to return."

It was a miserable voyage home—chilly winds for all eight days, and a severe storm in the mid-Atlantic. By the time they landed in New York, Tad had a cold and Mary's arthritic joints ached. The *New York Times* reported on their arrival: "Mrs. Lincoln is delighted to be in her native land. . . . Tad speaks English with a foreign accent."

THE LAST PHOTOGRAPH OF TAD, TAKEN JUST MONTHS BEFORE HIS DEATH

After arriving in Chicago in May, Mary and Tad settled into the Clifton House. Years later, the man who ran the hotel, W. A. Jenkins, remembered Tad as "a very lovable boy, quiet, gentle mannered, and good natured." Jenkins also remembered that Tad had a bad cough—a cough that grew worse. Soon, he could not breathe when lying down, and had to sleep sitting up. His mother bought him a special chair with a bar across the front to keep him from sliding to the floor when he nodded off. Still, she was hopeful. "The doctors," she told a friend, "assure me he is better. . . . They say that, thus far, his lungs are not diseased, although water has formed on his left lung." In fact, Tad was suffering from pleurisy, an accumulation of fluid in the pleural sacs around the lungs.

Tad did improve for a few weeks. His breathing eased and his color returned. But with the arrival of July, he grew worse again. Judge David Davis visited the sick teenager and went away with a sad heart. "Tad," he wrote his wife, "is dangerously ill. If he recovers it will be almost a miracle."

For the next two weeks, Mary watched helplessly as Tad fought for breath. He sat in his chair day and night, his chest heaving and his legs swollen. He turned blue. He choked and gasped. And yet, recalled Robert, he never complained. Instead, he suffered "with marvelous fortitude."

Finally, on July 15, 1871, the teenager's suffering ended. Slumping forward against the railing of his chair, eighteen-year-old Tad Lincoln died.

ANOTHER DEATH IN THE FAMILY

The day after Tad's death, a simple funeral was held in Robert's home. Friends, relatives, classmates—all came to pay their respects to the youngest son of Abraham Lincoln. All the while, Mary sat on a nearby sofa. Recalled one mourner, "She looked truly the woman of sorrow that she was."

While she managed to get through the service, she did not travel to Springfield to see her son interred in the Lincoln tomb. Instead, she took to her bed, where she fell into a deep depression. "I feel there is no life left to me," she sobbed. "Now in *this* world, there is only the deepest anguish and desolation."

RESTLESS, WANDERING YEARS

Mary did not know what to do with herself. Interested in little, she never stayed in one place long enough to make friends or cultivate new hobbies. Instead, she wandered from place to place, searching for solace. Below is just a partial list of places Mary lived between the fall of 1871 and the spring of 1875:

St. Charles, Illinois, 1871
Waukesha, Wisconsin, 1872
Moravia, New York, 1872
Boston, Massachusetts, 1872
Chicago, Illinois, 1872
Buffalo, New York, 1873
Niagara Falls, Canada, 1873
Chicago, Illinois, 1874
Chattanooga, Tennessee, 1874
Savannah, Georgia, 1875
Jacksonville, Florida, 1875
Chicago, Illinois, 1875

MARY BELIEVED THAT THIS PHOTOGRAPH, TAKEN BY A SPIRIT PHOTOGRAPHER IN 1872, WAS PROOF THAT LINCOLN'S GHOST HOVERED PROTECTIVELY AROUND HER.

After Tad's death, Mary grew determined to scale the wall between the living and the dead. She truly believed that "the spirits of our loved ones are with us always," and she craved a family reunion with her husband and three sons.

In search of this reunion, she moved to St. Charles, Illinois, a center for spiritualists thirty miles from Chicago. Here clairvoyants gathered to induce trances and serve as spirit guides. In her hotel the darkened parlors were said to resonate with mysterious tappings and ghostly appearances.

But Mary's search did not end here. She also traveled to Moravia, New York, where rumor had it that spirits congregated, drawn to a house whose cupola made it easy for them to enter and exit the world of the living. During a séance here, Mary claimed to have seen twenty-two spirit faces, including Tad's.

And still Mary moved on. In Boston she sought out a well-known medium on Washington Street. At one séance during her two-week stay, she claimed that her dead husband appeared. Even though she called herself Mrs. Tundall and wore a heavy veil so the medium would not recognize her (Mary liked to test mediums by appearing as an anonymous widow), she claimed the president instantly recognized her. Lovingly, he placed his arms on her shoulders.

Mary was so moved by this reunion, she hurried to the studio of William Mumler, a spirit photographer. He snapped this picture of Mary (the last taken during her life), then superimposed an image of the president onto the negative. Mary, however, believed Mumler had actually managed to photograph her husband's spirit. She cherished the print for the rest of her life and saw it as absolute proof that her loved ones were hovering just within reach.

➤ THE WARRANT FOR MARY'S ARREST ➤

In March 1875, Mary returned to Chicago, and for the next three months she occupied herself in the stores. Carrying $57,000—about a million dollars in today's money—in stocks and bonds in a secret pocket sewed into her skirt, she became a recognized eccentric in the downtown area. Many store clerks thought Mary Lincoln odd because she talked too much. In their experience, proper ladies rarely spoke to the people who waited on them. But this woman bargained for lower prices and told her life's history to anyone who would listen. Even more peculiar was her habit of buying multiples of the same item: ten pairs of white gloves because they reminded her of the presidential inauguration, five yards of red ribbon to recall her days as a lady of fashion, a dozen rugs to decorate a nonexistent house.

Her behavior embarrassed proper, respectable Robert, especially now that he was venturing into politics. (In just six years, his political connections would land him the position of secretary of war in President James A. Garfield's cabinet.) It was time, he decided, that she "be placed under . . . some control which will prevent her from making herself talked of by everybody."

On the morning of May 19, Mary, who was expecting the delivery of eight pairs of lace curtains, opened her door to find two Chicago policemen and an attorney named Leonard Swett standing on the threshold. Surprised, she asked the gentlemen what she could do for them.

Swett waved an arrest warrant. She had to go to the courthouse that afternoon, he told her. A jury was waiting to judge her sanity. According to state law, she had to be there to hear the charge, and to defend herself if possible.

Mary could not grasp what he was saying.

Swett tried again. "Your friends," he said, "have come to the conclusion that the troubles you have been called to pass through have been too much and have produced mental disease."

"You mean to say I am crazy?" Mary replied. "I am much obliged to you, but I am abundantly able to take care of myself. Where is my son Robert?"

Robert was waiting at the courthouse. Not only was he the person who had applied to the court to have her declared a lunatic, but he had organized the case against her. Over the past month, he had called in favors from judges, paid hotel employees and store clerks to testify to his mother's peculiarities, and hired private detectives to spy on her. Just one week earlier he had met with six doctors who, for a professional fee, had signed statements declaring Mary insane, even though they had never examined her. "You must go with me," Swett told Mary, "or I will turn you over to the police officers and let them take you."

At this, Mary "threw up her hands and with tears streaming down her cheeks prayed to the Lord and called upon her husband to help her," recalled Swett. Then she lifted her chin and "conducted herself like a lady in every regard."

Through the hotel they went, and out into the street. But when Swett tried to help Mary into the carriage, she drew back. "I ride with you from compulsion," she said, "but I beg you not to touch me."

ROBERT TODD LINCOLN TESTIFIES AT HIS MOTHER'S TRIAL.

When Leonard Swett flung open the big mahogany door to the courtroom that same afternoon, Mary shrank back. The place was crowded with witnesses, officials, reporters, and curious spectators. Taking her seat next to Isaac Arnold–the lawyer hired by Robert to defend her–Mary looked straight ahead. Behind her, people stared and whispered.

The judge banged his gavel. But before the proceedings could begin, Arnold suddenly had second thoughts about his participation in what some historians have since called "a kangaroo court," and he declined to serve as Mary's counsel. Swett was outraged. "You will put into her head that she can get some mischievous lawyer to make us trouble and defend her," he told Arnold. "Do your duty!"

Arnold did as he was told. But during the three-hour trial, he barely said a word. Not once did he object or cross-examine any of the seventeen witnesses who paraded across the stand. One hotel employee declared, "Mrs. Lincoln's manner was often nervous and excitable. She was not like ladies in general." Another recalled her closet "piled full of packages which were unopened, just as they came from the stores." And a store clerk described her shopping habits as "crazy."

In the late afternoon, Robert took the stand. Under questioning from the prosecutor (none other than Swett), he was seen to have tears in his eyes. "I have no doubt my mother is insane," he said. "She has long been a source of great anxiety to me. She has no home and no reason to make so many purchases."

With this statement, the case rested. Minutes later the jury–which had been assembled by Robert's close friend Judge David Davis–declared itself "satisfied that the said Mary Lincoln is insane, and is a fit person to be sent to a state hospital." Additionally, Robert was given control of all Mary's money, and she was forced to hand over her bonds. (She tore them angrily out of her skirt.) As the crowd gathered around to gape at her, she covered her face with her hands and cried, "Oh, Robert, to think that my son would do this to me."

HEADLINES IN THE CHICAGO TRIBUNE THE DAY AFTER MARY'S TRIAL

Newspapers across the country blared the news: Mrs. Lincoln was a lunatic! For Mary, the shame and humiliation must have been unbearable.

A SAD REVELATION

MRS. MARY LINCOLN, THE WIDOW OF THE LATE PRESIDENT, ADJUDGED INSANE.

AT LAST THE STRANGE FREAKS OF THE PAST TEN YEARS ARE UNDERSTOOD

AND THE UNFRIENDLY CRITICISM WILL CHANGE TO HEARTFELT COMMISERATION

THE POOR LADY A VICTIM TO MANY STRANGE AND STARTLING HALLUCINATIONS

WALLS HAD VOICES, INDIANS TROUBLED HER SCALP, AND SHE HAD A MANIA FOR SHOPPING.

A SORROWFUL SPECTACLE IN COURT.

INSANE OR NOT?

In the nineteenth century, mental illness was something few people understood. Even in the medical community, doctors made no distinction between persons who were obviously insane and those who were merely eccentric or nonconformist. All could be locked away in an asylum.

Women were especially susceptible. In Illinois in 1875, the law stated that "married women may be detained in hospitals at the request of the husband without evidence of insanity." Taking advantage of this law, dozens of men had their wives locked up for being annoying, improper, or unconventional, or for behaving in ways they did not approve.

Mary was probably a victim of this sort of treatment. As one historian wrote, "She was always more bewildering than bewildered, and more sickening (especially to her son) than sick." She shopped to make herself feel better, to escape her unhappy life, to fill her time. And while Mary's behavior was annoying, improper, and unnatural, she was a danger neither to herself nor to others. Hers was "not an instance of medical or legal insanity," wrote her biographer Jean Baker.

BELLEVUE PLACE IN BATAVIA, ILLINOIS, WHERE MARY WAS COMMITTED

Bellevue Sanitarium.

The morning after her trial, Mary was taken to an insane asylum twenty-five miles from Chicago. From the moment she arrived, she began thinking of ways to gain her freedom—freedom from her tiny room on the second floor, freedom from the hospital's self-proclaimed "modern management of mental disease by rest, diet, fresh air, occupation, diversion, change of scene, an orderly life, and no more medicine than necessary"; freedom from the private attendant who did her laundry, brought her meals, and (unknown to Mary) spied on her through the wooden slats between their rooms. While Bellevue Place was a private hospital that emphasized a "family atmosphere," it was still filled with seriously ill people. There was Mrs. Wheeler, who raved and pounded and screamed all night; Mrs. Munger, who grabbed another patient's scissors and stabbed herself; and Mrs. Johnson, who urinated on the floor with the explanation that "God imposes higher duties than cleanliness."

Mary had to get out. To do this, she knew she needed a lawyer. But that was easier said than done. Dr. Patterson, the hospital's director, censored her mail. Everyone Mary wrote to or received letters from had to be approved by him. Not to be defeated, Mary wrote two letters, enclosing both in an envelope addressed to an approved correspondent. She then directed the approved person to mail the second letter. It was weeks before Dr. Patterson uncovered her plan. When he did, he wrote in his treatment notes, "Mrs. Lincoln's lying and deceit should be put down to her insanity."

What he didn't know was that one smuggled letter had arrived at the home of a unique and influential woman named Myra Bradwell, whom Mary knew from her days in Chicago.

MYRA BRADWELL, THE WOMAN WHO TOOK ON MARY'S CASE

One June afternoon in 1875, a carriage pulled into Bellevue Place's circular drive, and out stepped Judge James Bradwell, along with his wife, Myra. They had come to visit Mrs. Lincoln.

Dr. Patterson was not pleased to see them. Both Bradwells were politically powerful. James, a former Chicago judge, now served in the Illinois General Assembly. Myra was an attorney, too, though the Illinois Supreme Court had denied her the right to practice because she was a woman. Instead, she had made it her life's work to advocate for women's rights. When she had received Mary's scribbled note, she wondered whether Mary was really crazy or just another victim of male injustice.

After this and several other lengthy visits with the former First Lady at Bellevue Place, Myra concluded, "Mrs. Lincoln is quite well, and I think not insane." She set to work to gain Mary's release.

First, Myra sent a reporter from the *Chicago Tribune* to interview Mary at the asylum. The published piece described how the reporter "had engaged Mrs. Lincoln in conversation on a wide range of topics, pleasant and painful," and had found "no abnormal manifestations of mind."

Next, Myra traveled to Springfield and persuaded Mary's sister Elizabeth Edwards to invite Mary to live with her. Myra believed she could convince Dr. Patterson to release Mary if she could "secure for her a quiet home."

Finally, Judge Bradwell played his part by threatening Robert with another court hearing that would "open the prison doors and unveil [his] treachery to the entire world."

In the face of bad publicity, Robert gave in. On September 11, Mary was released from Bellevue Place. She had been there only three months and three weeks—one of the shortest confinements in the asylum's history.

After Myra Bradwell's visit, Elizabeth Edwards decided to open her home to Mary. "If you bring her to me," she said, "I promise to do all in my power for her comfort and recovery."

Elizabeth was as good as her word. Putting Mary in the comfortable second-story bedroom (with the spare room next door reserved for her trunks), Elizabeth took her out to tea parties and card parties. "She . . . is cheerful and happy and in good health," Elizabeth reported to Robert. "She is very entertaining in conversation, enjoys the society of her friends, returns and receives calls."

Mary spent the next year in Springfield. But she was not quite as content as Elizabeth portrayed her. Because the law said a person convicted of lunacy could not have his or her property returned for a year after the conviction, Robert still controlled the purse strings. Mary could do nothing without her son's consent. She couldn't go on a trip, buy a new dress, or even subscribe to the Chicago newspapers. The situation infuriated her.

A FURIOUS LETTER TO ROBERT

On June 16, 1876—the same day the court restored her money—Mary lashed out at her son. She wrote, "You have tried your game of robbery long enough. . . . [Return] *all* my paintings . . . my silver set . . . and other articles your wife appropriated. Send my diamonds, my jewelry . . . [my] double lace shawls." In happier times, Mary had given his family these things. But now she wanted it all back. In a postscript, she remembered her engravings and favorite books—"Whittier, Pope . . . other books you have of mine." She signed the letter "Mrs. A. Lincoln."

Robert did not return the diamonds or the silver, though he did send back the books and a few other items on the advice of his attorney, Leonard Swett, who claimed "it would be impossible to return so many things from baby clothes to dress materials."

Mary, meanwhile, returned everything Robert had ever given her—a single set of Charles Dickens's works.

THIS LETTER AND TWENTY-FOUR OTHERS FROM MARY WERE RECENTLY DISCOVERED IN A STEAMER TRUNK OWNED BY THE CHILDREN OF ROBERT TODD LINCOLN'S ATTORNEY.

After her death, Robert admitted to trying to burn all Mary's letters written during and after the insanity trial, particularly those exchanged with the Bradwells. Historians believed he had succeeded. "None of Mrs. Lincoln's letters to the Bradwells remain and there is reason to believe Robert had theirs to her destroyed, so damning were they to him," wrote one historian in 1972. But in 2006, these lost letters were discovered in a dusty Maryland attic. They show Mary as calm, rational, and cogent, questioning both her son's motives and her own religious faith.

"It does not appear that God is good to have placed me here," she wrote in one letter to Myra Bradwell dated August 1875. "I endeavor to read my Bible . . . but my afflicted heart fails me and my voice often falters in prayer. I have worshipped my son and no unpleasant word ever passed between us, yet I cannot understand why I should have been brought out here." Of particular note is a letter from Elizabeth Edwards agreeing with Myra Bradwell's assessment that Mary should never have been put in Bellevue but should instead have had a "protector" and "companionship." "Had

I been consulted," Elizabeth wrote, "I would have remonstrated earnestly against the step taken."

Other letters show Mary's actions to secure her freedom, her estrangement from Robert, and her life in Europe afterward. Taken together, they write a new chapter on the insanity episode and prove that there are still undiscovered facts waiting to be learned about the Lincolns.

PAU, THE EUROPEAN TOWN THAT WAS MARY'S HOME FROM 1876 TO 1880

In the summer of 1876, while other Americans celebrated the nation's one hundredth birthday, Mary Lincoln made plans to flee the country. She no longer felt safe in the United States. That "monster of mankind son," as she called Robert, could send out his doctors, lawyers, and judges at any time. He had locked up his mother once before. What was to stop him from doing it again? Besides, she could no longer bear the stares and whispers of friends and strangers alike. People, she said, "will never cease to regard me as a lunatic. I feel it in their soothing manner. If I should say the moon is made of green cheese, they would heartily and smilingly agree with me. . . . I cannot stay. I would be much less unhappy in the midst of strangers."

Mary sailed on October 1, 1876. Her destination was Pau, a popular resort town in southwestern France. She had decided to live there because of the town's reputation as a health resort. By this time, she was riddled with ailments—arthritis, bladder problems, heart palpitations, cataracts, migraines. She hoped the fresh air and sunshine would help. For the next four years, Mary lived a bleak existence in Pau, rarely going out and inviting few friends in. Her only companion was her maid, who cleaned her rented rooms and helped her to bed at night. "I live," she wrote her grandnephew in 1877, "very much alone."

By 1880, sixty-two-year-old Mary had to come home. Weighing only a hundred pounds and racked with arthritic

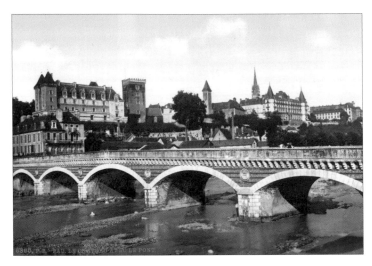

pain, she had fallen from a ladder while trying to hang a picture. Now barely able to walk, she wrote her sister, "I cannot trust myself any longer away from you all. I am too ill and feeble in health."

She arrived at New York City's docks four years, almost to the day, after she had left. Unnoticed, leaning heavily on her grandnephew's arm (he had been sent from Springfield to meet her), she tried to limp across the street. At that moment, a carriage pulled to the curb. Had people remembered Mary Lincoln after all? But no. The carriage had come to pick up the famous actress Sarah Bernhardt. Curtly, a policeman ordered Mary to stand aside until the actress had driven off.

A FORGETFUL SON?

Curiously, Robert Lincoln seemed to forget all about his mother's four-year exile in Europe. In 1914 he told a publisher:

My father's death deranged my mother so much that she became dangerous to herself. She was placed in a private asylum and after a prolonged stay there she went to my aunt's. Her health seemed to improve so much there that my aunt undertook to care for her in her house. This she did until my mother's death in 1882.

The Edwards home in Springfield, where Mary lived out the last of her days

In 1881, Mary Lincoln returned to Springfield, to her sister and brother-in-law's house on the hill and her lonely bedroom on the second floor. There she remained, with the shades always drawn because her eyes could bear only the faintest candlelight. She never went out and received few visitors. When she slept, she was careful to lie on only one side of the bed because—she said—she wanted to leave a place for her husband. Outside, neighborhood children pointed up at her window and whispered that "a crazy woman" lurked inside. Mary was waiting to die. And, she complained to a friend, "the waiting is so long."

On the afternoon of July 15, 1882 (the anniversary of Tad's death), Mary collapsed in her bedroom. The next day, July 16, she died of a stroke.

Suddenly, Mary Lincoln was somebody again. People streamed through the Edwardses' parlor to get a final glimpse of the president's wife. In her coffin—placed in the exact spot where she had taken her marriage vows forty years earlier—a faint smile touched her lips. And on her finger glowed her wedding band, so thin and worn that the words "Love is eternal" could barely be read.

Three days later, Springfield honored her in death as it had never done during her life. The mayor declared a holiday, stores were closed, and thousands of people lined the streets. Even the newspapers, which had insulted her so often in the past, printed black bands around their columns. In their obituaries, they called her "intelligent," "dignified," and "much maligned." The *New York Tribune* declared that she had never "received the credit due her for either her loyalty or her kindness of heart."

In the First Presbyterian Church, elaborate flower displays filled the apse and the transept. Among them was an immense arrangement shaped like a book "made of carnations," remembered Elizabeth, "with the words 'Mary Lincoln' emblazoned in forget-me-nots on the open pages." This display was none other than "the loving offering of the people of Springfield."

After the choir sang "Nearer, My God, to Thee," the Reverend James A. Reed eulogized Mary. He spoke of two stately pines growing so close together that their branches and roots were intertwined. When one was struck by lightning, the other wasted away. "With the one that lingered," said the minister, "it was only slow death from the same cause. . . . When Abraham Lincoln died, she died."

Then, with Robert Lincoln leading the long line of carriages (his wife and children did not attend), the procession moved slowly off to Oak Ridge Cemetery. There Mary's casket was placed in the tomb alongside those of her sons and her husband.

Time does not soften my grief, nor can I ever be reconciled to my loss until the grave closes over the remembrance and I am again with him.

—Mary Lincoln, 1882

BOOKS ABOUT THE LINCOLNS FOR YOUNG READERS

More books have been written about the Lincolns than any other Americans. Below is just a tiny sampling of the many wonderful books written specifically for young readers.

Bail, Raymond. *Where Lincoln Walked*. New York: Walker & Co., 1997.

Brenner, Martha. *Abe Lincoln's Hat*. New York: Step into Reading, Random House, 1994.

Freedman, Russell. *Lincoln: A Photobiography*. New York: Clarion Books, 1987.

Gross, Ruth Belov. *True Stories About Abraham Lincoln*. New York: Lothrop, Lee & Shepard Books, 1993.

Harness, Cheryl. *Young Abe Lincoln: The Frontier Days, 1809-1837*. Washington: National Geographic Society, 1996.

——. *Abe Lincoln Goes to Washington: 1837-1865*. Washington: National Geographic Society, 1997.

Hopkinson, Deborah. *Abe Lincoln Crosses a Creek*. New York: Schwartz & Wade Books, Random House, 2008.

Meltzer, Milton, ed. *Lincoln in His Own Words*. San Diego: Harcourt Brace, 1993.

Rinaldi, Ann. *An Unlikely Friendship: A Novel of Mary Todd Lincoln and Elizabeth Keckley*. New York: Harcourt, Inc., 2007.

LINCOLN WEB SITES

www.mrlincolnswhitehouse.org
This well-documented site, prepared by the Lincoln Institute, examines places and events that were pivotal to the Lincolns' time in Washington. It also provides detailed and fascinating biographies of the people who worked with the president.

www.mrlincolnandfriends.org
Another site prepared by the Lincoln Institute, this is devoted to chronicling the friendships Lincoln made throughout his life, and analyzing how they affected both his character and his career.

www.abrahamlincolnsclassroom.org
With quizzes and quotes of the day, as well as a cartoon corner, a map room, and links to other Lincoln sites, this is a fun-filled and informative Web site.

http://lincoln.lib.niu.edu
This site, prepared by the Abraham Lincoln Historical Digitization Project, presents historical documents from Lincoln's Illinois years (1830-1861), including his writings, his speeches, and photographs of his friends, his family, and places of interest.

www.civil-war.net
One of the largest and most comprehensive collections of Civil War-related material online, this site provides links to hundreds of other sites on related subjects, such as abolition and slavery, and to letters and diaries. More than 1,100 photographs, as well as battle reports from the official records of both the Union and Confederate armies, make this site a historical treasure trove.

A LITTLE BIT ABOUT THE RESEARCH

Any biography of the Lincolns should be founded on their own words. For Abraham, the most authoritative source is the *Collected Works of Abraham Lincoln*, eight volumes of his undisputed words and writings. Equally important are the Abraham Lincoln Papers at the Library of Congress, which include not only correspondence sent to him but also drafts and copies of his own letters and messages. Happily, these documents are now available online at http://memory.loc.gov/ammem/alhtml/malhome.html.

Even with all these sources, however, pinning down Lincoln's exact words is difficult. There have been, and continue to be, long debates over what Lincoln actually said at any given moment. Even for the Gettysburg Address, there are two slightly differing drafts, several later copies in Lincoln's hand, and varying versions reported by newspapers of the day and eyewitnesses at the event. In the numerous cases where historical sources contradict each other, I have done my best to present an accurate, if not word-perfect, version of events.

Mary's own words are more difficult to uncover. In 1932, Robert Todd Lincoln destroyed reams of his mother's papers, including most of the correspondence between her and her husband. Luckily, six hundred letters survived, and were compiled by Justin and Linda Turner in their wonderful book *Mary Todd Lincoln: Her Life and Letters*. Because of their work, I was able to follow Mary's evolution from Southern belle to bereaved widow—an intriguing portrait, painted by Mary's own pen.

Particularly helpful were the many recollections written by people who knew the Lincolns. These engaging accounts opened a window into the Lincolns' personal life and provided some of my favorite anecdotes: Tad and Willie's circus performance in the White House attic, Mary's childhood desire to help runaway slaves, Abraham's attendance at a séance. Especially useful were the reminiscences of:

Noah Brooks, a journalist and close friend of Abraham's whose books *Washington in Lincoln's Time* and *Personal Recollections of Lincoln* provided me with a candid portrait of the president's daily interactions with his friends and associates.

Elizabeth Grimsley, a cousin of Mary's who lived for a time at the White House. Her memoir *Six Months at the White House* gave me a glimpse of the First Lady before she was burdened with scandal and grief.

Elizabeth Keckly, Mary's seamstress and confidante, who

wrote a riveting and gossipy account of life at the White House called *Behind the Scenes*. Her vivid descriptions of the First Family's private thoughts and deeds truly brought the Lincolns to life.

Julia Taft Bayne, who was invited to the White House to look after her brothers, playmates of the Lincolns' sons. She eventually wrote *Tad Lincoln's Father*, a refreshing look at the Lincolns through the eyes of a sixteen-year-old.

Gideon Welles, secretary of the navy, who left behind his diaries, which provided an in-depth look at the day-to-day events of the nation.

John G. Nicolay, Lincoln's chief personal secretary, who knew the president as well as anyone outside the family. In his book *An Oral History of Abraham Lincoln*, he interviewed Lincoln's acquaintances in Springfield and Washington. The result was a work filled with little-known Lincoln details.

Assistant Secretary John Hay, whose books *Inside Lincoln's White House* and *At Lincoln's Side* provided marvelous insight into Lincoln's personality, as well as pithy, humorous observations of other important people of the day.

I relied heavily on the work of Mary's niece Katherine Helm, who gathered together the recollections of her aunt's friends and neighbors in Lexington. Published in a book called *Mary, Wife of Lincoln*, this enlightening account allowed me to understand and envision Mary's childhood.

I also relied on the work of Lincoln's law partner William Herndon. After Lincoln's death, Herndon traveled the country, interviewing anyone who had known the president. He prodded their memories, then painstakingly recorded their recollections. His work, which runs to several thousand pages, is flavorful and evocative and helped me see the Lincolns in the closest detail—including, for example, how Lincoln ate an apple, or how Mary's eyes flashed when she was angry.

A startling amount of information also came from my own travels. In the last three years I have journeyed from Fort Sumter in Charleston, South Carolina, to the Soldiers' Home in Washington, D.C. I have walked the battlefields of Gettysburg and strolled through the Todd family burial plot in Lexington, Kentucky. I've stood on the ramparts of Fort Stevens; marked the spot in Petersburg, Illinois, where Abraham completed his first surveying job; sat in the first row at Ford's Theater; fed grass to a horse at New Salem; sat on the back step of the house at Eighth and Jackson; collected rocks in Knob Creek; peered into the cabin believed to be Abraham's birthplace; walked the route from Mary's childhood home to the Lexington slave market; talked my way into an apartment building in Batavia, Illinois, that once was the insane asylum where Mary was held; and paid my respects at the Lincolns' final resting place in Oak Ridge Cemetery. Everywhere I went, I talked with archivists and curators. I uncovered new facts and discovered new truths. But best of all, as I walked in their footsteps, I felt the Lincolns begin to take shape for me. They began to form in my heart and in my mind until they were no longer merely historical figures but human beings, solid and concrete.

BACKWOODS BOY

"It is a . . .": John Scripps to William Herndon, 24 June 1865, Herndon-Weik Collection, Library of Congress.

The Wilds of Kentucky

"one could scarcely . . .": Louis A. Warren, *Lincoln's Youth* (Indianapolis: Indiana Historical Society Press, 2002), 20.

"In a few . . .": Jean H. Baker, *Mary Todd Lincoln: A Biography* (New York: W. W. Norton & Company, 1987), 5.

Thomas Lincoln

"a tinker—a piddler . . .": Nathaniel Griggs to William Herndon, 12 September 1865, Herndon-Weik Collection, Library of Congress.

"wandering, laboring boy": Abraham Lincoln, *The Collected Works of Abraham Lincoln*, ed. Roy P. Basler, 8 vols. (New Brunswick, N.J.: Rutgers University Press, 1953), 3:511.

"never did more . . .": Ibid., 4:61.

Nancy Hanks

"remarkable keen perception . . .": Eleanor Atkinson, "Dennis Hanks Interview," *American Magazine*, February 1908, 36.

"seemed enough time . . .": Ibid.

Thomas and Nancy's Marriage Document

"too shiftless, too . . .": Ibid.

"maple sugar lumps . . .": Ida Tarbell, *The Life of Abraham Lincoln*, 4 vols. (New York: Lincoln History Society, 1898), 1:10.

Cabin at Sinking Spring

"Nancy got a . . .": Atkinson, "Dennis Hanks Interview," 40.

"I cut and . . .": Ibid.

"layin' thar in . . .": Ibid.

A Sister

"crazy fer the tot": Ibid.

"little Abe": Ibid.

"he didn't feel scaired" and "Yessiree": Ibid.

A Glimpse

"Well, now, he looked . . .": Dennis Hanks to William Herndon, 13 June 1865, Herndon-Weik Collection, Library of Congress.

Cumberland Trail

"no small part . . .": F. B. Carpenter, *Six Months at the White House with Abraham Lincoln* (New York: Hurd & Houghton, 1866), 312.

A Close Call

"Abe and I . . .": David Plowden, ed., *Lincoln and His America* (New York: Viking Press, 1970), 22.

The Lincolns' Indiana Cabin

"eighteen-hundred-and-froze-to-death": Dennis Hanks to William Herndon, 13 June 1865, Herndon-Weik Collection, Library of Congress.

"When first my . . .": Lincoln, *Collected Works*, 1:386.

"From then . . .": Ibid., 4:62.

Young Scribe

"He set everybody . . .": John Locke Scripps, *The First*

Published Life of Abraham Lincoln Written in the Year MDCCCLV (Detroit: Cranbrook Press, 1900), 16.

"wrote words and . . .": Ibid.

"little Abraham was . . .": Ibid.

"It was a heady . . .": Warren, *Lincoln's Youth*, 25.

Wild Turkey

"shot through a . . .": Lincoln, *Collected Works*, 4:62.

"My early start . . .": Ibid.

Nancy Lincoln's Funeral

"I am going . . .": Warren, *Lincoln's Youth*, 54.

"She was my . . .": Joshua F. Speed, *Reminiscences of Abraham Lincoln and Notes of a Visit to California* (Louisville, Ky.: John P. Morton & Company, 1884), 19.

Consoling His Sister

"She'd get so . . .": Warren, *Lincoln's Youth*, 58.

Sarah Bush Lincoln

"Well, Miss Johnston . . .": Ward Hill Lamon, *The Life of Abraham Lincoln: From His Birth to His Inauguration as President* (Boston: J. R. Osgood, 1872), 51.

"She soaped—rubbed . . .": Dennis Hanks to William Herndon, 13 June 1865, Herndon-Weik Collection, Library of Congress.

"Cracky, but Aunt . . .": Ibid.

"I never gave . . .": Mrs. Thomas Lincoln to William Herndon, 8 September 1865, Herndon-Weik Collection, Library of Congress.

"She had been . . .": Charles H. Colman, *Abraham Lincoln and Coles County, Illinois* (New Brunswick, N.J.: Scarecrow Press, 1955), 199.

Favorite Books

"hankered after books . . .": Atkinson, "Dennis Hanks Interview," 40.

"though not as . . .": Mrs. Thomas Lincoln to William Herndon, 8 September 1865, Herndon-Weik Collection, Library of Congress.

"He kept . . . Aesop's . . .": David Turnham to William Herndon, n.d., Herndon-Weik Collection, Library of Congress.

"Abe could easily . . .": Emanuel Hertz, ed., *The Hidden Lincoln: From the Letters and Papers of William H. Herndon* (New York: Viking Press, 1928), 350.

Man's Best Friend

"My best friend . . .": Lincoln Quotes, www.literacytrust.org.uk/Database/quote.html.

Sum Book

"When he came . . .": Mrs. Thomas Lincoln to William Herndon, 8 September 1865, Herndon-Weik Collection, Library of Congress.

"Abraham Lincoln/his . . .": Facsimile of Lincoln's exercise book, n.d., Abraham Lincoln Papers, Library of Congress.

Little Pigeon Creek

"They had the . . .": Warren, *Lincoln's Youth*, 53.

"By cracky, but . . .": Dennis Hanks to William Herndon, 13 June 1865, Herndon-Weik Collection, Library of Congress.

Father and Son

"he would slash . . .": Ibid.

"farming, grubbing . . ." Alfred J. Beveridge, *Abraham Lincoln, 1809-1858,* 2 vols. (Boston: Houghton Mifflin, 1928), 1:67.

"He was lazy . . .": Dennis Hanks to William Herndon, 8 September 1865, Herndon-Weik Collection, Library of Congress.

"He was awful . . .": Elizabeth Crawford to William Herndon, 7 September 1865, Herndon-Weik Collection, Library of Congress.

"loving everyone and . . .": Ibid.

"[My father] grew up . . .": Lincoln, *Collected Works,* 4:61.

"did nothing more . . .": Ibid.

"there was absolutely . . .": Ibid., 3:511.

"cramped life": Doris Kearns Goodwin, *Team of Rivals* (New York: Simon & Schuster, 2005), 53.

"If we could . . .": Lincoln, *Collected Works,* 2:96-97.

"Unable to simulate . . .": Ibid.

First Dollar

"two men with . . .": Carpenter, *Six Months at the White House,* 97-98.

"I could scarcely . . .": Ibid.

Backwoods Comedian

"my father wants . . ." Scripps, *The First Published Life,* 20.

"Abe would take . . ." Matilda Johnston Moore to William Herndon, 8 September 1865, Herndon-Weik Collection, Library of Congress.

"He was so . . .": "Dennis Hanks to William Herndon, 13 June 1865, Herndon-Weik Collection, Library of Congress.

"it was hard . . .": Arthur and Morgan, New Lighton Lincoln's Boyhood," *Atlantic Monthly,* February 1920, 218.

"Abe was always . . .": Dennis Hanks to William Herndon, 8 September 1865, Herndon-Weik Collection, Library of Congress.

"pleased and proud . . ." Ibid.

"laughed to burst . . ." Ibid.

Thinking About God

"taken with the . . .": Warren, *Lincoln's Youth,* 116.

"recited certain Bible . . .": Ibid., 32.

"Fit and prepare . . .": Ibid.

"Abe had no . . .": Mrs. Thomas Lincoln to William Herndon, 8 September 1865, Herndon-Weik Collection, Library of Congress.

"Doctrine of Necessity": David Herbert Donald, *Lincoln* (New York: Simon & Schuster, 1995), 15.

"the human mind . . .": Ibid.

Grieving for Sarah

"I will never . . .": Warren, *Lincoln's Youth,* 173.

"From that moment . . .": J. T. Hobson, *Footprints of Abraham Lincoln* (Dayton, Ohio: Otterbein Press, 1909), 24.

"laughing, then crying . . .": Joseph C. Richardson to William Herndon, 14 September 1865, Herndon-Weik Collection, Library of Congress.

Growing Up with Slavery

"naturally anti-slavery . . .": Lincoln, *Collected Works,* 7:281.

"not only declare . . .": Donald, *Lincoln,* 31.

"unsettling and overwhelming": Lincoln, *Complete Works,* 2:320.

"Negroes in chains . . .": Tarbell, *The Life of Lincoln,* 1:57.

"satisfy themselves that . . .": Ibid.

"By God, boys . . .": Ibid.

"Against this inhumanity . . .": William H. Herndon and Jesse W. Weik, *Herndon's Lincoln: The True Story of a Great Life,* 3 vols. (Chicago: Bedford-Clarke, 1890), 1:63.

Saves His Dog

"out of obligation . . .": Donald, *Lincoln,* 36.

"painfully slow and . . .": Ibid.

"But I could not . . .": Ibid.

"His frantic leaps . . .": Ibid.

Good-by to Ma and Pa

"Saying good-by . . .": Carl Sandburg, *Lincoln: The Prairie Years* (New York: Harcourt, Brace and Company, 1926), 59.

New Salem

"I was a . . ." Herndon, *Herndon's Lincoln,* 1:79.

"He had his . . .": Earl Schenk Miers, ed., *Lincoln Day by Day,* 3 vols. (Washington, D.C.: Lincoln Sesquicentennial Commission, 1960), 1:14.

Announces Candidacy

"When he talked. . . .": Robert L. Wilson to William Herndon, 29 May 1865, Herndon-Weik Collection, Library of Congress.

"Lincoln had nothing . . ." Donald, *Lincoln,* 42.

"I was born . . .": Lincoln, *Collected Works,* 1:5.

Discharge Paper

"Halt! This company will . . .": Stefan Lorant, *Lincoln: A Picture Story of His Life* (New York: Harper & Brothers, 1952), 29.

"had a good . . .": Lincoln, *Collected Works,* 1:510.

Berry-Lincoln Store

"[me] to speak . . ." Ibid., 4:62.

"winked out": Ibid., 4:65.

"the national debt": Ibid., 4:64.

Postmaster Letter

"I never saw . . .": Donald, *Lincoln,* 50.

Struggling

"went at it": Lincoln, *Collected Works,* 4:65.

"foxed" and "protect his more . . .": Ibid., 4:66.

"When any dispute . . .": Robert L. Wilson to William Herndon, 28 May 1865, Herdon-Weik Collection, Library of Congress.

First Love

"was a beautiful . . .": Tarbell, *Life of Lincoln,* 1:116.

"slept not . . .": James G. Randall, *Lincoln the President,* 4 vols., (New York: Dodd, Mead & Co., 1945-1955), 2:322.

"that he could . . .": Mrs. E. Abell to William Herndon, 15 February 1867, Herndon-Weik Collection, Library of Congress.

Mary Owens

"was tall, portly . . .": Oliver R. Carruthers and R. Gerald McMurtry, *Lincoln's Other Mary* (Chicago: Ziff Davis Publishing, 1946), i.

"If ever that . . .": Beveridge, *Abraham Lincoln,* 1:155.

"I suppose you . . .": Hertz, *Hidden Lincoln,* 46.

"You're plenty smart . . .": Ibid.

"Mr. Lincoln was . . .": Herndon, *Herndon's Lincoln,* 1:148.

"Now when I . . .": Lincoln, *Collected Works,* 1:117-18.

"I had told . . .": Ibid.

"dry and stupid": Ibid., 1:55.

"I now say . . .": Ibid., 1: 118-19.

"My vanity was . . .": Ibid.

"never again think . . .": Ibid.

Pay Stub

"Boys, if that . . .": J. R. Herndon to William Herndon, 28 May 1865, Herdon-Weik Collection, Library of Congress.

"by the highest . . .": Lorant, *Lincoln,* 35.

New Evidence

"Lincoln invested in . . .": Ann Gorman, "Digging into Abe's Past: Archeologists Look for artifacts at New Salem," *The State Journal Register* (Springfield, Ill.), April 30, 2006.

"We will have . . .": Ibid.

Lawyer Lincoln

"bloviate and bluster": Herndon, *Herndon's Lincoln,* 1:142.

"borrowed books from . . .": Lincoln, *Collected Works,* 4:65.

New Hometown, Springfield

"It is all prairie . . .": Paul Angle, *Here I Have Lived: A History of Lincoln's Springfield* (1935; rpt., Chicago: Abraham Lincoln Bookshop, 1971), 86.

Joshua Speed

"I never saw . . .": Tarbell, *Life of Lincoln,* 1:148.

"It is probably . . .": Ibid.

"Everlasting friends": Ibid.

BLUEGRASS GIRL

"My whole childhood . . .": Mary Lincoln to Eliza Stuart Steele, 23 May 1871, in Justin G. Turner and Linda Levitt Turner, eds., *Mary Todd Lincoln: Her Life and Letters* (New York: Fromm International Publishing Corporation, 1987), 588.

Parade Through Lexington

"I cannot educate . . .": Baker, *Mary Todd Lincoln,* 55.

"Athens of the west": Ibid.

What Did Mrs. Todd Do?

"read a few romances . . .": William Levy, "A Memoir of Lexington and Its Vicinity," *Register of Kentucky Historical Society,* July 1942, 257.

A Glimpse

"Mary in those . . .": Katherine Helm, *Mary, Wife of Lincoln* (New York: Harper & Brothers, 1928), 19.

Doll

"squeaked entrancingly . . .": Ibid., 30.

"lovely, sheer, embroidered . . .": Ibid.

"I made [the doll] . . .": Ibid.

"[Mary] used her . . .": Ibid.

Indian Attacks

"but this seemed . . .": Ibid., 33.

"Hide me, oh . . .": Ibid.

Eliza Todd's Funeral
"his residence on . . .": Duff's Funeral Notices Scrapbook
    1806-1911, Kentucky Room, Lexington Public Library.
"resurrection in heaven . . .": Baker, *Mary Todd Lincoln*, 23.

Elizabeth Humphreys Todd
"It takes seven . . .": Ibid., 29.
"bundle of nervous . . .": Helm, *Mary, Wife of Lincoln*, 17.
"an April day . . .": Ibid., 32.
"willful and original . . .": Ibid., 17.
"a limb of Satan": Ibid., 47.
"abandoned, unloved and . . .": Ibid.

Godey's Lady's Book
"became fascinated by . . .": Ibid., 26.
"What a fright . . .": Ibid., 28.
"She thought she . . .": Ibid., 29.
"a standing joke . . .": Ibid., 30.

Stepgrandmother Humphreys
"If I can only be . . .": Ibid., 34-35.

Crab Orchard Springs
"How exciting we . . .": Ibid., 54.

The Book That Changed Mary's Future
"a substantial rather . . .": Baker, *Mary Todd Lincoln*, 36.
"If you do not . . .": Ibid.

Mary's First School
"complete system . . .": Ibid., 38.
"her book with . . .": Ibid., 37.
"pored over her . . .": Helm, *Mary, Wife of Lincoln*, 20.
"far in advance . . .": Ibid., 21.

A Continuing Education
"At different times . . .": Ibid., 53.
"forever reciting" and "This was the cause . . .": Ibid., 32.
"Mary Todd was . . .": Ibid., 53.
"cotillions, rounds, and . . .": Jennifer Fleischner, *Mrs. Lincoln
    and Mrs. Keckly* (New York: Broadway Books, 2003), 62.
"my early home . . .": Mary Lincoln to Elizabeth Keckly, 29
    October 1867, in Turner and Turner, eds., *Letters*, 447.

Charlotte Mentelle
"has no amiable . . .": Baker, *Mary Todd Lincoln*, 42.
"morals, temper and . . .": Ibid.

Henry Clay
"I can't help . . .": Helm, *Mary, Wife of Lincoln*, 2-3.
"mistress of the . . .": Ibid., 5.

Andrew Jackson
"ordinary as the . . .": Ibid., 41.
"I wouldn't think . . .": Ibid., 43.

Thinking About God
"we will be . . .": Baker, *Mary Todd Lincoln*, 23.
"What is to be . . .": Helm, *Mary, Wife of Lincoln*, 111.
"always with me": Baker, *Mary Todd Lincoln*, 220.

Growing Up with Slavery
"a jewel of . . .": Helm, *Mary, Wife of Lincoln*, 23.
"white folks' church": Ibid.
"ole satan" and "just like an old male cow": Ibid., 24.
"Am I a fox?": "Mary Todd Lincoln—A Profile," pamphlet
    about temporary exhibit at Mary Todd Lincoln House,
    Lexington, Ky.

"You a smart . . .": Ibid.
"How could we do . . .": Ibid., 39.
"That might be . . .": Ibid., 24-25.
"a monstrous wrong": Ruth Painter Randall, *Mary Lincoln:
    Biography of a Marriage* (Boston: Little, Brown & Company,
    1953), 323.

Cholera
"They would not . . .": Helm, *Mary, Wife of Lincoln*, 49-50.

Lexington Cotillion
"clear blue eyes . . .": Ibid., 62.
"her figure was . . .": Baker, *Mary Todd Lincoln*, 51.
"too sharply, and . . .": Helm, *Mary, Wife of Lincoln*, 63.
"She won the debate . . .": Ibid.
"when friends were . . .": Baker, *Mary Todd Lincoln*, 52.

No Beau
"hypocritical": Ibid., 82.
"frivolous in their . . .": Ibid.
"uninteresting" and "hard bargains": Ibid.
"Among [those] who . . .": Helm, *Mary, Wife of Lincoln*, 55.
"His manners were . . .": Ibid., 55-56.
"That limb of . . .": "Mary Todd Lincoln—A Profile," pamphlet
    about temporary exhibit at Mary Todd Lincoln House,
    Lexington, Ky.

Springfield Family
"relentless persecution": Baker, *Mary Todd Lincoln*, 75.
"quality hill": Fleischner, *Mrs. Lincoln and Mrs. Keckly*, 92.
"Anyone with ambitions . . .": Angle, *Here I Have Lived*, 83.
"the happiest of . . .": Baker, *Mary Todd Lincoln*, 10.

THE HAPPIEST STAGES OF LIFE

"Nothing new here . . .": Goodwin, *Team of Rivals*, 101.
"I believe a . . .": Mary Lincoln to Mary Harlan Lincoln, 22
    March 1869, in Turner and Turner, eds., *Letters*, 504.

Abraham When Mary Met Him
"This thing of . . .": Lincoln, *Collected Works*, 4:78.
"because I should . . .": Ibid.
"Oh boys, how . . .": Baker, *Mary Todd Lincoln*, 89.
"utterly classless": Donald, *Lincoln*, 84.

Mary When She Met Abraham
"the Coterie" and "the Edwards clique": Turner, *Letters*, 10.
"Mary could make . . .": Baker, *Mary Todd Lincoln*, 79.

Cotillion Invitation
"the plainest man . . .": Ibid., 83.
"Miss Todd, I want . . .": Helm, *Mary, Wife of Lincoln*, 74.

Why Mary?
"the most congenial . . .": Mrs. Ninian Edwards to William
    Herndon, 10 January 1866, Herndon-Weik Collection,
    Library of Congress.
"Mary led the . . .": Ibid.

Why Abraham?
"almost immediately intrigued . . .": Helm, *Mary, Wife of
    Lincoln*, 72.
"such a rough . . .": Ibid., 81.
"Imagine what joy . . .": Ibid., 81-82.
"lover's eyes": Baker, *Mary Todd Lincoln*, 85.

Why Not Abraham?

"Unsuitable. Opposite in . . .": Randall, *Mary Lincoln*, 41.

"I am opposed . . .": Ibid.

"His future is . . .": Ibid.

The Fatal First

"panic-stricken": Helm, *Mary, Wife of Lincoln*, 87.

"Don't write, that . . .": Joshua F. Speed to William Herndon, n.d., Herndon-Weik Collection, Library of Congress.

"he loved Mary . . .": Randall, *Mary Lincoln*, 47.

"the 'Fatal First'": Baker, *Mary Todd Lincoln*, 90.

"felt as always": Mrs. Ninian Edwards to William Herndon, 10 January 1866, Herndon-Weik Collection, Library of Congress.

"crazy as a loon": Randall, *Mary Lincoln*, 35.

Suicide Poem

"I am the . . .": Lincoln, *Collected Works*, 1:228.

"reduced and emaciated . . .": Baker, *Mary Todd Lincoln*, 91.

"to remove razors . . .": Joshua F. Speed to William Herndon, n.d., Herdon-Wcik Collection, Library of Congress.

"Yes! I've resolved . . .": Abraham Lincoln, "The Suicide's Soliloquy," *Sangamo Journal*, 25 August 1841, 6.

Brokenhearted Mary

"[Abraham] deems me . . .": Mary Lincoln to Mercy Ann Levering, June 1841, in Turner and Turner, eds., *Letters*, 25.

"I was much . . .": Baker, *Mary Todd Lincoln*, 92.

Matchmaking

"Be friends again": Herndon, *Herndon's Lincoln*, 2:227.

Marriage Certificate

"looked and acted . . .": James Matheny to William Herndon, 3 May 1866, Herndon-Weik Collection, Library of Congress.

"To hell, I suppose": Herndon, *Herndon's Lincoln*, 2:229.

"for better for . . .": Randall, *Mary Lincoln*, 65.

"Love is eternal": Turner and Turner, eds., *Letters*, 30.

Globe Tavern

"she lived quietly . . .": Helm, *Mary, Wife of Abraham*, 96.

Lexington Observer & Reporter

"A.L.": William H. Townsend, *Lincoln and the Bluegrass: Slavery and Civil War in Kentucky* (Lexington: University Press of Kentucky, 1955), 82.

Happy Birthday

"I am so . . .": Randall, *Mary Lincoln*, 68.

Robert Todd Lincoln

"precious son": Randall, *Mary Lincoln*, 70.

"my darling husband . . .": Baker, *Mary Todd Lincoln*, 102.

"He has a . . .": Ruth Painter Randall, *Lincoln's Sons* (Boston: Little, Brown & Company, 1955), 12.

"Bobbie's lost . . .": Ibid., 13.

"learned his sums . . .": Ibid.

"He is quite . . .": Ibid., 12.

"cockeye": Ibid., 26.

"uncomfortable reserve and . . .": Ibid.

"act a bit . . .": Ibid., 21.

New Home

"Our furnishings remain . . .": Wayne Temple, *By Square and Compasses: The Building of Lincoln's Home and Its Saga* (Bloomington, Ill.: Ashalar Press, 1984), 52.

New Business

"Billy, do you . . .": Donald, *Lincoln*, 100.

"a laborious, studious . . .": Ibid., 101.

"Billy" and "Mr. Lincoln": Ibid.

Lincoln & Herndon Law Office

"a somewhat dilapidated . . .": Paul Angle, *Where Lincoln Practiced Law* (Springfield, Ill.: Lincoln Centennial Association, 1927), 32.

"If you can't . . .": Ibid.

"his desk and . . .": John Duff, *A. Lincoln: Prairie Lawyer* (New York: Rinehart & Co., 1960), 117.

"lost or destroyed . . .": Angle, *Where Lincoln Practiced Law*, 32.

"The Widow Reed . . .": Duff, *Lincoln: Prairie Lawyer*, 213. *Lincoln Legal Papers* (Springfield: Illinois Historic Preservation Agency, 2001), 2.

Eighth Circuit

"Indeed, he was . . .": Lorant, *Lincoln*, 65.

Hardships on the Circuit

"with 20 men . . .": Duff, *Prairie Lawyer*, 198.

"in a homemade . . .": Lorant, *Lincoln*, 65.

"halfway between his . . .": Ibid.

"he was the . . .": Ibid.

"pretty tough coffee": Duff, *Prairie Lawyer*, 198.

Court Days

"assault and battery . . ." Donald, *Lincoln*, 105.

"he took pains . . .": Lorant, *Lincoln*, 66.

Murder!

"slung shot": Duff, *Prairie Lawyer*, 354.

"in the bright . . .": Ibid.

"Now I will . . .": Ibid.

"took the jury . . .": Ibid., 359.

"Gentlemen, I appear . . .": Ibid.

Rules for Being a Good Lawyer

"Persuade your neighbors . . .": Lincoln, *Collected Works*, 10:20.

Hardworking Woman

"Illinois is Heaven . . .": Randall, *Mary Lincoln*, 76.

The Light of the Home

"The perfection of . . .": *Godey's Lady's Book*, July 1860, 71.

"angelic countenance": Ibid.

"Your error lies . . .": Ibid., December 1841, 16.

"I feel exhausted . . ." Turner and Turner, eds., *Letters*, 60.

Mary in the Kitchen

"waffles, batter cakes . . .": Mary Lincoln to Edward Lewis Baker Jr., 4 October 1879, in Turner and Turner, eds., *Letters*, 690.

All Alone

"If my husband . . .": Baker, *Mary Todd Lincoln*, 108.

Ladies Guide

"When it comes . . .": Ellen Hatch to O. M. Hatch, 6 February 1860, Hatch Papers, Abraham Lincoln Presidential Library and Museum, Springfield, Ill.

"boil the roots . . .": Baker, *Mary Todd Lincoln*, 115.

"unspeakably dull and . . .": Randall, *Mary Lincoln*, 84.

Patterns Like These from *Godey's*

"a white fur . . .": Mary Lincoln to Elizabeth Dale Black, 17 September 1853, in Turner and Turners, eds., *Letters*, 42.

"could not endure . . ."; Randall, *Mary Lincoln*, 82.

"calico . . . cross barred . . .": Ibid.

"white silk with . . .": Helm, *Mary, Wife of Lincoln*, 109.

"fine feathers enough . . .": Ibid.

Ambitious Abraham

"His ambition was . . .": Randall, *Mary Lincoln*, 86.

"to nothing beyond . . .": Lincoln, *Collected Works*, 1:114.

"How hard, oh . . .": Donald, *Lincoln*, 163.

Ambitious Mary

"very ambitious": Randall, *Mary Lincoln*, 65.

"My husband is . . .": *The American Experience: Abraham and Mary Lincoln: A House Divided*, PBS DVD Gold, 2001.

"But nobody knows . . .": Miers, *Lincoln Day by Day*, 172.

"Such a sucker . . .": Ibid.

"[Mary] is my . . .": Baker, *Mary Todd Lincoln*, 148.

What Is a Whig?

"I am always . . .": Lincoln, *Collected Works*, 3:512.

Guess Who Wants

"That assemblage offers . . .": Lorant, *Lincoln*, 53.

"Why shouldn't I . . .": Ibid.

"Now if you . . .": Lincoln, *Collected Works*, 1:306-7.

A New Baby

"He is very . . .": Randall, *Mary Lincoln*, 86.

The Campaign Must Go On

"All who desire . . .": Lorant, *Lincoln*, 53.

Funding a Campaign

"I made the . . .": Henry E. Pratt, *The Personal Finances of Abraham Lincoln* (Springfield, Ill.: Abraham Lincoln Association, 1943), 24.

Shocking!

"Mrs. L., I am told . . .": David Davis to Sarah Walker Davis, 8 August 1847, David Davis Papers, Abraham Lincoln Presidential Library and Museum, Springfield, Ill.

"She wishes to . . .": Ibid.

"Will you be a . . .": Abraham Lincoln to Mary Lincoln, May 1848, in Turner and Turner, eds., *Letters*, 38.

Family Vacation

"To my mind . . .": Helm, *Mary, Wife of Lincoln*, 100.

"I remember thinking . . .": Ibid.

"So this is . . .": Ibid.

"Aunt Betsey, I was . . .": Ibid., 101.

"we hated to . . .": Ibid.

Washington, D.C., the Year the Lincolns Arrived

"with a bed . . .": Randall, *Mary Lincoln*, 95.

"graham bread, apples . . .": Ibid., 96.

"very retiring": Ibid.

Not All It's Cracked Up to Be

"going out and . . .": Miers, *Lincoln Day by Day*, 219.

Absence Makes the Heart Grow Fonder

"What did Bobby . . ." Abraham Lincoln to Mary Lincoln, May 1848, in Turner and Turner, eds., *Letters*, 38.

"Do not fear . . .": Mary Lincoln to Abraham Lincoln, May 1848, in Turner and Turner, eds., *Letters*, 37.

"I want to see . . .": Randall, *Mary Lincoln*, 97.

"I feel very . . .": Mary Lincoln to Abraham Lincoln, May 1848, in Turner and Turner, eds., *Letters*, 37.

"In this troublesome . . ." Turner and Turner, eds., *Letters*, 36, n.d.

"How much I . . .": Mary Lincoln to Abraham Lincoln, May 1848, in Turner and Turner, eds., *Letters*, 37.

Spot Resolutions

"the blood of . . .": James D. Richardson, ed., *A Compilation of Messages and Papers of the President*, 4 vols. (Washington, D.C.: Government Printing Office, 1897), 4:534.

"whether the particular . . .": Lincoln, *Collected Works*, 1:421-22.

"treasonable assault . . .": Donald, *Lincoln*, 131.

"Out, damned spot" and "Old Spotty": Ibid.

"allow the president . . .": Ibid.

Abraham's Patent

"whittled away on . . .": Tarbell, *Life of Lincoln*, 2:21.

Licking Political Wounds

"If you collect . . .": Lincoln, *Collected Works*, 2:19.

Sad News

"no time, nor room . . .": Baker, *Mary Todd Lincoln*, 125.

Eddie's Death

"Eat, Mary, for . . .": Octavia Roberts, *Lincoln in Illinois* (Boston: Houghton Mifflin, 1918), 65.

"Angel boy . . .": "Mary Lincoln," *Illinois Journal*, February 1850, 5.

"We miss him . . .": Lincoln, *Collected Works*, 2:77.

TUMULTUOUS TIMES

"As a nation . . .": Donald, *Lincoln*, 189.

"You must not . . .": Mary Lincoln to Emilie Todd, 23 November 1856, in Turner and Turner eds., *Letters*, 46.

The Compromise of 1850

"this glorious day . . .": Mary Beth Norton, ed., *A People and a Nation* (Boston: Houghton Mifflin Company, 1982), 343.

"settled forever": Donald, *Lincoln*, 167.

Fugitive Slave Act

"barbaric practice": Lincoln, *Collected Works*, 2:266.

"you're too rampant . . .": Donald, *Lincoln*, 167.

Uncle Tom's Cabin

"the little lady . . .": Lincoln, *Collected Works*, 2:282.

Willie Lincoln

"a very beautiful . . .": Randall, *Lincoln's Sons*, 7.

"I know every . . .": Donald, *Lincoln*, 159.

"formed a special . . .": Randall, *Lincoln's Sons*, 7.

"comfort" and "Mother's boy": Ibid.

"chuckling with the . . .": Ibid., 32.

"This town is . . .": Ibid., 43.

"everything changed": Ibid., 57.

Peeking into a Marriage

"merry hell": Fleischman, *Mrs. Lincoln and Mrs. Keckly*, 153.

"he'd trot the . . .": Ibid.

"Mr. Lincoln may . . .": Herndon, *Herndon's Lincoln*, 2:296.

"Molly" and "Mother": Turner and Turner, eds., *Letters*, 39.

"My child wife": Ibid.

"but he only . . .": Helm, *Mary, Wife of Lincoln*, 106.

Thomas Lincoln

"completely engaging with . . .": Randall, *Lincoln's Sons*, 44.

"like a small thunderbolt": Ibid.

"I love you . . .": Ibid.

"Hurrah for Old Abe!": Ibid., 60.

"thought it adorable . . .": Ibid.

Good Neighbors

"The tall, gaunt . . .": Randall, *Mary Lincoln*, 132.

Pa

"Mr. Lincoln was . . .": Randall, *Lincoln's Sons*, 29.

"the dear codgers": Ibid., 10.

"little devils": William Herndon to Jesse Weik, 6 January 1866, Herndon-Weik Collection, Library of Congress.

"Those children would . . .": William Herndon to Jesse Weik, 19 November 1885, Herndon-Weik Collection, Library of Congress.

"We never controlled . . .": Baker, *Mary Todd Lincoln*, 120.

Ma

"darling sons [who were] . . .": Randall, *Mary Lincoln*, 87.

"the Lincoln brats": Baker, *Mary Todd Lincoln*, 120.

"What those children . . .": William Herndon to Jesse Weik, 16 January 1866, Herndon-Weik Collection, Library of Congress.

"looked pleased as . . .": Ibid.

"[My sons] never . . .": Mary Lincoln to Alexander Williamson, 15 June 1865, in Turner and Turner, eds., *Letters*, 251.

"It was Mrs. Lincoln's . . .": William Herndon to Jesse Weik, 16 January 1866, Herndon-Weik Collection, Library of Congress.

"in being too . . .": Mary Lincoln to Alexander Williamson, 15 June 1865, in Turner and Turner, eds., *Letters*, 251.

"children's gala for . . .": Helm, *Mary, Wife of Lincoln*, 108.

"I feel it . . .": Fleischner, *Mrs. Lincoln and Mrs. Keckly*, 159.

"Take that!" and "*En garde* . . .": Randall, *Lincoln's Sons*, 34.

"Gramercy, brave knights . . .": Baker, *Mary Todd Lincoln*, 121.

"she went to . . .": Fleischner, *Mrs. Lincoln and Mrs. Keckly*, 159.

"as usual, screaming . . .": Ibid.

"a happy, loving . . .": Mary Lincoln to Emilie Todd Helm, 20 September 1857, in Turner and Turner, eds., *Letters*, 50.

Kansas-Nebraska Act

"thunderstuck and stunned": Lincoln, *Collected Works*, 2:282.

"natural death": Ibid.

"as I had never . . .": Ibid.

"monstrous injustice" and "cancer": Ibid.

"in a nation . . .": Ibid.

"if all earthly . . .": Ibid., 2:255.

Lincoln Wins . . .

"[We were] down on . . ." William Jayne to William Herndon, 15 August 1886, Herndon-Weik Collection, Library of Congress.

"the best Christmas . . .": Donald, *Lincoln*, 180.

. . . Then Loses

"It was hard . . .": Lincoln, *Collected Works*, 2:307.

"cold, selfish treachery": Mary Lincoln to Hannah Shearer, 26 June 1859, in Turner and Turner, eds., *Letters*, 56-57.

"pretended not to . . .": Julia Trumbull to Lyman Trumbull, 14 April 1856, Trumbull Papers, Library of Congress.

The Crisis Grows . . .

"Physical rebellions and . . .": Donald, *Lincoln*, 188.

"more effective channels": David Herbert Donald, *Lincoln's Herndon* (New York: Alfred A. Knopf, 1948), 81.

Preston Brooks Attacking Senator Charles Sumner

"it symbolized the . . .": David M. Potter, *The Impending Crisis, 1848-1861* (New York: Harper Perennial, 1977), 168.

. . . And the Lincoln Home Grows

"Stranger, do you . . .": James Ghourley to William Herndon, n.d., Lamon Manuscripts, Huntington Library, San Marino, Calif.

"The air of . . .": Donald, *Lincoln*, 198.

Fido

"wanted a dog-cat-rat . . .": Randall, *Lincoln's Sons*, 35.

"hobby": Ibid.

Look Who's a Republican

"I have been . . .": Lincoln, *Collected Works*, 2:126.

Mary, Political Consultant

"special intuition in . . .": Baker, *Mary Todd Lincoln*, 134.

"full-fledged, home based . . .": Ibid.

"Mary, now listen . . .": Mrs. B. S. Edwards interview with Ida Tarbell, n.d., Tarbell Collection, Sophia Smith Collection, Smith College, Northampton, Mass.

"Saying so-and-so . . .": Ibid.

"usurper" and "meddling hag": Baker, *Mary Todd Lincoln*, 135.

"a domestic woman . . ." Ibid.

Lincoln's First Great Republican Speech

"buckling on the . . .": Lincoln, *Collected Works*, 2:333.

"as though transfixed . . .": Herndon, *Herndon's Lincoln*, 2:384.

"ready to fuse . . .": Lincoln, *Collected Works*, 2:341.

"Liberty and Union . . .": Ibid.

"full of fire . . .": Herndon, *Herndon's Lincoln*, 2:384.

"If Mr. Lincoln . . .": Ibid.

Short History of Secession

"as people": Eric Foner and John A. Garraty, eds., *The Reader's Companion to American History* (Boston: Houghton Mifflin, 1991), 972.

"disunion": Ibid.

Supreme Court and Dred Scott

"were not intended . . .": Mary Beth Norton, ed., *A People and a Nation: A History of the United States* (Boston: Houghton Mifflin, 1982), 292.

"We are now . . .": Don E. Fehrenbacher, *The Dred Scott Case: Its Significance in American Law and Politics* (New York: Oxford University Press, 1978), 177.

"Where will it . . .": Ibid.

Lincoln on Dred Scott

"universal and eternal . . .": Lincoln, *Collected Works*, 2:404.

"House Divided" Speech

"were too much . . .": John Armstrong to William Herndon, n.d., Herndon-Weik Collection, Library of Congress.

"It is true . . .": Herndon, *Herndon's Lincoln*, 2:398.

"It will make . . .": Arthur C. Cole, *Lincoln's House Divided Speech* (Chicago: Chicago Historical Society, 1923), 14.

"a house divided . . .": Lincoln, *Collected Works*, 461-62.

"a pledge to . . ." Cole, *Lincoln's House Divided Speech*, 18.

"If I had . . .": Lincoln, *Collected Works*, 2:464.

A Brilliant Politician

"Mr. Lincoln manifested . . .": Robert L. Wilson to William Herndon, 10 February 1866, Herndon-Weik Collection, Library of Congress.

A Political Wife

"business or politics": Turner and Turner, eds., *Letters*, 135.

And the Candidates Are . . .

"broad shoulders, a large . . .": Lincoln, *Collected Works*, 2:506.

"wiry, jet-black . . .": Lloyd Ostendorf, *Lincoln's Photographs* (Dayton, Ohio: Rockywood Press, 1998), 23.

"clad in a . . .": Donald, *Lincoln*, 215.

The Great Debates

"best show going . . .": Edwin Earle Sparks, *Lincoln-Douglas Debates* (Springfield: Trustees of the Illinois State Historical Library, 1908), 75.

"fizzle-gigs and fireworks": Randall, *Mary Lincoln*, 153.

"vote, and eat . . .": Ibid.

"If you think . . .": Kenneth Davis, *Don't Know Much About the Civil War* (New York: William Morrow, 1992), 128-29.

"Mr. Douglas seems . . .": Ibid., 129.

"the real issue . . .": Abraham Lincoln, *The Lincoln-Douglas Debates of 1858,* ed. Robert W. Johannson (New York: Oxford University Press, 1965), 319.

"the most interesting . . .": Thomas Reilly, "Lincoln-Douglas Debates of 1858 Forced New Role on the Press," *Journalism Quarterly*, winter 1979, 734.

Mary's Scrapbooks on the Debates

"Belle of Washington": Baker, *Mary Todd Lincoln*, 155.

"a very little giant": Helm, *Mary, Wife of Lincoln*, 140.

Election Results

"I feel like . . .": Lorant, *Lincoln*, 77.

"One feels better . . .": Randall, *Mary Lincoln*, 155.

Biographical Sketch

"people want to . . .": Osborn Hamiline Oldroyd, *The Lincoln Memorial: Album–Immortelles* (Boston: D. L. Guernsey, 1882), 474.

"Herewith is . . .": Lincoln, *Collected Works*, 3:511-12.

Cooper Union Speech

"weird, rough and . . .": Donald, *Lincoln*, 238.

"the long, ungainly . . .": Ibid.

"Let us have . . .": Lincoln, *Collected Works*, 3:550.

"went off passably well": Abraham Lincoln to Mary Lincoln, 4 March 1860, in Lincoln, *Collected Works*, 3:555.

"It was the . . .": Hiram Barney to Abraham Lincoln, 28 February 1860, Abraham Lincoln Papers, Library of Congress.

Side Trip

"man of the people": Goodwin, *Team of Rivals*, 266.

"Robert, you ought . . .": John S. Goff, *Robert Todd Lincoln: A Man in His Own Right* (Norman: University of Oklahoma Press, 1969), 32.

"Isn't it too . . .": Donald, *Lincoln*, 240.

"got hold of . . .": Marshall S. Snow, "Abraham Lincoln: A Personal Reminiscence," *Magazine of History*, February 1910, 65.

"my father centered . . .": Randall, *Lincoln's Sons*, 53.

"closest father and . . .": Ibid.

***Harper's* Sketch of Men Most Likely**

"What is the . . .": Helm, Mary, *Wife of Lincoln*, 144.

"The taste is . . .": Lincoln, *Collected Works*, 4:45.

Lincoln for President!

"new in the field": Ibid., 4:34.

"not the first . . .": Ibid.

"Stop Seward": Goodwin, *Team of Rivals*, 244.

"There was a . . .": Ibid., 249.

"I arise, Mr. Chairman . . .": Murat Halstead, *Three Against Lincoln: Murat Halstead Reports the Caucuses of 1860,* ed. William B. Hesseltine (Baton Rouge: Louisiana State University Press, 1960), 170.

"rose to their . . .": Goodwin, *Team of Rivals*, 249.

"between 20,000 . . .": Ibid.

"Lincoln for president!": Halstead, *Three Against Lincoln*, 210.

Springfield Celebrates

"Abe, we did . . .": Lorant, *Lincoln*, 93.

"Gentlemen, there is . . .": Charles Zane, "Lincoln as I Knew Him," *Sunset Magazine*, October 1912, 438.

"It is all . . .": Mary Lincoln to Hannah Shearer, 20 October 1860, in Turner and Turner, eds., *Letters*, 66.

Candidate Receives Well-Wishers

"shut up in Springfield": Baker, *Mary Todd Lincoln*, 159.

The Four Presidential Candidates

"I trust I have . . .": Jeffrey A. Jenkins, *Running to Lose: John C. Breckinridge and the Presidential Election of 1860* (College Park, Md.: Department of Government and Politics, University of Maryland, 2006), 4.

"is it 'Abraham' . . .": Donald, *Lincoln*, 253.

"Imagine a veritable . . .": Editorial in the *New Orleans Crescent*, November 13, 1860, 5.

"Do Nothing" and "Old Man's": Davis, *Don't Know Much*, 138.

Mary Lincoln: Celebrity

"amicable and accomplished . . .": "A Report from Springfield," *New York Times*, May 25, 1860.

"kitchen cabinet": Walter B. Stevens, *A Reporter's Lincoln* (Lincoln: University of Nebraska Press, 1998), 49.

Why a Beard?

"You would look . . .": Lincoln, *Collected Works*, 4:129-30.

"Do you not . . .": Ibid.

"Old Abe is . . .": Ostendorf, *Lincoln's Photographs*, 67.

Newspaper Headlines Proclaim the News

"You used to . . .": Mary Lincoln to Hannah Shearer, 20 October 1860, in Turner and Turner, eds., *Letters*, 66.

"It is well . . .": Helm, *Mary, Wife of Lincoln,* 152.

"Mary! Mary! We . . .": Stevens, *A Reporter's Lincoln,* 46.

Charleston Mercury Announces

"Let the consequences . . .": Russell Freedman, *Lincoln: A Photobiography* (New York: Clarion, 1987), 65.

A Commitment

"practically pulled his . . .": Herndon, *Herndon's Lincoln,* 2:241.

"I will suffer . . .": Lincoln, *Collected Works,* 4:146.

"The concept of . . .": Donald, *Lincoln,* 269.

"He was a . . .": William Herndon, "Mrs. Lincoln's Denial, and What She Says," broadside dated January 12, 1874, Massachusetts Historical Society, Boston.

Mary Goes Shopping

"delighted" and "excellent spirits": Randall, *Mary Lincoln,* 191.

Farewell to Springfield

"My friends—No one . . .": Lincoln, *Collected Works,* 4:190.

AND THE WAR CAME

"In your hands . . .": Draft copy of inaugural address, February 1861, Abraham Lincoln Papers, Library of Congress.

"Washington is perfectly . . .": Mary Lincoln to Hannah Shearer, 28 March 1861, in Turner and Turner, eds., *Letters,* 81.

Presidential Train Trip

"I have always . . .": Ibid., 4:218.

"Where's the Missus . . .": Randall, *Mary Lincoln,* 180.

"an awful and . . .": Ibid.

Baltimore Cartoon

"an invalid passenger": Norma B. Cuthbert, ed., *Lincoln and the Baltimore Plot* (San Marino, Calif.: Huntington Library, 1949), xvi.

"PLUMS ARRIVED HERE . . .": Ibid.

"the flight of Abraham": George Temple Strong, *The Diary of George Temple Strong: The Civil War, 1860-1865,* ed. Allan Nevins and Milton Halsey Thomas (New York: Macmillan Co., 1952), 102.

"nocturnal dodging and . . .": Ibid.

"I did not . . .": Cuthbert, *Lincoln and the Baltimore Plot,* xvi.

"damned cowardly"; William Herndon to Norman B. Judd, 1866, Herndon-Weik Collection, Library of Congress.

President of the Confederate States

"I am sure . . .": Haskell M. Monroe Jr. and James T. McIntosh, eds., *The Papers of Jefferson Davis,* 10 vols. (Baton Rouge: Louisiana State University Press, 1971), 7:22.

"inferior, fitted expressly . . .": Ibid., 6:331.

"Upon my weary . . .": Ibid., 7:27.

Washington in 1861

"To make a . . .": Baker, *Mary Todd Lincoln,* 177.

Inauguration Day

"Lincoln will be . . .": F. L. Bullard, ed., *The Diary of a Public Man* (Chicago: Abraham Lincoln Bookshop, 1945), 117.

"one ray of hope"; Frederick Douglass, *The Narrative and Selected Writings,* ed. Michael Meyer (New York: Modern Library, 1984), 369.

"There goes that . . .": Bullard, ed., *Diary of a Public Man,* 117.

"Sea of upturned . . .": Elizabeth Todd Grimsley, "Six Months in the White House," *Journal of the Illinois State Historical Society,* April-July 1926, 45.

White House, 1861

"It's mine, my . . .": Ronald D. Rietveld, "The Lincoln White House Community," *Journal of the Abraham Lincoln Association,* summer 1990, 2.

"had the air . . .": William O. Stoddard, "White House Sketches No. 1," *New York Citizen,* April 18, 1866, 24.

"unchanged from George . . .": Grimsley, "Six Months in the White House," 46.

"rats, mildew and . . .": Stoddard, "White House Sketches," 26.

The New President

"When an attempt . . .": Lorant, *Lincoln,* 113.

"Mr. Lincoln, you . . .": Ibid.

The New First Lady

"standing with the . . .": Mary Lincoln to Mr. Anthony, November 1861, in Turner and Turner, eds., *Letters,* 116.

What to Do About Fort Sumter

"We are in . . .": Allan Nevins, *The War for the Union, Vol. 1: The Improvised War, 1861-1862* (New York: Charles Scribner's Sons, 1959), 58.

What to Do About a Dressmaker

"bright rose-colored silk": Fleischner, *Mrs. Lincoln and Mrs. Keckly,* 206.

All the President's Men

"save my freedom . . .": Lorant, *Lincoln,* 118.

"He is a . . .": John M. Taylor, *William Henry Seward: Lincoln's Right Hand Man* (New York: Harper Collins, 1991), 89.

"his trust in . . .": Charles A. Dana, *Recollections of the Civil War* (New York: D. Appleton & Company, 1898), 158.

"Chase resented the . . .": Donald, *Lincoln,* 478.

"In times of . . .": Goodwin, *Team of Rivals,* 286.

"no system, no . . .": Edward Bates, *The Diary of Edward Bates, 1859-1866,* ed. Howard K. Beale (Washington, D.C.: Government Printing Office, 1933), 280.

"Had no aptitude . . .": Ibid.

"incapable either of . . .": John G. Nicolay, *With Lincoln in the White House: Letters, Memoranda, and Other Writings of John G. Nicolay, 1860-1865,* ed. Michael Burlingame (Carbondale: Southern Illinois University Press, 2000), 59.

"wholly and honestly . . .": Benjamin P. Thomas and Harold Hyman, *Stanton: The Life and Times of Lincoln's Secretary of War* (New York: Alfred A. Knopf, 1962), 221.

"Stanton was for . . .": Ibid.

"Old Mars": Philip B. Kunhardt, Jr., *Lincoln: an Illustrated Biography* (New York: Alfred A. Knopf, 1992), 301.

"fool": Allan Thorndike Rice, ed., *Reminiscences of Abraham Lincoln by Distinguished Men of His Time* (New York: North American Review, 1888), 56.

☞ "Well, if Mr. Stanton . . .": Ibid., 57.

"restless mischief-maker . . .": Noah Brooks, *Washington, D.C., in Lincoln's Time* (New York: Century Co., 1895), 41.

"a most contentious . . .": John Hay, *Inside Lincoln's White House: The Complete Civil War Diary of John Hay,* ed. Michael Burlingame and John R. Turner Ettlinger (Carbondale: Southern Illinois University Press, 1999), 233.

"where there was . . .": Thurlow Weed, *Autobiography of Thurlow Weed,* ed. Harriet A. Weed (Boston: Houghton Mifflin & Company, 1883), 611.

Mary on the Cabinet

"My husband places . . .": "The President Talked to by a Strong-Minded Woman," *The Columbus Crisis,* 10 October 1861.

"she would have . . .": Ibid.

"an utter thief": Mary Lincoln to James Gordon Bennett, 4 October 1862, Abraham Lincoln Papers, Library of Congress.

"not to be trusted": Ibid.

"a little firecracker": Ibid.

"Father, you will . . .": Elizabeth Keckley, *Behind the Scenes* (Chicago: Lakeside Press, 1998), 115.

"If I listened . . .": Fleischner, *Mrs. Lincoln and Mrs. Keckly,* 250.

A Few More Good Men

"utterly unconscious that . . .": Burlingame, *Hay Diary,* 179.

"smart, and he knew . . .": William O. Stoddard, *Lincoln's Third Secretary* (New York: Exposition Press, 1955), 166.

"The Boys" and "the Ancient": Donald, *Lincoln,* 310.

"the Tycoon" and "John": Ibid.

Mary vs. "the Boys"

"There soon arose . . .": Helen Nicolay, *Lincoln's Secretary* (New York: Longmans, Green & Co., 1949), 191-92.

"her Satanic Majesty": Ibid.

"I think she . . .": Ibid.

"She is, indeed . . .": Stoddard, *Lincoln's Third Secretary,* 169.

Bombardment of Fort Sumter

"keeled over": Nevins, *The War for the Union,* 58.

"The shells were . . .": Mary Chestnut, *A Diary of Dixie* (New York: Gramercy, 1997), 29.

A War by Any Other Name

"civil war" and "rebellion": Donald, *Lincoln,* 302.

"so-called Confederate States": Ibid.

Robert E. Lee

"very best soldier . . .": Goodwin, *Team of Rivals,* 350.

"Will you take . . .": Ibid.

"Mr. Blair, I . . .": Ibid.

"It would have come . . .": Ibid.

Recruiting Poster

"wound up to . . .": Lorant, *Lincoln,* 146.

Sixth Massachusetts Regiment in Baltimore

"Our men are . . .": Lincoln, *Collected Works,* 4:342.

"Why don't they . . .": John G. Nicolay and John Hay, *Abraham Lincoln: A History,* 10 vols. (New York: Century Co., 1890), 4:152.

"Thousands of soldiers . . .": Randall, *Mary Lincoln,* 202.

Tramples on Civil Liberty

"You are engaged . . .": Lincoln, *Collected Works,* 4:428.

"in cases of rebellion . . .": Constitution of the United States, Charters of Freedom Collection, National Archives.

"such extreme tenderness . . .": Lincoln, *Collected Works,* 4:430.

Three Tales About Mary

"This illustrates an . . .": Julia Taft Bayne, *Tad Lincoln's Father* (Lincoln: University of Nebraska Press, 2001), 20.

"a whit for discipine": Grimsley, "Six Months in the White House," 53.

"unspeakable . . . immoral . . . mercy . . .": Ibid.

"Think, father, if . . .": Ibid., 54.

"By request of . . .": Ibid.

"First Lady of . . .": Baker, *Mary Todd Lincoln,* 180.

A Cartoon About Abraham

"an ill-bred, ravenous crowd": Donald, *Lincoln,* 285.

"At least the . . .": John G. Nicolay to Therena Bates, 12 April 1861, Nicolay Papers, Digital Archives Library, Virginia Polytechnic Institute and State University, Blacksburg, Va.

"seldom if ever . . .": John G. Nicolay to Therena Bates, 11 April 1861, Nicolay Papers, Digital Archives Library, Virginia Polytechnic Institute and State University, Blacksburg, Va.

"They do not . . .": Henry Wilson to William Herndon, 30 May 1867, Herndon-Weik Collection, Library of Congress.

Mischief in the White House

"Tyrant of the White House": Randall, *Lincoln's Sons,* 109.

"I promised never . . .": Dorothy Meserve Kunhardt and Philip B. Kunhardt Jr., *Twenty Days: The Authoritative Account of Lincoln's Assassination, the Conspiracy and the Aftermath* (North Hollywood, Calif.: Newcastle Publishing, 1985), 75.

"Get out of . . .": Randall, *Lincoln's Sons,* 125.

"Tell dear Tad . . .": Abraham Lincoln to Mary Lincoln, 28 April 1864, Abraham Lincoln Papers, Library of Congress.

"circus": Bayne, *Tad Lincoln's Father,* 48.

"Come help, Julie . . .": Ibid., 48-50.

"threw back his . . .": Randall, *Lincoln's Sons,* 77.

"What is that . . .": Bayne, *Tad Lincoln's Father,* 58-59.

"The Doll Jack . . .": Kunhardt and Kunhardt, *Twenty Days,* 76.

The Other Son

"Any great intimacy . . .": Randall, *Lincoln's Sons,* 210.

Mrs. Lincoln's Flub Dubs

"one fine porcelain . . .": Harry Pratt and Ernest East, "Mrs. Lincoln Refurbishes the White House," *Lincoln Herald,* February 1945, 12.

"stink in the land . . .": Benjamin Brown French, *Witness to the Young Republic* (Hanover, N.H.: University Press of New England, 1989), 382.

"We cannot afford that": Ibid., 384.

Memorandum of Military Policy

"concentration and intensity . . .": Brooks, *Washington, D.C., in Lincoln's Time,* 217.

General George McClellan

"Little Mac": Lorant, *Lincoln*, 128.

"He looks as . . .": Orville Hickman Browning, *The Diary of Orville Hickman Browning*, 2 vols., ed. Theodore C. Peases and James A. Randall (Springfield: Illinois State Historical Library, 1933), 1:516.

"The President is . . .": George B. McClellan, *The Civil War Papers of George B. McClellan*, ed. Stephen W. Sears (New York: Ticknor & Fields, 1989), 85.

"The supreme command . . .": Ibid.

"I can do . . .": Hay, *Inside Lincoln's White House*, 33.

"nothing more than . . .": McClellan, *Civil War Papers*, 106.

"meddling, officious, incompetent": Ibid., 107.

"a fool" and "old woman": Ibid., 113.

THIS AWFUL BURDEN

"If there is . . .": William K. Golrick, ed., *Rebels Resurgent: Fredericksburg to Chancellorsville* (New York: Time-Life Books, 1985), 92.

"Can life be endured?": Randall, *Mary Lincoln*, 256.

The Lincolns' Reception

"Half the city . . .": John Nicolay to Therena Bates, 2 February, 1862, Nicolay Papers, Digital Archives Library, Virginia Polytechnic Institute and State University, Blacksburg, Va.

"Are the President . . .": Fleischner, *Mrs. Lincoln and Mrs. Keckly*, 230.

"the most superb . . .": *Washington Star*, 6 February 1862, 2.

One of the Last Photographs of Willie

"weaker and more . . .": Keckley, *Behind the Scenes*, 82.

"All that human . . .": Mary Lincoln to Julia Ann Sprigg, 29 May 1862, in Turner and Turner, eds., *Letters*, 127.

"Well, Nicolay, my . . .": Goodwin, *Team of Rivals*, 419.

"The pale face . . .": Keckley, *Behind the Scenes*, 88.

"Please, Ma, don't . . .": French, *Witness to the Young Republic*, 391.

"He was too . . .": Keckley, *Behind the Scenes*, 87.

A Father's Sorrow

"That blow overwhelmed . . .": Goodwin, *Team of Rivals*, 423.

"my lost boy . . .": Ibid.

A Mother's Sorrow

"The mere mention . . .": Keckley, *Behind the Scenes*, 87.

"so dark that . . .": Walt Whitman, *Complete Writings* (New York: Putnam, 1902), 1:325.

"Always, she must . . .": Baker, *Mary Todd Lincoln*, 216.

"I had become . . .": Mary Lincoln to Hannah Shearer, 20 November 1864, in Turner and Turner, eds., *Letters*, 188-89.

Just Pa and Me

"Just Pa and me . . .": Randall, *Lincoln's Sons*, 255.

"tossed with typhoid": Randall, *Mary Lincoln*, 253.

"the moment [the president] . . .": Ibid., 254.

"Tad was always . . .": Randall, *Lincoln's Sons*, 106.

"When this is over . . .": Kunhardt, *Lincoln*, 293.

Ghosts in the White House

"Oh, it is . . .": Randall, *Mary Lincoln*, 263.

"surround us like . . .": Baker, *Mary Todd Lincoln*, 219.

"made wonderful revelations . . .": Ibid., 220.

"I have seen . . .": Prior Melton, "A Readable Sketch: Spiritualism at the White House," *Herald Progress*, May 1863, 8.

"Willie lives . . .": Helm, *Mary, Wife of Lincoln*, 227.

Lincoln's General War Order

"Do not allow . . .": Lorant, *Lincoln*, 134.

"The entire country . . .": Donald, *Lincoln*, 341.

Peninsula Campaign

"I think you . . .": Lincoln, *Collected Works*, 5:182.

"I was tempted . . .": Donald, *Lincoln*, 351.

"Have no fear . . .": Lorant, *Lincoln*, 142.

A Few Words

"It is hard . . .": Lincoln, *Collected Works*, 5:194.

"McClellan is a . . .": Keckley, *Behind the Scenes*, 116.

Mary's Greatest Social Cause

"with a great . . .": Ibid., 93.

"tents, blankets, ends . . .": Fleischner, *Mrs. Lincoln and Mrs. Keckly*, 241.

"The transition from . . .": Keckley, *Behind the Scenes*, 94.

"The cause of . . .": Mary Lincoln to Abraham Lincoln, 3 November 1862, in Turner and Turner, eds., *Letters*, 141.

Writing the Emancipation Proclamation

"[He] would look . . .": Donald, *Lincoln*, 363.

"You need more men . . .": Ibid.

"Slavery is the real . . .": Lincoln, *Collected Works*, 5:436.

Lincoln Reads Draft of Emancipation Proclamation

"resolved upon this . . .": Carpenter, *Six Months*, 21.

"written in . . . the . . .": Adam Gurowski, *Diary from March 4, 1861, to November 12, 1862* (Boston: Lee & Shephard, 1862), 278.

"resign and go home": Goodwin, *Team of Rivals*, 466.

"the last measure . . .": Ibid., 468.

"We mustn't issue . . .": Carpenter, *Six Months*, 22.

Frederick Douglass

"any authentic record . . .": Frederick Douglass, *Narrative of the Life of Frederick Douglass, an American Slave* (Boston: Anti-Slavery Office, 1845), 78.

"we were separated . . .": Ibid.

"it will make . . .": Goodwin, *Team of Rivals*, 331.

"Anything to get . . .": Douglass, *Narrative*, 86.

"What to the American . . .": Sandra Thomas, *Frederick Douglass, Abolitionist/Editor* (Rochester, N.Y.: University of Rochester Press, 2000), iii.

"Some thought we . . .": Frederick Douglass, editorial in *Douglass Monthly*, April 1861, 2.

"The negro is the . . .": Fleischner, *Mrs. Lincoln and Mrs. Keckly*, 233.

"tardy, hesitating and . . .": Frederick May Holland, *Frederick Douglass: The Colored Orator* (New York: Funk and Wagnalls Company, 1895), 212.

"a genuine representative . . .": John J. Dwyer,

☞ "Misconceptions About Lincoln," www.lewrock.com/orig3.dwyer6.html.

A Sly Approach

"thus liberated": Lincoln, *Collected Works*, 5:219.

"My paramount object . . .": Ibid., 5:388-89.

Battle of Antietam

"a complete success": Ibid., 5:443.

Lincoln Visits Antietam

"over-cautiousness": Donald, *Lincoln*, 388.

"Will you pardon . . .": Lincoln, *Collected Works*, 5:474.

"case of the slows": Lorant, *Lincoln*, 158.

General Ambrose Burnside

"I am not . . .": Kunhardt, *Lincoln*, 193.

Cartoon of Lincoln Writing the Proclamation

"There are some . . .": C. Peter Ripley, *Witness for Freedom: African American Voices on Race, Slavery, and Emancipation* (Chapel Hill: University of North Carolina Press, 1993), 257.

"radical fanatic": Donald, *Lincoln*, 380.

"an act of Revolution": Ibid.

"doing the devil's . . .": Rufus Rockwell, *Lincoln in Caricature* (New York: Horizon Press, 1953), 193.

Good Result of Antietam

"added or changed . . .": Carpenter, *Six Months*, 22.

"fixed it up . . .": Lincoln, *Collected Works*, 5:420.

"but a first step": John Hope Franklin, "The Emancipation Proclamation: An Act of Justice," *National Geographic*, February 2003, 22.

"I can only . . .": Lincoln, *Collected Works*, 5:438.

An Awful Burden

"wrung by the . . .": Donald, *Lincoln*, 372.

"weary, care-worn and troubled": Goodwin, *Team of Rivals*, 461.

"almost ready to . . .": Donald, *Lincoln*, 372.

"Engage the enemy": Abraham Lincoln to George McClellan, 1 June 1862, Abraham Lincoln Papers, Library of Congress.

"Pursue them": Lorant, *Lincoln*, 178.

"defeat them": Ibid., 179.

"force a surrender": Ibid., 236.

"Let us die . . .": Julia Ward Howe, "The Battle Hymn of the Republic," *Atlantic Monthly*, February 1862, 10.

Disappearing Act

"I consider myself . . .": Baker, *Mary Todd Lincoln*, 226.

Lincoln Signs Emancipation Proclamation

"I never in . . .": Donald, *Lincoln*, 407.

"Now this signature . . .": Ibid.

"If my name . . .": Freedman, *Lincoln: A Photobiography*, 91.

Whom Did the Proclamation Free?

"That on the . . .": Abraham Lincoln, "Emancipation Proclamation," Featured Documents of the National Archives, www.archives.gov/exhibits/featured_document/emancipation_proclamation.

"[The president] has . . .": *New York World*, January 3, 1863, 1.

"We show our . . .": www.civilwarhome.com/

☞ lincolnandproclamation.htm.

"It changed forever . . .": Goodwin, *Team of Rivals*, 502.

"Whatever [flaws] it . . .": *Boston Daily Evening Transcript*, 3 January 1863, 5.

A Grudging Good Word

"Strange phenomenon in . . .": Goodwin, *Team of Rivals*, 501.

Mary and Emancipation

"coming from an . . .": Helm, *Mary, Wife of Lincoln*, 209.

"to the quick": Ibid.

"[Mrs. Lincoln] is more . . .": Randall, *Mary Lincoln*, 323.

"the oppressed colored race": Mary Lincoln to Charles Sumner, 5 April 1864, in Turner and Turner, eds., *Letters*, 174.

"She could talk . . .": Helm, *Mary, Wife of Lincoln*, 194.

The President, 1863

"considerable call": Ostendorf, *Lincoln's Photographs*, 129.

"Can it be . . .": Ibid.

General Joseph Hooker

"It is neither . . .": Davis, *Don't Know Much*, 279.

"May God have . . .": Lorant, *Lincoln*, 172.

107th Colored Infantry

"I saw 25 Negroes . . .": Davis, *Don't Know Much*, 347.

"Once let the . . .": Frederick Douglass, *Douglass' Monthly*, August 1863, 1.

Civil War Draft Notice

"a rich man's . . .": Davis, *Don't Know Much*, 314.

Laughing Lincoln

"so funny he . . .": James Matheny to William Herndon, November 1866, Herndon-Weik Collection, Library of Congress.

"I laugh because . . .": "The Wit and Wisdom of Abraham Lincoln," www.suite101.com/article.cfm/presidents_and_first_ladies/94636.

"He took aim . . .": Alexander K. McClure, *Lincoln's Yarns and Stories* (New York: Bengal Press, 1980), 121.

"If I had . . .": Karen E. Crummy, "Politicans Work to Win Laughs," *Denver Post*, 23 April 2007, 16.

"People who like . . .": Richard J. Carwardine, *Lincoln* (New York: Pearson Education, 2003), 16.

"I suppose your . . .": Kunhardt, *Lincoln*, 324.

"There are two . . .": Abraham Lincoln's Classroom, "Abraham Lincoln's Stories and Humor," www.abrahamlincolnsclassroom.org/Library/newsletter.

Joke Book Ad

"I don't make . . .": Ibid.

General and Mrs. Tom Thumb

"down and down . . .": Kunhardt, *Lincoln*, 205.

"the President led . . .": Ibid.

"Mother, if you . . .": Randall, *Lincoln's Sons*, 120.

Lincoln Napping

"recited some poem . . .": Grimsley, "Six Months in the White House," 55.

"at all times . . .": William D. Stoddard, *Inside the white House in War Times* (New York: Charles L. Webster & Co., 1890), 62.

"complete picture of . . .": Keckley, *Behind the Scenes*, 102.

Blue Room Salon

"my beau monde . . .": Baker, *Mary Todd Lincoln*, 231.

"if you could . . .": John W. Forney, *Anecdotes of Public Men* (Ann Arbor: Scholarly Publishing Office, University of Michigan, 2006), 367.

"très chic": Ibid.

"affable, insinuating and . . ." Welles, *Diary*, 2:122.

Battle of Chancellorsville

"outgeneraled": Goodwin, *Team of Rivals*, 520.

"My God! My God! . . .": Brooks, *Washington, D.C., in Lincoln's Time*, 57.

General George Meade

"He is not . . .": Henry Livermore Abbott, *Fallen Leaves: The War Letters of Major Henry Livermore Abbott*, ed., Robert Garth Scott (Kent, Ohio: Kent State University Press, 1991), 216.

Anderson Cottage

"It's odd . . .": Anne Colver, *Mr. Lincoln's Wife* (New York: Holt, Rinehart & Winston, 1943), 280.

"sense of misery": Mary Lincoln to Elizabeth Blair Lee, 25 August 1865, in Turner and Turner, eds., *Letters*, 267.

"How I dearly . . .": Ibid.

Gettysburg

"The [bullets] were . . .": Geoffrey C. Ward, *The Civil War: An Illustrated History* (New York: Random House, 1990), 224.

"The hoarse and . . .": Ibid., 225.

"It was all . . .": Ibid., 235.

"Do not let . . .": Lincoln, *Collected Works*, 6:319.

"If I had . . .": Ibid., 6:329.

"My dear general . . .": Ibid., 6:327-28.

Ulysses S. Grant

"rescued": Davis, *Don't Know Much*, 185.

"We must cut . . .": Ibid.

"Senseless" and "horrific": T. Harry Williams, *Lincoln and His Generals* (New York: Alfred A. Knopf, 1952), 84.

"butcher Grant": Keckley, *Behind the Scenes*, 116.

"I can't spare . . .": Williams, *Lincoln and His Generals*, 86.

Armory Square Hospital

"I am sitting . . .": Mary Lincoln to Mrs. Agen, 10 August 1864, in Turner and Turner, eds., *Letters*, 179.

Battle of Vicksburg

"I cannot, in . . .": Howard K. Beale and Alan W. Browns word, eds., *Diary of Gideon Welles, Secretary of the Navy Under Lincoln and Johnson* (3 Vols.; New York: W. W. Norton 4 Co., 1960), 1:364.

A Poem by the President

"General Lee's invasion . . .": Donald, *Lincoln*, 447.

Gettysburg Address

"a few appropriate remarks": Lorant, *Lincoln*, 187.

"his audience in . . .": Donald, *Lincoln*, 464.

"Four score and . . .": Lincoln, *Collected Works*, 7:21.

"so astonished . . .": Donald, *Lincoln*, 465.

"The few words . . .": Ibid.

"the remarks by . . .": Ibid.

Thanksgiving Proclamation

"Would it not . . .": Mike Bellah, "She Helped Give Us Thanksgiving," www.bestyears.com/sarah_hale.html.

The End of a Long Year

"I feel as . . .": Randall, *Mary Lincoln*, 304.

Rebels in the White House

"rebel family": Helm, *Mary, Wife of Lincoln*, 221.

"with the warmest . . .": Ibid.

"It comes between . . .": Ibid., 224.

"We whipped the . . .": Ibid., 229-31.

"Oh, Emilie . . .": Ibid., 234.

Tad's Confederate Cousin

"This is the . . .": Ibid., 232.

Proclamation of Reconstruction

"re-establish a state . . .": Lincoln, *Collected Works*, 7:53.

"They should pay . . .": P. J. Staudenraus, ed., *Mr. Lincoln's Washington: The Civil War Dispatches of Noah Brooks.* (South Brunswick; N.J.: Thomas Yoseloff, 1967), 271.

"let [the rebels] up . . .": Lamon, *Recollection*, 167-68.

WITH CHARITY FOR ALL

"Doesn't it seem . . .": Donald, *Lincoln*, 514.

"I live in fear . . .": Randall, *Mary Lincoln*, 333.

Why a Second Term?

"I confess that . . .": Donald, *Lincoln*, 540.

Salmon Chase

"mad dash for . . .": Hay, *Inside Lincoln's White House*, 79.

"feebleness of will . . .": Donald, *Lincoln*, 481.

"more of the . . .": Ibid., 482.

"It is so . . .": Ibid., 481.

"Chase is a . . .": Ibid.

"You and I . . .": Ibid., 508.

"[Chase] and I . . .": Ibid., 552.

Grant's Appointment

"It is an . . .": Brooks, *Washington in Lincoln's Time*, 290.

"With Grant in . . .": Nicolay, *Lincoln's Secretary*, 196.

"Why, here is . . .": Ibid., 194.

"That night Mr. Lincoln . . .": Ibid.

General Sherman

"Tecumseh was a . . .": Davis, *Don't Know Much*, 385.

"like a well-oiled . . .": Brooks, *Washington in Lincoln's Time*, 294.

Grant's Course

"no more shilly-shallying": Lorant, *Lincoln*, 198.

"I will concentrate . . .": Ibid.

"[He] is the . . .": Nicolay, *Lincoln's Secretary*, 196.

Robert Todd Lincoln and Family

"I am determined . . .": Donald, *Lincoln*, 571.

"shirker" and "coward": Ibid.

"as though I . . .": Abraham Lincoln to Ulysses S. Grant, 19 January 1865, Abraham Lincoln Papers, Library of Congress.

Battle of the Wilderness

"More desperate fighting . . .": Kunhardt, *Lincoln*, 274.

Battle of Spotsylvania Court House

"his long arms . . .": Rice, *Reminiscences,* 337.

Cold Harbor

"It was not . . .": Joan Waugh, "Carnage in Rural Virginia," *Virginia Quarterly Review,* spring 2001, 62.

"I regret this . . .": Ibid., 64.

"Those poor fellows . . .": Ibid.

Siege at Petersburg

"Hold on with . . .": Kunhardt, *Lincoln,* 280.

Mary on Grant

"He is a . . .": Keckley, *Behind the Scenes,* 116-17.

Andrew Johnson

"The delegates have . . .": Brooks, *Washington in Lincoln's Time,* 422.

"His written speeches . . .": Ibid., 423.

"Wish not to . . .": Lincoln, *Collected Works,* 7:376.

Raid on Washington

"with a long . . .": Donald, *Lincoln,* 519.

"Get down, you . . .": Kunhardt, *Lincoln,* 294.

"cloud of dust . . .": Goodwin, *Team of Rivals,* 643.

"Mrs. Lincoln, I . . .": Ibid., 644.

Doom, Gloom

"The month of . . .": Michael Burlingame, ed., *Lincoln Observed: Civil War Dispatches of Noah Brooks* (Baltimore: Johns Hopkins University Press, 1998), 129.

"wild for peace": Hay, *Inside Lincoln's White House,* 238.

"our bleeding, bankrupt . . .": Brooks, *Washington in Lincoln's Time,* 368.

"the tide is . . .": Donald, *Lincoln,* 529.

"you think I . . .": Ibid.

Atlanta Is Ours

"Atlanta is ours . . .": Goodwin, *Team of Rivals,* 654.

"the glorious achievement . . .": Lincoln, *Collected Works,* 7:533.

"In the name . . .": Kunhardt, *Lincoln,* 288.

"You might as . . .": Ibid.

"We all know . . .": Ibid., 289.

And So Is the Shenandoah Valley

"To make the . . .": Ibid., 294.

"peel the land": Ibid.

"Give 'em hell . . .": P. H. Sheridan, *Personal Memoirs of P. H. Sheridan* (New York: Charles L. Webster, 1888), 461.

"went whirling back . . .": Ibid., 466.

"With great pleasure . . .": Kunhardt, *Lincoln,* 294.

Mood Swing

"Three weeks ago . . .": Nicolay and Hay, *Abraham Lincoln,* 9:221.

Political Broadside, 1864 Campaign

"peace at any price": Welles, *Diary,* 2:136.

"no peace without . . .": Ibid.

"There are but . . .": Donald, *Lincoln,* 541.

Anti-Lincoln Biography

"*Only Authentic Life* . . .": Lorant, *Lincoln,* 212.

"Mr. Lincoln stands . . .": Ibid.

Mary's Plan

"In a political . . .": Keckley, *Behind the Scenes,* 127.

"insinuating and unreliable": Welles, *Diary,* 2:114.

"Can you sway . . .": Mark E. Neely Jr., "Thurlow Weed, the New York Custom House, and Mrs. Lincoln's Treasure," *Lincoln Lore,* January 1978, 4.

"If anyone can . . .": Ibid.

Campaign Button

"If it could . . .": William F. Zornow, *Lincoln and the Party Divided* (Norman: University of Oklahoma Press, 1954), 202.

"The President has . . .": Welles, *Diary,* 2:151.

Long Abraham

"Dispatches kept coming . . .": Hay, *Inside the White House,* 233-34.

Premonition

"It was just . . .": Brooks, *Washington in Lincoln's Time,* 199.

Abraham's Best Boots

"Dr. Zacharie's boots . . .": Lorant, *Lincoln,* 204.

Stovepipe Hat

"Madam, I could . . .": P. M. Zall, ed., *Abe Lincoln Laughing: Humorous Anecdotes from Original Sources by and About Abraham Lincoln* (Berkeley: University of California Press, 1982), 134.

Home Cookin'

"keel over from . . .": Randall, *Mary Lincoln,* 303-4.

Still in Love

"He [is] my . . .": Mary Lincoln to Sally Orne, 12 December 1869, in Turner and Turner, eds., *Letters,* 533.

"My wife is . . .": Baker, *Mary Todd Lincoln,* 196.

Mrs. Lincoln Travels

"The President's wife . . .": *New York Herald,* 19 October 1861, 6.

"pure pleasure": Ibid.

"I really wish . . .": Lincoln, *Collected Works,* 6:283.

"Such female vigor!": *Frank Leslie's Illustrated Newspaper,* October-November 1862, 6.

"wayward impulsive moods": Randall, *Mary Lincoln,* 311.

Threats

"May the hand": "Night of Assasination," temporary exhibit, Abraham Lincoln Presidential Library and Museum, 1 April to 1 September 2004.

"Abe you must . . .": Ibid.

"you have been . . .": Ibid.

"I know I . . .": Donald, *Lincoln,* 550.

"It would never . . .": Carpenter, *Six Months,* 62-63.

"but it must . . .": *The American Experience: Abraham and Mary Lincoln: A House Divided,* PBS DVD Gold, 2001.

"Mr. Lincoln's life . . .": Ibid.

Consoling Words

"Dear Madam . . .": Lincoln, *Collected Works,* 8:116-17.

A Hopeful Ending

"I beg to . . .": William T. Sherman to Abraham Lincoln, 25 December 1864, Abraham Lincoln Papers, Library of Congress.

"I almost tremble . . .": Davis, *Don't Know Much,* 393.

The President

"so jaded and . . .": Speed, *Reminiscences,* 26-28.

"Poor Mr. Lincoln . . .": Keckley, *Behind the Scenes*, 157.

"Nothing touches the . . .": Brooks, *Washington, D.C., in Lincoln's Time*, 55.

And the First Lady

"an Indian removing . . .": Kunhardt, *Lincoln*, 394.

"nervous affliction": Baker, *Mary Todd Lincoln*, 269.

Sitting Beside Vice President Johnson

"were in a . . .": Brooks, *Washington, D.C., in Lincoln's Time*, 213.

"Cheer upon cheer . . .": Ostendorf, *Lincoln's Photographs*, 400.

"burst forth in . . .": Brooks, *Washington, D.C., in Lincoln's Time*, 213.

"to both North . . .": Lincoln, *Complete Works*, 8:333.

Planning the Future

"he intended to . . .": William Herndon interview with Mary Lincoln, 5 September 1866, Herndon-Weik Collection, Library of Congress.

Thirteenth Amendment

"only a question . . .": Charles M. Segal, ed., *Conversations with Lincoln* (New York: G. P. Putnam's Sons, 1961), 362.

"The passage of . . .": Ibid.

"The greatest measure . . .": Fawn Brodie, *Thaddeus Stevens: Scourge of the South* (New York: W. W. Norton & Co., 1959), 204.

"this great historic occasion": *American Experience: Abraham and Mary Lincoln: A House Divided*.

"The greatest job . . .": Ibid.

Telegram from Grant

"I think the rest . . .": Ulysses S. Grant to Abraham Lincoln, 20 March 1865, Abraham Lincoln Papers, Library of Congress.

Mary's Meltdown

"vile names": Goodwin, *Team of Rivals*, 712.

"Poor Mr. Lincoln . . .": Adam Badeau, *Grant in Peace* (New York: Appleton, 1887), 365.

Another Premonition

"a death-like stillness . . .": Lamon, *Recollections*, 114.

"terror from [that] . . .": Randall, *Mary Lincoln*, 341.

Three Little Kittens

"Where is your . . .": Carl Sandburg, *Abraham Lincoln: The War Years* (New York: Harcourt Brace, 1939), 146.

Behind Enemy Lines

"While Richmond's fall . . .": Ernest B. Furguson, *Ashes of Glory* (New York: Alfred A. Knopf, 1996), 117.

"Quickly from mouth . . .": *London Times*, 25 April 1865, 2.

"Pale women and . . .": Davis, *Don't Know Much*, 398.

"in exile": Ibid.

Lincoln Entering Richmond

"Bless the Lord . . .": Donald, *Lincoln*, 576.

"Thank God I . . .": Kunhardt, *Lincoln*, 268.

A Soldier's Observation

"I witnessed his . . .": Margarita Spalding Gerry, ed., *Reminiscences of Colonel William H. Crook, Bodyguard to President Lincoln* (New York: Harper & Brothers, 1910), 51.

Terms of Surrender

"There is nothing . . .": Davis, *Don't Know Much*, 402.

"with reference to . . .": Lorant, *Lincoln*, 238.

"I must make . . .": Goodwin, *Team of Rivals*, 725.

"The war is . . .": Lorant, *Lincoln*, 239.

"I love you . . .": Goodwin, *Team of Rivals*, 726.

Glorious News

"General Lee surrendered . . .": Ulysses S. Grant to Abraham Lincoln, 9 April 1865, Abraham Lincoln Papers, Library of Congress.

"Mr. L.–told . . .": Mary Lincoln to Charles Sumner, 10 April 1865, in Turner and Turner, eds., *Letters*, 216.

Front Page of the *New York Times*

"The country seems . . .": Brooks, *Washington, D.C., in Lincoln's Time*, 252.

Joyful Words

"In honor of . . .": Ibid.

"Guns are firing . . .": Welles, *Diary*, 2:278.

"I have always . . .": Adolphe de Chambrun, *Impressions of Lincoln and the Civil War* (New York: Random House, 1952), 82.

Lincoln's Last Speech

"Reuniting our country . . .": Lincoln, *Collected Works*, 8:401.

"the very intelligent . . .": Ibid., 404.

"Lincoln's talking nigger . . .": William Hanchett, *The Lincoln Murder Conspiracies* (Urbana: University of Illinois Press, 1983), 37.

John Wilkes Booth

"one of the greatest . . .": Frances Wilson, *John Wilkes Booth: Fact and Fiction of the Lincoln Assasination* (Boston: Houghton Mifflin Company, 1929), 51.

"By God": Hanchett, *The Lincoln Murder Conspiracies*, 37.

That Fateful Day

"His face that . . .": Keckley, *Behind the Scenes*, 137-38.

"It is a good . . .": Randall, *Mary Lincoln*, 342.

"Didn't our chief . . .": Goodwin, *Team of Rivals*, 732.

"look happier than . . .": Ibid.

"playfully and tenderly . . .": Mary Lincoln to Mary Jane Welles, 11 July 1865, in Turner and Turner, eds., *Letters*, 257.

"dear, loving letters": Ibid.

"Dear husband, you . . .": Mary Lincoln to Charles Bicknell Carpenter, 15 November 1865, in Turner and Turner, eds., *Letters*, 284-85.

"We must *both* . . .": Ibid.

"His mind was . . .": Ibid.

"Come back, boys . . .": Tarbell, *The Life of Lincoln*, 4:235.

"Lincoln got to . . .": Ibid.

"The President stepped . . .": E. R. Shaw, "The Assassination of Lincoln," *McClure's Magazine*, December 1908, 181.

"seemed to take . . .": George Bryan, *The Great American Myth* (New York: Carrick & Evans, 1940), 176.

"Don't know the . . .": Donald, *Lincoln*, 596.

"*sic semper tyrannis*": Goodwin, *Team of Rivals*, 739.

"They have shot . . .": Donald, *Lincoln*, 597.

"Oh, doctor . . .": Lorant, *Lincoln*, 261.

"Where is my . . .": Randall, *Mary Lincoln*, 344.

"How can it . . .": Elizabeth Dixon to Laura Wood,

☛ 25 April 1865 (copy), on display at Abraham Lincoln Presidential Library and Museum.

"Take that woman . . .": John K. Lattimer, *Kennedy and Lincoln: Medical and Ballistic Comparison* (New York: Harcourt Brace Jovanovich, 1980), 32.

"was struggling with . . .": Elizabeth Dixon to Laura Wood, 25 April 1865.

"Oh, my God . . .": Randall, *Mary Lincoln*, 345.

"Now he belongs . . .": Bryan, *Great American Myth*, 189.

Final Contents of Pockets

"banished": "Artifacts of Assassination," American Treasures of the Library of Congress, www.loc.gov/exhibits/treasures/trm012.html.

"All those who . . .": Ibid.

BLIND FROM WEEPING

"No place is . . .": Mary Lincoln to Elizabeth Blair Lee, 25

Now He Belongs to the Ages

August 1864, in Turner and Turner, eds., *Letters*, 268.

"That dreadful house . . .": Kunhardt, *Lincoln*, 93.

"Not there! Oh . . .": Randall, *Mary Lincoln*, 345.

"The sudden and . . .": Benjamin Brown French diaries, 15 April 1865, Library of Congress.

"Alas, all is . . .": Keckley, *Behind the Scenes*, 181.

Tad

"Don't cry so . . .": Ibid., 176.

"Pa is dead . . .": Ibid., 179-80.

Robert Todd Lincoln Letter

"In all my plans . . .": Randall, *Lincoln's Sons*, 168.

An Engraving of the Catafalque

"Temple of Death": Kunhardt, *Lincoln*, 368.

"gave [Mary] spasms . . .": Turner, *Letters*, 248.

Funeral on Pennsylvania Avenue

"All were sad . . .": Brooks, *Washington, D.C., in Lincoln's Time*, 279.

Springfield Funeral

"in some quiet place": Turner and Turner, eds., *Letters*, 240, n.d.

"I shall have . . .": Mary Lincoln to Richard J. Oglesby, 10 June 1865, in Turner and Turner, eds., *Letters*, 244.

"I know'd they . . .": *American Experience: Abraham and Mary Lincoln: A House Divided*.

Mary in Mourning

"was in a daze . . .": Margarita Spalding Gerry, ed., *Through Five Administrations: Reminiscences of Colonel William H. Crook, Bodyguard to President Lincoln* (New York: Harper & Brothers, 1910), 71.

What of the Assassin

"[I have been] . . .": John Wilkes Booth diary, 21 April 1865, on display at Ford's Theater Museum, National Park Service.

"became terribly swollen . . .": Ibid.

"Providence": Bryan, *Great American Myth*, 201.

"Tell Mother I . . .": Kunhardt, *Twenty Days*, 176.

Mary's Assassination Theory

"That inebriate had . . .": Mary Lincoln to Sally Orner, 18 March 1866, in Turner and Turner, eds., *Letters*, 345.

"desecrating": Ibid., 380.

Too Many Trunks

"Packing afforded quite . . .": Keckley, *Behind the Scenes*, 183.

"burn all your plunder": Ibid., 187.

"a passion for . . .": Ibid.

"Every day, even . . .": Kunhardt, *Lincoln*, 396.

Goodbye, Washington

"felt really very . . .": French diaries, 24 May 1865, Library of Congress.

"so unlike the . . .": Keckley, *Behind the Scenes*, 187.

Hello, Chicago

"After the many . . .": Mary Lincoln to Simon Cameron, 6 April 1866, in Turner and Turner, eds., *Letters*, 351.

"Tad was a . . .": Keckley, *Behind the Scenes*, 194.

"I would almost . . .": Ibid.

"my mother's gloom . . .": Robert Todd Lincoln to David Davis, 2 January 1866, Davis Papers, Abraham Lincoln Presidential Library and Museum.

Lizzy Goes Home

"Lizzy, you are . . .": Keckley, *Behind the Scenes*, 193.

"I had listened . . .": Ibid., 194.

"first class nurse . . .": Fleischner, *Mrs. Lincoln and Mrs. Keckly*, 294.

What Mary Did for Money

"settling the Lincoln estate": Turner and Turner, eds., *Letters*, 244.

"a pittance . . . a mere . . .": Mary Lincoln to David Davis, 24 February 1867, in Turner and Turner, eds., *Letters*, 410.

"I could starve . . .": Ibid., 247.

"With a stroke . . .": Baker, *Mary Todd Lincoln*, 260.

"I absolutely refuse . . .": Pratt, *Personal Finances of Abraham Lincoln*, 139.

"Mrs. Clarke of Chicago": Turner and Turner, eds., *Letters*, 430.

"$75 from the . . .": *New York World*, 3 October 1867, 2.

"Mrs. Lincoln's Second-Hand . . .": Baker, *Mary Todd Lincoln*, 275.

"Mrs. Lincoln has . . .": Mary Lincoln to Elizabeth Keckly, 13 October 1867, in Turner and Turner, eds., *Letters*, 442.

"Mrs. L. will . . .": Baker, *Mary Todd Lincoln*, 278.

"the people of . . .": Mary Lincoln to Elizabeth Keckly, 13 October 1867, in Turner and Turner, eds., *Letters*, 442.

William Herndon Invents a Love Story

"this beautiful, amiable . . .": From a pamphlet bearing the text of William Herndon's fourth lecture, photocopy in Abraham Lincoln Presidential Library and Museum.

"It was always . . .": Mary Lincoln to Mary Jane Welles, 6 December 1865, in Turner and Turner, eds., *Letters*, 296.

Keckly's Tell-All Book

"dear [Lizzy]": Mary Lincoln to Elizabeth Keckly, 13 October 1867, in Turner and Turner, eds., *Letters*, 442.

"She is my . . .": Ibid.

"illiterate, ungrammatical twaddle": Keckley, *Behind the Scenes,* lxix.

"the back-stairs gossip . . .": Fleischner, *Mrs. Lincoln and Mrs. Keckly,* 317.

"a traitorous eavesdropper": Keckley, *Behind the Scenes,* xviii.

"ignorant and vulgar": Ibid.

Robert's Bride

"The terror of . . .": Mary Lincoln to Rhoda White, 19 August 1868, in Turner and Turner, eds., *Letters,* 481.

"not to look . . .": Mary Lincoln to Eliza Slataper, 27 September 1868, in Turner and Turner, eds., *Letters,* 485.

"elegantly decorated with . . .": Randall, *Lincoln's Sons,* 198.

"a rich glowing . . .": Ibid.

"the very personification . . .": Ibid.

"the after effects . . .": Mary Lincoln to Eliza Slataper, 27 September 1868, in Turner and Turner, eds., *Letters,* 485.

Frankfurt

"To avoid persecution . . .": Randall, *Mary Lincoln,* 373.

"I came face-to-face . . .": Mary Lincoln to Eliza Slataper, 17 February 1869, in Turner and Turner, eds., *Letters,* 501-2.

"dear, old Frankfurt": Randall, *Lincoln's Sons,* 206.

A Difficult Daughter-in-Law

"other choice little things"; Mark E. Neely Jr. and R. Gerald McMurtry, *The Insanity File: The Case of Mary Todd Lincoln* (Carbondale: Southern Illinois University Press, 1986), 165.

"Don't mope around . . .": Mary Lincoln to Mary Harlan Lincoln, 2 April 1870, ibid., 171.

"If I was . . .": Mary Lincoln to Mary Harlan Lincoln, 16 September 1870, ibid., 170-71.

"Have fun; be . . .": Mary Lincoln to Mary Harlan Lincoln, n.d., ibid., 168.

"blessed baby" and "Little Mamie": Randall, *Lincoln's Sons,* 378.

"My mother became . . .": Neely, *The Insanity File,* 36.

Widow's Pension

"Sir: I herewith . . .": Mary Lincoln to the United States Senate, December 1868, in Turner and Turner, eds., *Letters,* 493.

"If the Senate . . .": *Congressional Globe, Forty-first Congress, Second Session,* 5560.

"harsh" and "indecent": Ibid., 5563.

"Surely the honorable . . .": Ibid., 5398.

"not a muttering . . ." Mary Lincoln to Sally Orne, 17 August 1870, in Turner and Turner, eds., *Letters,* 575.

Tad at Fifteen

"Taddie is my . . .": Randall, *Lincoln's Sons,* 203.

"It is impossible . . .": Turner and Turner, eds., *Letters,* 421.

"air of restraint": Randall, *Lincoln's Sons,* 202.

"the little white . . .": Ibid.

"[Tad's] presence has . . .": Mary Lincoln to Mary Harlan Lincoln, 22 March 1869, in Turner and Turner, eds., *Letters,* 504.

"almost wild to . . .": Baker, *Mary Todd Lincoln,* 303.

"Mrs. Lincoln is . . .": Ibid., 306.

Photograph of Tad Before Death

"a very lovable . . .": Randall, *Lincoln's Sons,* 208.

"The doctors assure . . .": Mary Lincoln to Rhoda White, 8 June 1871, in Turner and Turner, eds., *Letters,* 570.

"Tad is dangerously . . .": David Davis to Ward Lamon, 12 July 1871, David Davis Papers, Abraham Lincoln Presidential Library and Museum.

"with marvelous fortitude . . .": Randall, *Lincoln's Sons,* 209.

Another Death

"She looked truly . . .": Ibid., 210.

"I feel there . . .": Randall, *Mary Lincoln,* 382.

Spirit Photograph

"the spirit of . . .": Baker, *Mary Todd Lincoln,* 291.

Arrest Warrant

"be placed under . . .": Neely, *Insanity File,* 14.

"Your friends have . . .": Leonard Swett to David Davis, 24 May 1875, David Davis Papers, Abraham Lincoln Presidential Library and Museum.

"You mean to . . .": Ibid.

"You must go . . .": Ibid.

"threw up her . . .": Ibid.

"I ride with . . .": Ibid.

Robert Todd Lincoln Testifies

"a kangaroo court": Neely, *The Insanity File,* 17.

"You will put . . .": Leonard Swett to David Davis, 24 May 1875, David Davis Papers, Abraham Lincoln Presidential Library and Museum.

"Mrs. Lincoln's manner . . .": Neely, *The Insanity File,* 16.

"piled full of . . .": Ibid., 15.

"crazy": Baker, *Mary Todd Lincoln,* 320.

"I have no . . .": *Chicago Inter Ocean,* 20 May 1875, photostat in records of the Chicago History Museum.

"satisfied that the . . .": Turner, *Letters,* 611.

"Oh, Robert, to . . .": Baker, *Mary Todd Lincoln,* 325.

Insane or Not?

"married women may . . .": *General Laws of the State of Illinois, Passed by the Seventeenth General Assembly* (Springfield: Lanphier & Walker, 1851), 98.

"She was always . . .": Baker, *Mary Todd Lincoln,* 332.

"not an instance . . .": Ibid.

Bellevue Place

"modern management of . . .": Ibid.

"family atmosphere . . .": Ibid.

"God imposes higher . . .": Ibid., 333.

"Mrs. Lincoln's lying . . .": Bellevue Patient Progress Reports, 30 July 1875, photostat in files of Batavia (Ill.) Historical Society.

Myra Bradwell

"Mrs. Lincoln is . . .": Neely, *Insanity File,* 60.

"had engaged Mrs. Lincoln . . .": Ibid., 63-64.

"secure for her . . .": Ibid., 70.

"open the prison . . .": Baker, *Mary Todd Lincoln,* 341.

Sister to the Rescue

"If you bring . . .": Neely, *Insanity File,* 67.

"She . . . is cheerful . . .": Ibid., 78.

Furious Letter

"You have tried . . .": Mary Lincoln to Robert Todd Lincoln, 19 June 1876, in Turner and Turner eds., *Letters,* 615.

👉 "it would be . . .": Baker, *Mary Todd Lincoln*, 350.

Discovered Letters

"None of Mrs. Lincoln's . . .": Jason Emerson, "The Madness
of Mary Lincoln," *American Heritage*, June/July 2006, 11.

"It does not . . .": Mary Lincoln to Myra Bradwell, August
1875, Abraham Lincoln Papers, Library of Congress.

"protector" and "companionship": Emerson, "Madness of
Mary Lincoln," 13.

"Had I been consulted . . .": Ibid.

Pau

"monster of mankind son": Baker, *Mary Todd Lincoln*, 349.

"will never cease . . .": Helm, *Mary, Wife of Lincoln*, 298.

"I live very . . .": Mary Lincoln to Elizabeth Edwards, 19
March 1877, in Turner and Turner, eds., *Letters*, 627.

"I cannot trust . . .": Mary Lincoln to Edward Lewis Baker
Jr., 7 October 1880, in Turner and Turner, eds.,
Letters, 703.

Forgetful Son

"My father's death . . .": Baker, Mary Todd Lincoln, 363.

Mary's Obituary

"intelligent" and "dignified": *Louisville Courier-Journal*,
17 July 1882, photostat in files of Kentucky Room,
Lexington Public Library.

"much maligned": Ibid.

"made of carnations . . .": Randall, *Mary Lincoln*, 398.

"the loving offering . . .": Ibid.

"With the one . . .": Carl Sandburg, *Mary Lincoln, Wife and
Widow* (New York: Harcourt, Brace & World, Inc., 1932),
326.

Final Photographs

"Time does not . . .": Mary Lincoln to Elizabeth Blair Lee, 25
August 1865, in Turner and Turner, eds., *Letters*, 268.

PICTURE CREDITS

All photographs and illustrations not specifically credited below
were provided by the Library of Congress. All contributors are
herewith gratefully acknowledged.

Abraham Lincoln Library and Museum of Lincoln Memorial
University, Harrogate, Tennessee: 2 (bottom left), 31 (right),
38 (right), 103 (top right)

Abraham Lincoln Presidential Library and Museum:
5 (top left), 6 (right), 13, 14 (bottom left), 15, 17 (top), 29,
33, 34, 39, 49, 55 (bottom), 57 (top), 59, 63 (bottom right),
66 (left), 67 (top), 87 (bottom right), 116, 140 (bottom left),
141 (top), 151, 152, 155 (bottom), 156 (top)

Allegheny College, Tarbell Collection: 32

American Antiquarian Society: 85

Batavia Historical Society: 153 (left)

Chicago History Museum: 43, 52 (bottom), 53, 86 (top left),
87 (top left), 144

Collection of Keya Morgan, LincolnImages.com, New York
City: 44 (left), 54, 55 (top), 76 (left), 86 (top right), 126
(bottom right), 127

Collection of the Museum of American History, Smithsonian
Institution: 124 (right)

Collection of the New-York Historical Society: 70 (bottom left),
82 (right)

Collection of Professor and Mrs. Gabor S. Boritt: 124 (top)

Filson Historical Society: 17 (bottom)

Gilder Lehrman Institute of American History: 92 (bottom),
132 (top), 156 (bottom right)

Hildene, the Lincoln Family Home, Manchester, Vermont: 146
(right), 147 (right)

Indiana Historical Society: 141 (bottom right)

Kansas State Historical Society: 58 (top left)

Lexington Public Library Kentucky Room: 19 (bottom),
20 (top), 21, 22 (top right), 35 (bottom), 113

Lincoln Boyhood National Memorial: 2 (bottom right), 9 (top),
10

Lincoln Home National Historic Site: 37 (top)

The Lincoln Museum, Fort Wayne, Indiana: 6 (top left), 7, 9
(bottom), 12, 36, 66 (right), 123 (bottom right), 142 (right),
149, 150

McLean County Historical Society: 44 (right), 60

Michigan State University: 41 (left)

National Archives: 48, 88, 96, 128, 148

National Library of Medicine: 28 (top)

Anson Nichols: 37 (right)

Northern Illinois University Libraries: 28 (right)

Old State Capitol, Springfield, Illinois: 16

Pennsylvania State Archives: 104 (bottom right)

Picture History: 70 (top left), 77 (bottom right), 140 (top left)

Print Collection, Miriam and Ira D. Wallach Division of Art,
Prints and Photographs, New York Public Library, Astor,
Lenox and Tilden Foundation: 58 (bottom left)

Eric Rohmann: 38 (left), 63 (left), 117 (bottom)

Smithsonian Institution Libraries on Display: 42 (top)

Transylvania University, J. Winston Coleman, Jr.,
Photographic Collection: 19 (top)

Transylvania University, Special Collections, Mentelle
Collection: 24

University of Kentucky, Townsend Collection: 23 (bottom),
26 (top), 27 (bottom right)

University of North Carolina at Chapel Hill Libraries,
Documenting the American South: 146 (left)

University of Vermont: 42 (bottom)

Virginia Historical Society: 95 (bottom), 120 (bottom right)